The Red Virgin

Memoirs of Louise Michel

Louise Michel, drawn from life, 1880. (Photo. Bibl. nat. Paris)

The Red Virgin
Memoirs of
Louise Michel

edited and translated by

Bullitt Lowry

and

Elizabeth Ellington Gunter

The University of Alabama Press
University, Alabama

Publication of this book has been assisted by a

grant

from the National Endowment for the

Humanities.

Library of Congress Cataloging in Publication Data

Michel, Louise, 1830–1905.
　The Red Virgin: Memoirs of Louise Michel

　Translation of Mémoires de Louise Michel, écrits par elle-même.
　Bibliography: p.
　Includes index.
　1. Michel, Louise, 1830-1905. 2. Paris—History—Commune, 1871—Sources. 3.
Revolutionists—France—Biography. 4. New Caledonia—Description and travel. 5.
Political prisoners—France—Biography. I. Lowry, Bullitt, 1936– II. Gunter, Elizabeth
Ellington, 1942– III. Title
DC342.8.M64A313　　944.081'2'0924 [B]　　80-23073
ISBN 0-8173-0062-7
ISBN 0-8173-0063-5 (pbk.)

To Anne, Ross, and Sheila

Acknowledgments

The translators wish to express their appreciation to *Stonecloud* (1975), which published an earlier version of Chapter 18, "Women's Rights," and to *The Phoenix* (Summer and Fall, 1977), which published abridged versions of Chapter 4, "The Making of a Revolutionary," Chapter 10, "After the Commune," and Chapters 12–14 on New Caledonia.

Contents

	Translators' Introduction	viii
1.	Introduction	1
2.	Vroncourt	4
3.	The End of Childhood	15
4.	The Making of a Revolutionary	24
5.	Schoolmistress in the Haute-Marne	31
6.	Schoolmistress in Paris	38
7.	The Decaying Empire	45
8.	The Siege of Paris	56
9.	The Commune of Paris	63
10.	After the Commune	69
11.	The Trial of 1871	81
12.	Voyage to Exile	89
13.	Numbo, New Caledonia	95
14.	The Bay of the West	104
15.	Nouméa and the Return	115
16.	Speeches and Journalism, November 1880–January 1882	123
17.	The Death of Marie Ferré	135
18.	Women's Rights	139
19.	Speeches Abroad, 1882–1883	143
20.	Speeches in France, 1882–1883	150
21.	The Trial of 1883	158
22.	Prison	172
23.	My Mother's Death	179
24.	Final Thoughts	190
	Epilogue	198
	Bibliography	202
	Translators' Note	204
	Appendix I. Chapter List Showing Source in Original Text	206
	Appendix II. Table of Poems in Original Text	207
	Index	209

Translators' Introduction

Even today, Louise Michel, who won fame as the "Red Virgin" during the Paris Commune of 1871, remains a heroine to the French Left. While Karl Marx sat in the British Museum writing tracts, Michel was facing French government troops across the barricades of Paris. While her contemporaries were just beginning to decry colonialism, she, as a convict in New Caledonia, was involved in the Kanaka uprising of 1878. Freed by the amnesty of 1880 from her exile at the other end of the earth, she returned to France and the speaker's platform, and except for several periods in prison she continued her revolutionary exhortations until her death in 1905.

Born illegitimately on 29 May 1830, Louise Michel was brought up by her mother and paternal grandparents in a half-ruined, fortified manor house in the Haute-Marne. Her paternal grandfather, Etienne-Charles Demahis, was descended from nobility and had changed his name from De Mahis to the less grand Demahis in republican sympathy with the French Revolution of 1789. Although impoverished, he was serving as mayor of the village of Vroncourt when Louise was born to a servant of the household, Marie Anne (or Marianne) Michel, and his son Laurent, of whom no further record exists. Louise was raised as if she had been a legitimate Demahis granddaughter, and after her paternal grandparents died, she became a schoolmistress, teaching first in the Haute-Marne and later in Paris. She turned to revolutionary dreams and became deeply involved in radical affairs during the twilight of France's Second Empire, the gaslit Paris of Louis Napoleon. During the Franco-Prussian War of 1870 and the Prussian siege of Paris, she was a leading member of the revolutionary groups controlling Montmartre, that squalid and colorful district which has been inhabited by the disaffected poor for centuries. During the Paris Commune of March to May 1871, when the citizens of Paris rebelled against the government because they believed it was trying to steal their republic, Michel became even more deeply involved in events, emerging as one of the leaders of the insurrection.

When the forces of the Versailles Government crushed the Commune in May 1871, Michel was captured, tried, and sentenced to exile. She was transported to New Caledonia on a prison ship in 1873. For six years she lived under harsh conditions in the prison colony near the capital, Nouméa, and later she lived in the capital itself, with a limited amount of freedom. Following the general amnesty of 1880, which the government gave to the Communards in response to public pressure, she returned to France and public acclaim.

Though massive public gatherings greeted Michel upon her return, it was difficult for her to find a place in revolutionary circles. She was ignorant of events that had taken place in France during the preceding decade, and the persons who had risen to power and influence in radical circles had no great interest in relinquishing their position to any legend. But her popular support from the working people of France remained immense, and her speeches in Paris, the provinces, and abroad during the next few years were heavily and tumultuously attended.

In 1882 Michel was arrested for disturbing the peace and spent two weeks in jail. Then, in the spring of 1883, after a demonstration at les Invalides, she led a crowd across Paris under the black flag of anarchism. She was arrested and tried for rioting and for inciting her followers to loot bakeries. Offering no real defense at her trial, she was sentenced to six years in prison. Pardoned three years later, she resolutely continued her speeches and writing, the radical public honoring her as "la grande citoyenne." From 1890 to 1905 she spent the greater part of her time in England in self-imposed exile, although she made a number of speaking tours in France and elsewhere. She was engaged in one of those speaking tours in 1905 when she died, her funeral becoming an occasion for a massive outpouring of sentiment from three generations of revolutionaries.

Louise Michel declares in her memoirs that she was an anarchist, having come to the faith after she passed through her youthful, vague sympathy for the downtrodden and her later ill-defined devotion to a Utopian revolution. She claimed later that her transformation to anarchism came on her voyage to New Caledonia aboard the prison ship *Virginie,* during which time she was caged for four months with Natalie Lemel, who converted her. In her memoirs Michel states that the anarchist "Manifesto of Lyon" of January 1883 precisely expressed her political beliefs. "I share *all* of the ideas written there," she writes in her memoirs, and she quotes the complete text of that document.

But Michel's anarchism was emotional, not theoretical. In fact, she was surprisingly ill read in contemporary and historical revolutionary writings. That she had read Lamennais is certain; that she had read Proudhon is likely. It is less probable that she had read either Blanqui or Bakunin, although she certainly knew of their ideas, which were in the air at the time. Marxism dismayed her, but played little part in her memoirs because her full exposure to Marxism did not come until the 1890s, several years after her memoirs were published. What is remarkable are her omissions. For example, she never mentions Babeuf and his "Manifesto of the Equals." She writes about close friends and associates who made theoretical and practical contributions to radical doctrine— Kropotkin, Guesde, and Pouget, who was her codefendant in 1883—but she never mentions their writings.

That her commitment to anarchism was emotional did not produce intellectual inconsistency. Indeed, after her Utopian phase she was entirely consistent in her view of property, her perception of exploitation, her claims for the role of science, and her vision of the basic good in mankind. Similarly, in her encomiums to the Social Revolution she was consistent regarding its form and nature: It would be a spontaneous rising of the people against injustice and exploitation.

That emphasis on the spontaneous uprising of the people kept her, indirectly, from demanding the use of terror, a step many anarchists took. Michel mentions assassination as a tool only occasionally. Once, she discusses murdering Louis Napoleon Bonaparte; another time, she talks about assassinating Adolphe Thiers. Yet she never made any concrete preparations to carry out plans to murder the two. Similarly, her only use of explosives was an abortive attempt to blow up a statue. "Tyrannicide," she writes, "is practical only when tyranny has a single head, or at most a small number of heads. When it is a hydra, only the Revolution can kill it."

She was vague about what would happen the day after the Social Revolution, other than offering images of dawns and fireworks. She does comment that it would be better if all the leaders of the Revolution should perish in achieving it, for then the people would not have to contend with a surviving general staff. But somehow the anarchist dream would be fulfilled.

Anarchism, "the logical conclusion of the romantic doctrine," to use E. H. Carr's felicitous phrase,[1] is perilously difficult to define. Yet its core—an insistence on the importance of the individual, a hatred of all forms of political organization, a belief in the innate goodness of man—fitted so providentially with Michel's thinking that it is hard to decide whether Michel found anarchism or anarchism found Michel. At the time when she wrote her memoirs she believed implacably that progress was inevitable, that people were innately good, and that governments, any governments, were evil. Her statement that "power is evil" forms the nucleus of every anarchist system, but neither she nor any other anarchist ever found a ready answer to George Bernard Shaw's irritating question. If man is so good, he asked, "how did the corruption and oppression under which he groans ever arise?"[2]

Michel avoided the question. She saw history as the story of free people being somehow enslaved; the details were vague. But her interest in the past was as great as her hope for the future. Romantic though her vision of the past may have been, full of myth and monster, yet it was in easy accord with her romantic dream for the future. To her, past and future were indissolubly linked.

Unfortunately for Michel's hopes—and historical reputation—the romantic dream of anarchism was a waning force not the wave of the future. While it is true that anarchism's greatest influence in France, numerically at least, followed the outrages of the 1890s and lasted until the outbreak of the Great War, in those decades the simple and direct force of anarchism was absorbed into the Bourses de Travail, the protean Confédération Générale du Travail, and factional infighting. The anarchism that Louise Michel dreamed of, the formless uprising leading to the Social Revolution and the end of exploitation, disappeared into irreconcilable bickering over detail and method. The dream diffused, then disappeared like a wisp of smoke.

Michel was no more an organizer than she was a theorist. Not for Michel the shabby, ill-lit rooms where intriguers and plotters put together demonstrations and organizations. "All revolutions have been insufficient because they have been political," she said in a speech in 1882. She believed organization unnecessary because she was adamantly of the opinion that at some near moment the poor and exploited would rise up spontaneously, and through sheer numbers, force of will, and the decency of their cause, they would force the old order to shrivel up before them. In this vein, Michel's most typical act was in 1883, when, with no particular objective, she led the crowd of self-proclaimed anarchists across Paris.

Neither theorist nor organizer, Michel filled another role for the French radicals. "Nearly Joan of Arc," Verlaine called her.[3] And Victor Hugo, no anarchist, although surely a romantic, had named the first draft of a poem "Louise Michel"; in this lengthy poem, retitled "More Than a Man," Hugo wrote,

> Those who know . . .
> Your days, your nights, your cares, your tears, given to everyone,
> Your forgetfulness of yourself in helping others,
> Your words like the flames of apostles,
>
> ....
>
> Your long look of hatred to all those who are inhuman,
> And the feet of children which you warm between your hands, . . .

He would realize Michel was incapable of anything not heroic or virtuous. Michel had, Hugo concluded:

> . . . two spirits intermingled
> . . . the divine chaos of starlike things
> Seen at the bottom of a great and stormy heart
> . . . a radiance seen in a flame.[4]

Every movement needs prophets and lawgivers, sinners and apostates, martyrs and saints. For French anarchists, Michel was martyr and saint—the Red Virgin.

Michel's intellectual curiosity was immense, her thirst for knowledge unquenchable. Throughout her memoirs runs an amazing assortment of subjects: music, musical instruments, teaching techniques, cruelty to animals, the status of women, the money used in the Canary Islands, insects, Kanakan anthropology, the weather, botany—the list is endless. As a child she collected animal skeletons in her tower; as a schoolmistress in Paris, in spite of her busy teaching schedule, she attended classes on physics, chemistry, history, and even law; in prison she wrote books and poetry; in New Caledonia she catalogued flora and fauna and experimented with vaccinating papaya trees against jaundice.

The inner life she reveals in her memoirs was surely a remarkable one. Legends, beasts, and folk heroes mingled in her fantasies, and she never distinguished between her fantasies and reality. Her early life, she says, was "made up of dreams and study," a preparation for the second part of her life, "the period of struggle." But according to her account, she acted during the waking world of the Siege and Commune as she had seen herself act in her dreams. Dream and action were the same, and, in her mind, apparently indistinguishable. The gallows speeches she invented in her childhood she delivered to her judges in 1871.

People make their own dramas and then star in them, and Michel gave the impression of playing herself. She saw herself as druidess, valkyrie, vestal virgin, moving through a life that contained far more—strange demons and mystic visions—than the eye could see. On one occasion in the 1860s she walked with her friend Victorine through the deep woods near her childhood home. Near the pair, padding along almost silently through the forest, a wolf paced their steps, she claims. Was the wolf really there? Probably not. In the 1860s the number of wolves, even in the Haute-Marne, was small, but the beast existed in Michel's mind certainly and truly.

When Michel is narrating events of public record she is surprisingly accurate, considering that the main preparation of the text took place in prison cells. After her return from New Caledonia she was followed daily by police agents when she was not in jail. Their reports have survived, so her life from 1881 to 1883 and from 1886 to 1889 has a corroborative record, if not an objective one.[5] But for her childhood and her years as a schoolmistress almost the only record is her memory, and some of the attitudes she describes do not ring true. Perhaps Michel constructed her fantasy and then lived it out; it seems more likely that she lived her life and then superimposed her fantasy onto it retrospectively. Few people other than memoirists have the chance to live their lives over again.

Michel is astonishingly free of the self-aggrandizement memoirs are prone to, even to the point of neglecting her own importance. She was, after all, the chairman of the Women's Vigilance Committee during the Commune. During the Siege she had been responsible for the day-to-day welfare of some two hundred children, a task which she did very well, thanks to the assistance of Georges Clemenceau; no mention of her effort appears in her memoirs, although it is obliquely referred to at one of her trials. After her return from exile in New Caledonia, she represented France at Kropotkin's international gathering in London; she mentions the trip, but says nothing of her role there.

From time to time misdirection, whether conscious or unconscious, appears in her memoirs. She points with a grand gesture to an inviting vision that is simply not true. Still, the misdirections of 1886 indicate either the way that Louise Michel truly saw her own life or the way she wanted others to see it. The effect is almost the same, and perhaps she was unaware of the difference. The revolutionary, a fifty-six-year-old woman, had sacrificed everything to the Revolution. Perhaps to justify what she had become she had no choice other than to make her youthful self into the revolutionary she was later.

Some of her misdirection is harmless. She subtracts five or six years from her true age, and when she writes of her childhood adventures, she paints herself as a mischievous hoyden. She was fifteen when her grandfather died, and twenty when her paternal grandmother died and the half-ruined manor house where she had grown up was sold. The majority of the childhood stories concern the period while her grandfather was still living, and she says comparatively little that can be dated with certainty to the period from his death until her grandmother's, although her stories of the *écrègnes,* the gatherings of village women, probably belong to those years.

She was apparently a properly religious child, despite her attempt to show herself as determinedly anticlerical from the first Voltairian teachings of her grandfather. Contradicting her attempts to don this mantle are hints of her attraction to mystical Catholicism through the fervent teachings of her devout aunt. Even Michel's story of instructing her pupils in Audeloncourt to boycott the mandated prayer for the Emperor rings false in view of a strong recommendation by a local curé which appears in her application to certify her school.[6] Even without that document as proof, much of the verse she wrote in the 1850s—verse which she does not quote in her memoirs—was ardently Christian.

Similarly, her memoirs would have the reader believe that she taught in Audeloncourt for several years and then left for Paris. That is not true. After a limited formal education she received her diploma in September 1852, taught in Audeloncourt for a year, went to Paris for a first and unmentioned period beginning in January 1854, and then returned to the Haute-Marne the following fall because her mother was ill. She tried to reopen her school at Audeloncourt, but failed because her former pupils had gone elsewhere. Then she tried to open a school at Clefmont; whether she succeeded is unclear, but in 1855 she and Julie Longchamps opened a school at Millières, where Michel taught for two

years before going to Paris a second time. Possibly the reason for
Michel's lack of clarity on this subject stems from embarrassment over
admitting a succession of failures or only partial successes.

Perhaps still fearing governmental reprisals, Michel lies about the
demonstration of 22 January 1871, suggesting that it was intended to be
a gentle and unarmed protest. In fact, it was planned as a direct
confrontation with the Government of National Defense. She also omits
the information that she was dressed in a National Guard uniform and
was carrying a rifle. Similarly, she minimizes her role in the councils of
the Commune and is a bit elliptical when she discusses what part she
played in military events. For example, she was a member of the 61st
Battalion of the National Guard, which was commanded by Eudes, the
husband of her friend, Victorine Louvet.

Her narrative of her arrest, confinement, and trial are straightfor-
ward, as is her account of the voyage to New Caledonia in 1873. The
captain of the prison ship, the *Virginie,* was deeply concerned, his reports
show, with the well-being of the deportees aboard; and the trip, while
certainly unpleasant, was not unnecessarily arduous.[7]

Michel makes light of the physical discomfort of the prison camps on
the Ducos Peninsula at Numbo and later at the Bay of the West.
Conditions there were far less easy than she suggests, but she reserves
her criticism for the jailers and their policy of repression, not the poor
food and inadequate medical facilities.

She was certainly involved peripherally in the Kanakan uprising of
1878 in New Caledonia, yet her comments on it are scanty. Indeed, her
account of these events, in which she hints broadly that she knows more
than she chooses to tell, is the only place in her memoirs where she is coy
with the reader. Certainly the authorities might have taken notice of an
open confession, but when she writes about the Siege and the Commune, she simply avoids indictable revelations.

Upon her return to France, Michel plunged into radical politics almost
without pausing. Her account of these events is anecdotal and episodic,
not systematic. Among the subjects on which she focuses is the incredible
effort of the Prefect of Police to establish a radical journal, his idea being
that such a publication would help him to keep track of revolutionaries
because they would congregate around it.[8] Michel also describes speaking tours she made to Belgium and England.

During those years her friend Marie Ferré died, but the climax of
events, for Michel, was the Trial of the Sixty-eight at Lyon, where the
government tried to break the anarchist movement by destroying many
of its leaders, among them Kropotkin and Gauthier. Michel had been in
England during the earlier part of the trial, but she was present at the
last phase, and she identified herself with the prisoners, although she
was not among those indicted. After the conviction of the Sixty-eight,

she felt she had to do something: "I would have been an accessory to cowardice if I did not use the liberty I was allowed—I don't know why—to call up a new and immense International which would stretch from one end of the earth to the other." She was searching for martyrdom when she found it at les Invalides in April 1883; the government reacted savagely and after a sham of a trial she was sentenced to six years of solitary confinement, a sentence so incommensurate with the crime that even conservative papers protested.

Her mother's declining health worsened. Michel was given parole to visit her while awaiting trial and at least twice after conviction. When she was in the Centrale Prison at Clermont she was also allowed to go see her mother, a most exceptional proceeding, although as Michel's biographer Edith Thomas notes when she discusses this episode, the nineteenth century was "a much more humane epoch than ours."[9] Michel gave credit to the authorities for transferring her to a Paris prison at the beginning of December 1884 so that she might be near her mother. Four days later the Minister of the Interior gave permission for Michel, guarded by two police inspectors, to stay at her mother's bedside. From Michel's memoirs it is hard to tell that she stayed with her mother almost a month, from 11 December 1884 until her mother's death on 3 January 1885.

Michel's emotions were always intense. The pages of her memoirs are sprinkled throughout with affection for her mother, and when she describes her childhood, she exhibits devotion to her older relatives. Later, as a young woman, she formed a close friendship with Julie Longchamps, who followed her to Paris. The two remained close into the 1860s, drifting apart only when Longchamps failed to follow Michel into radical politics.

Through the years Michel's affection for her pupils remained undimmed. She is bitter when she rebuts the government's claim, made at her first trial, that she had no pupils, yet she let far greater falsehoods stand unrefuted. She seems to have been a conscientious and imaginative teacher, and outside evidence corroborates that judgment. For example, her devotion to teaching the Kanakas in Nouméa earned a letter of commendation, a letter she quotes with obvious pride.

Michel's sympathies focused upon all who were helpless in society: the poor, the elderly, prisoners, and women. She developed a protofeminism, but it quickly merged into a more general radicalism. Michel saw the problems of society clearly, and she saw that many groups, not just women, were being exploited. Thus, a chapter in her memoirs concerning women changes its tone until it becomes a plea for both women and men "to move through life together as good companions" as they march toward the Social Revolution. After it occurs, "men and women together will gain the rights of all humanity." They will not argue any longer "about which sex is superior" any more than "races will argue about which race is foremost." Michel's aversion to cruelty to animals is connected with her sympathies for the helpless and exploited: "Everything fits together, from the bird whose brood is crushed to the humans whose nests are destroyed by war."

The most intense feelings in her memoirs, after those for her mother, are reserved for Théophile Ferré. She frequently refers to him and his execution, but it is hard to determine whether her feelings are for Ferré as a person or as a symbol of what repression could lead to. Whether Michel's warm friendship for Ferré's sister Marie was the product of her feelings for Théophile or independent of them is unclear, but Michel's and Marie Ferré's lives were permanently intertwined. Marie helped to care for Michel's mother while Michel was at meetings, exiled, traveling, or in prison, and the two maintained a lively correspondence through the years. It is to Marie that she owed her collection of poems and clippings, many of which are included in the memoirs. Shortly after Michel's arrest for the demonstration following the anniversary of Blanqui's death Marie died, and in the memoirs Michel includes an account of Marie's funeral and a eulogistic letter from Henri Rochefort.

But Michel's emotional life centered on her mother. Michel recognized that she had caused the greater part of her mother's sufferings, caused them because of opinions which her mother "didn't share." Throughout her life, her mother struggled to pay her daughter's debts and showered her with affection and little presents. In return, Louise tried to hide her misfortunes from her mother and to ease her last moments. "We revolutionaries bring so little happiness to our families," Michel laments. To pay tribute to her mother, Michel prints the account of her mother's funeral in full. What she failed to realize was that the many thousands who followed her mother's body through Paris to the graveyard at Levallois-Perret were honoring not only her mother but Louise herself.

For all practical purposes, Michel's memoirs end at the time of her mother's death, and with her spirit bleak from the loss she had suffered, she completed them for publication the following year. Reality is malleable, and to recall the processes of one's mind, which a memoirist must do, is to see past events through whatever sun or shadow exists at the moment when the recollection is called forth. Though Michel's devotion to the revolutionary cause and her optimism for the future remained steadfast, even under the shadow of the mother's death, it is possible that she would have shown less nostalgia and less sorrow for a lost past if she had not written her memoirs under the immediate impact of her grief.

It was sometime during Michel's third prison term, which began in 1883, that she started to write these memoirs, although documents for them had been collected earlier. She also had some earlier pieces, like a history of the Haute-Marne that she had begun during her childhood, and she makes one tantalizing reference to a "journal" she kept of the voyage to New Caledonia, which has disappeared.

In 1885, after her mother died, Michel suffered some sort of nervous collapse, which certainly was among the reasons for her memoirs' being fragmented and disjointed. Although a very rough chronological outline runs through the two parts, stories and anecdotes appear more through word association than from step-by-step narrative. Nor are the memoirs limited to factual accounts. They are filled with emotional descriptions of her dreams, stirring calls to action, and a number of poems. She flits from one idea to another "as they come to mind." Occasionally she seems aware of the problems she might be causing the reader. "Before speaking about my third arrest," she writes in the original text, "I ought to relate the first two." The memoirs oscillate wildly among nostalgia, exaltation, narrative, and prophecy.

As a consequence, the original memoirs are most difficult to follow, and we, as translators, decided that a direct rendering into English would be incomprehensible to modern readers. Therefore, we translated the original text completely, and then transposed Michel's words into a chronological narrative of her life, being careful to stay as true as possible to the thought and tone of the original.

Very little material has been eliminated. Frequently, there were several versions of one event, agreeing with each other in broad outline always, which is unusual, but each adding new details. Those versions were combined to make one account. Several poems were omitted because they added nothing to the narrative; furthermore, Michel's poetry is mediocre—Edith Thomas noted that Michel's "best poem is surely her life"—and those poems that were retained were kept to add information or color to the text. Parts of her long catalogue of the flora and fauna of New Caledonia have also been excised; it is frequently impossible to tell from her nonscientific descriptions which of several species she was writing about. A digression about a literary lawsuit brought by Grippa de Winter, in which Michel was not involved, was also omitted.

In the original text almost every chapter ends with a paean to the coming Revolution. Reducing the number of chapters from thirty-three (plus three appendices) to twenty-four left several extra paeans, and in any event, it seemed a bit monotonous to follow Michel's example, so they have been included only where they seemed most appropriate. Moreover, she frequently inserts parenthetical exclamations of grief at her mother's death; their number has been reduced, although enough of them have been retained to remind the reader of the emotional strain under which Michel was writing.

In summary, the words of these translated memoirs are Louise Michel's; the organization of those words is ours. The loss of the original texture and the feeling for how ideas were associated with each other in

Michel's mind is compensated for, we believe, by having an orderly memoir of her life to 1886.

We have added almost nothing to the narrative. In some places where it was possible to establish definitely the identity of some person mentioned, we have added a phrase identifying him, because persons who were familiar to Michel's readers in 1886 are now often obscure. We have occasionally added dates established from documents like the records of the prison ship that carried Michel to New Caledonia. On matters which she could not check in prison, we felt accuracy served the reader. Where she is inaccurate and we were uncertain whether that inaccuracy was deliberate, we left the material as it was written, noting major problems in italicized interpolations.

Michel clearly intended to write a continuation of these memoirs. A decade after she published this volume she talked about doing so, but nothing came of it. So, other than her poetry and letters, the volume here, the *Mémoires de Louise Michel écrits par elle-même*, is the main autobiographical offering of a fascinating woman, revolutionary, poet, and dreamer.

When she published these memoirs in 1886 she was fifty-six years old and still had nineteen years to live, one-third of her adult life. It is a pity she never wrote the second volume she spoke of, but the memoirs that she did write stand as a monument to human dreams. Motivated by compassion, not doctrine, Michel testified in her memoirs and by her life that an unattractive, illegitimate child from the fringe of nowhere could so love freedom that she was ready to sacrifice her own. There have been worse lives.

Notes

1. E. H. Carr, *Michael Bakunin* (New York: Octagon Books, 1975), p. 434.
2. George Bernard Shaw, "The Impossibilities of Anarchism," *Fabian Tract* 45 (1895): 14–15.
3. "Ballade en l'honneur de Louise Michel," in *Oeuvres complètes de Paul Verlaine* (Paris: Albert Messein, 1911) 2:39–40.
4. "Viro Major," in *Oeuvres complètes de Victor Hugo* (Paris: Albin Michel / Imprimerie Nationale, 1935) 12:82–83; notes, 12: 360–61, 404; and plate, 12:489.
5. Archives historiques de la préfecture de police, Ba 1183–87, Paris.
6. Edith Thomas, *Louise Michel ou la Velléda de l'anarchie* (Paris: Gallimard, 1971), p. 42.
7. Résumé du 2ᵉ voyage de circumnavigation de la Virginie, to Ministre de Marine et Colonies, 4 May 1874, Ministère de Marine, Paris.
8. L. Andrieux, *Souvenirs d'un préfet de police* (Paris: Jules Rouff, 1885), 1: 175, 337–41.
9. Thomas, *Louise Michel*, p. 265.

The Red Virgin

Memoirs of Louise Michel

Chapter 1

Introduction

People have often asked me to write my memoirs, but whenever I have tried to speak about myself I have felt the same repugnance I would feel about undressing in public. Today, in spite of these feelings, I have decided to put together a few of my memories. My life is full of poignant memories, and I will expose some very personal feelings. I will tell them randomly as they come to mind; if I give my pen the right to wander, I have paid very dearly for this right.

My life has been composed of two very distinct parts that form a complete contrast. The first was made up of dreams and study; the second of events, as if the aspirations of the calm period came alive during the period of struggle. I will go to some lengths to avoid mentioning the names of persons whom I lost sight of long ago, to spare them the disagreeable surprise of being accused of conniving with revolutionaries. It might become a crime for them to have known me, and my old acquaintances might be treated like anarchists when they don't know exactly what anarchism is.

I shall write boldly and frankly regarding everything that concerns me personally, leaving in the shadows they loved those people who brought me up in the old ruin of Vroncourt in the Haute-Marne. The Military Tribunals of 1871 investigated the very bottom of my cradle and still respected the privacy of my relatives, and I won't disturb their ashes. Moss has worn their names off their tombstones in the cemetery and the old château has fallen down, but once again I see the nest of my infancy, and I see those who brought me up brooding over me. Their images will appear often in this book. Alas, of the memories of the dead, of the fleeting thought, of the hour which has passed, nothing remains.

If a little bitterness drops onto these pages, no venom will ever fall. The human race as a whole is blameless if individuals waste away like animals in the struggle for existence. When the obstacles that fetter humanity finally are forced aside, humanity will pass beyond this anguish.

In this unceasing battle the lone human being is not and cannot be free. My life is not mine to live. I must fulfill my duty to the Revolution, and lead my life harshly, without comfort, so that it will all be over more quickly.

Perhaps these memoirs will have a great number of volumes. To tell all, one would write without end. In any case, I would do well to sketch the history of my prisons. Many brave hearts are found among those unfortunate prisoners whom people despise. People must see things as they are, and only someone who has lived through such experiences knows.

Some of these pages would be difficult to send out the gates of Saint-Lazare prison, which is where I am now writing. But to rescue these words from oblivion I intend to take advantage of an article in the regulations that states: "Attorneys can receive sealed letters from prisoners." One attorney understands that because these memoirs are, in a sense, my last will and testament, I have the right to say whatever I want in them and send them to him.

In these memoirs I want to include accounts of my three trials. I have taken reports of my first and third trial from the *Gazette des tribunaux*, which no one could suspect of being too favorable to me. The second trial took place only in a lower court, and so was not reported in the *Gazette;* I have included a newspaper account of it. For the masses, the great masses, my loves, I will add some observations that I didn't think it was proper to make to the judges at the time. For us revolutionaries, every trial is an act of war over which our flag is waving. May that flag cover my book, as it has covered my life, as it will wave over my coffin.

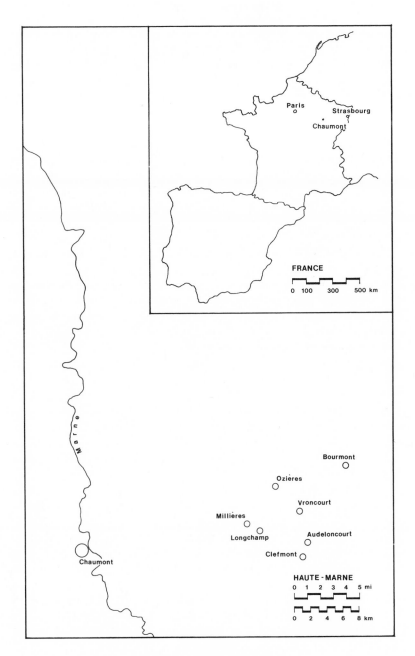

FRANCE

0 100 300 500 km

Marne

Bourmont

Ozières

Vroncourt

Millières

Longchamp

Audeloncourt

Clefmont

Chaumont

HAUTE - MARNE

0 1 2 3 4 5 mi

0 2 4 6 8 km

Detail of the Haute-Marne

Chapter 2

Vroncourt

My childhood nest was a tumbled-down château. At its corners, the same height as the main building, were four square towers with roofs like church steeples. The south side had no windows, only loopholes in the towers, which made the building look like a tomb or a castle, depending on the point of view. A long time ago, people called the place the Fortress, but when I lived there it was usually called the Tomb.

To the east lay a vineyard, and we were separated from the little village of Vroncourt by a grassy stretch as wide as a prairie. At the end of it, a brook flowed down the only street in the village, and in the winter the brook became so swollen that people in Vroncourt had to put stepping stones in it to make it passable.

Further to the east there was a screen of poplars, and the wind murmured sweetly as it blew through those trees; and then, rising behind everything, were the blue mountains of Bourmont. Many years later when I saw Sydney, Australia, surrounded by bluish peaks, I recognized on a larger scale the crests of the mountains I had seen in my childhood.

To the west were the hills and woods of Suzerin. When the snow was deep, wolves would creep from the woods into the Tomb through gaps in the wall, and they would howl in the courtyard. Our dogs would answer them, and this concert would last until the frozen morning. All was well at the Tomb, and I loved those nights.

I loved them especially when the north wind raged, and we read late, the whole family gathered in the old Great Hall. I loved the wintry setting and the frozen upper rooms. All of it—the white shroud of snow, the chorus of the wind, the wolves and dogs—would have made me a poet, even if all my family hadn't been poets from the cradle.

It was glacially cold in the Tomb's enormous rooms. Through that vast ruin the wind whistled, as it does through the rigging of a sailing ship. We huddled around the fire, my grandfather sitting in his easy chair situated halfway between his bed and a stack of all kinds of guns. In winter he threw a big cloak of white flannel over his clothes and wore wooden shoes trimmed with fleece. Often I sat on those wooden shoes in front of the fireplace, snuggling up to the cinders along with the dogs and cats.

Depending on the circumstances, my grandfather appeared like many different men to me. When he told me of the old, great days, the epic fights of the First Republic, he was passionate, so that he could relate to me the war of the giants, the war when "whites" and "blues," brave men fighting brave men, showed history how heroes died. Sometimes when he explained to me the various books we read together, he was ironic, like Voltaire, the master of his youth. At other times he was gay and witty, like Molière. Still other times, when our minds traveled across unknown worlds together, we spoke of things he saw stirring on the horizon. We looked at past stages of human development, and we discussed the future. Often I cried, touched in my heart by some quick image of progress, art, or science, and my grandfather, with great tears in his eyes, too, would put his hand on my head, which was more tousled than one of our dogs.

Both my grandmothers lived with us, and how different they were! One had a delicate, Gallic face framed by a headdress of white muslin gathered into tiny pleats, under which her hair was arranged in a large chignon on her neck. The other had eyes that were black like coal, and short hair; she was enveloped in an eternal youth which made me think of fairies in the old tales.

My mother was then a blonde, with soft and smiling blue eyes and long, curly hair. She was so fresh and pretty that her friends used to say to her laughingly, "It is impossible for this ugly child to be yours." As for me, I was tall, skinny, disheveled, wild, brazen, sunburned, and often decorated with torn clothing held together with pins. I knew how I looked, and I was amused at people finding me ugly, although my poor mother sometimes took offense at it.

Many animals lived in the Tomb. We had a big Spanish hound with long yellow hair, and two sheepdogs. All three dogs answered to the name of Presta. We also had a black and white dog named Médor, and a young bitch we named Doe in memory of an old mare named Doe that had died just before we got the bitch. When I gave the old mare an apronful of hay her manner would change remarkably. The thing I remember best about her was her stealing my bouquets; she would take them and then lick my face. When she died my grandfather and I wrapped her head in a white cloth, so no dirt would touch it, and buried her outside near the acacia.

We had legions of cats, too, especially male ones. We called all the male cats Lion or Darling and all our female cats Galta. Sometimes the cats would crowd us at the fire, and my grandfather would use the tongs to pick a glowing coal from the fireplace and wave it at them. The whole pack would run off, only to make a fresh assault soon after.

My mother, my aunt, and my grandmothers usually sat around the table. One read aloud, and the other knitted or sewed. Beside me as I write now is the sewing basket my mother kept her things in.

Friends often came to visit us. When Bertrand or M. Laumont, the old teacher from Ozières, came, the family sat up later than usual, reading aloud. They tried to send me to bed so they could finish reading the chapters they didn't want to read in front of me. Sometimes I obstinately refused, nearly always winning eventually, and other times when I was in a hurry to hear what they wanted to hide from me, I obeyed quickly, and then tiptoed back and hid behind the door to listen.

We called the schoolteacher Little Laumont to distinguish him from his relative, another Laumont, the doctor at Bourmont, whom we called Big Laumont. Big Laumont, the doctor, enveloped in a vast black coat that made him look like an Egyptian scarab, came on a stocky horse to spend every Tuesday with us. Little Laumont was always dressed in a short, gray frock coat and carried an enormously long cane. When he moved, his feet never seemed to touch the ground, and he was as intelligent as he was strange. He used to spend the winters with us. Long ago Little Laumont had given lessons to my aunt Agathe and my mother, and I think he had taught the whole countryside to read.

Those were the good days. My grandmother or I was at the piano, and my grandfather played his bass viol. Big Laumont sometimes carried a flute in his pocket, and when he played it, he played perfectly. All of us together would play music until we tired of it. Then in the dusk of the evening the doctor would leave swiftly, with his capacious black cloak floating around him. He looked like the black horseman of the legends.

Big Laumont asked me once, very seriously, the way he always spoke to me, why I didn't write some prose works. Following his suggestion, I began a story, *The Naughty Deeds of Helen*, which began, "Helen was very naughty and stubborn." It was a collection of my own wicked deeds, each of which I ended with an exemplary punishment for the sake of morality. For example, I described one episode in which Helen stole a small encyclopedia from an old doctor's house, a leather-bound volume in which were found the names of everything that could be learned. For punishment, Helen was condemned to spend a month with no book other than a huge grammar, which she certainly wouldn't have bothered to steal. "Oh, you little monster," said Big Laumont when he read this piece, "I thought it was you who had taken my book!"

That wasn't the only thing I took as a child. Each of us is capable of all the good or evil in his being. Without remorse I used to take money (when there was any), fruits, vegetables, and so on, and gave them away in my relatives' names. That caused some great scenes when the recipients tried to thank them. Incorrigible as I was, I laughed about it.

Once my grandfather offered me twenty sous a week if I would promise not to steal anything again, but I found I lost too much money on that deal and I refused. I had filed some skeleton keys to open the cupboards where pears and other fruits were kept, and I used to leave little notes there in place of what I had taken. I remember one that read: "You have the lock, but I have the key."

In the summer the Tomb filled up with birds that flew in through the broken windows. Swallows came back to their nests of former years, sparrows flew in and out of the broken windows, occasionally knocking on the unbroken panes, and the larks sang loudly with us. That is, they sang with us when we sang in a major key; when we changed to a minor key they would fall silent.

The birds weren't the dogs' and cats' only fellow-boarders. We had partridges, a tortoise, a roebuck, some wild boars, a wolf, barn-owls, bats, several broods of orphaned hares that we had raised by spoon-feeding—a whole menagerie. And of course, there was also the colt, Zéphir, and his grandmother Brouska. How old Brouska was I don't know—she had been with us so long that no one could remember her age. Brouska walked in and out of the rooms in order to take bread and sugar from the hands of people she liked. To people she didn't like, she would pull back her lips, showing all her huge yellow teeth as if she were laughing in their faces. And there were cows, too, the great white Bioné and the young Bella and Néra. I went to their stable to chat with them, and they answered me in their own way by looking at me with their soft eyes.

All these beasts lived on good terms with each other. The cats would lie curled up, following with a negligent eye the birds toddling about on the ground. Even more strange, I never saw a cat bother about a mouse, and mice lived in all the walls. In the Great Hall, behind the green tapestry that covered the walls, the mice ran around rapidly but unafraid, uttering little shrill cries as they went. The mice behaved perfectly, and never gnawed on papers or books and never placed a tooth on the violins, cellos, and guitars which were scattered about.

What peace there was in this place, and what peace there was in my life at this time! Maybe I didn't deserve it. How I love to dream of this little corner of the earth. If my mother had been able to survive my prison term, I would have liked to have spent some peaceful days near her, days such as she needed, with me working near her armchair, and the old Caledonian cats purring at the hearth.

Every time something important happened in my family, my grandmother would write a verse account of it. My grandfather added some pages of his own to that collection, which was kept in two large, looseleaf books. I wrapped those books in black crepe when my grandmother died.

The winds of adversity blow on things as well as people. Of all the pages my grandfather wrote, I have only one left, "A des antiquaires," and I have only one piece my grandmother wrote, "La Mort," which she wrote after the death of her husband. They are all that remain to me. Their sad tones are a feeble enough exhalation compared to the delicate verses that I no longer have. All has faded away, even my grandfather's guitar, which crumbled while I was in New Caledonia. My mother cried over it a long time.

In autumn, my mother, my aunts, and I used to go far into the forest. It was good to hear through the deep silence in our woods the heavy hammer of the smithy, and the sharp blows of the axe that made the branches shiver. Then, too, there were the songs of birds and the buzzing of insects under the fallen leaves. Often we would hear the little branches breaking where some old woman was gathering a pile of faggots. Sometimes we would hear the snort of a wild boar in the thickest woods, and other times it was a few poor roebucks flashing across our vision. Maybe they sensed the autumn hunts, when men cut the throats of animals to the sound of the hunting horn. Animals kill to live; the hunter destroys only to destroy.

On the road to Bourmont was Uncle Georges's old mill, which stood at the foot of a hill where there was an uncultivated vineyard. The grass was thick and cool in the meadow bordered by the millpond. The rosebushes rustled as the ducks moved through them or the wind pushed them. In the mill, the first room was dark even at midday, and it was there that Uncle Georges used to read every evening. How much he learned reading that way!

All those people, living and dead, here they are in this place of time gone by. Here are my grandmother Marguerite's sisters with their white headdresses, pins fastening scarves at their necks, the square bodices— the complete outfits of peasant women, which they wore coquettishly from their youth, when people called them beautiful girls, until their deaths. Like themselves, their names were simple: Marguerite, Catherine, Apolline.

One of my mother's sisters, Aunt Victoire, was with us later at Audeloncourt. She was very tall, with a thin face that had fine, regular features. My mother's other sister, my Aunt Catherine, lived in the Lagny area. Like my mother, both had an absolute cleanliness, a luxury of neatness, which allowed neither the shadow of a spot, nor a speck of dust, from their headdresses to the tips of their feet.

In the first flush of my Aunt Victoire's youth, some missionary preaching at Audeloncourt left behind a religious fanaticism that led many young girls into the convent. My aunt was one of them. She became a novice, or lay sister, at the hospice of Langres, but she broke her health by fasting and was forced to return to secular life. She came to live with us at Vroncourt, where she stayed until my grandparents died.

I never heard a more ardent missionary than my Aunt Victoire. From Christianity she had absorbed everything that sweeps a person away: somber hymns, evening visits to churches drowned in shadow, the lives of virgins, which recall druidesses or vestal virgins or valkyries. All her nieces were swept into this mysticism, me more easily than the others.

What a strange impression still remains with me. I used to listen at the same time to my Voltairian grandparents and my exalted Catholic aunt. Moved by strange dreams, I searched the way a bewildered compass-needle looks for north in a fierce storm.

My north, where my compass finally pointed, was the Revolution. My fanaticism changed from dream to reality; years later my friend Théophile Ferré told me I was consecrated to the Revolution, and it was true. All of us were its fanatics.

I read hungrily during those years, especially with Nanette and Josephine, two remarkably intelligent young women who had never left the district. We used to talk about everything. In good weather we carried out magazines and books to read in the tall grass: *Magasins pittoresques,* and *Musées des familles,* Hugo, Lamartine, and others. I have always wondered if Nanette and Josephine loved me better than their own children. I certainly loved them. One day, when I was perhaps six or seven years old, we drenched Lamennais's *Paroles d'un croyant* with our tears. From that day on, I belonged to the masses.

From that moment I climbed step by step from Lamennais to anarchy. Is there further to go? Of course, because there is always more to come, there is always further to go, always progress to make in light and liberty, in the development of new sensitivities of which we now have only the rudiments. There is a future which we imprisoned spirits cannot even glimpse.

In front of me are a few handfuls of memorabilia from my childhood. I take one at random, a description of Vroncourt my mother saved. How many things this little piece of yellowed paper has survived!

Vroncourt

Vroncourt lies on the slope of a mountain between the forest and the plain. You can hear the wolves howling, but you do not see the lambs' throats being cut. At Vroncourt, you're separated from the rest of the world. The wind rattles the old church tower and the towers of the château, and it bends the fields of ripe grain like ocean waves. All that you can hear is the formidable noise of the storm. It is great and beautiful.

This work, as well as my *Legendary Haute-Marne,* was illustrated with my own charcoal sketches. Responsible for a piece of that work was Marie Verdet, who must have been more than a hundred years old. "Say," she said to me, "it won't be worth the trouble to write your book on Vroncourt if you don't include the legend of the Three Washerwomen."

So I drew the Fountain of the Ladies. The shadow of willows lies on the water, and from this shadow the pale washerwomen emerge, three phantoms under the trees. According to Marie Verdet, one cries about the past, another moans for the days of the present, and the last mourns for tomorrow. They remind me of the legends of the Norns.

Another charcoal sketch in the same work depicted another custom, the Diableries of Chaumont, last held more than a century ago. My sketches of the Diableries are impressionistic and try to reproduce the feeling of the moonbeams, the forest, the snow, and the night.

Here is another fragment. It comes from my *Legendary Haute-Marne* and describes these Diableries of Chaumont which took place every seven years.

> The Diableries of Chaumont are related to history, fancy, and legend. The Diablerie is a dream which had a real existence, and traces of it were still visible at the end of the eighteenth century. Many bizarre customs disappeared at the end of the Middle Ages; the Diablerie of Chaumont was one that survived. . . . Every seven years, say the chroniclers of Champagne, twelve men would dress like devils, or as you would expect devils to dress, in all the old torn-up clothes of hell, where there are all sorts of disguises, even that of Jehovah. The devils of Chaumont got theirs at the shop of old Anne Larousse, at the sign of Brac et Joie: an immense pair of horns and a black hood. They accompanied the Palm Sunday procession to honor heaven and to represent hell there. After they had danced in the procession, for the love of God, our lords the devils spread out into the countryside, which they had the right to pillage, for the love of the devil, to their heart's content.
>
> Why did they choose the number twelve? The chroniclers say that it was in honor of the twelve apostles, although this method of honoring them wouldn't have suited them. Some scholars claimed that they stood for the twelve signs of the Zodiac, and others that they stood for the sons of Jacob.
>
> None of these suppositions was generally accepted. At each Diablerie the arguments arose anew among the scholars, clerks, and astrologers of the good town of Chaumont, who exhausted themselves in writing tracts on the question.

These men disguised as devils sang continuously "Quis ist iste rex gloriae" with as much spirit as those whose costumes they were wearing, but with less harmony, since the devil has an essentially musical ear.

The Diablerie of Chaumont lasted from Palm Sunday to the Nativity of St. John, and it ended with a representation of the main acts of the life of Saint John, presented on ten stages so that the faithful could watch.

The celebration was concluded with a ceremonial death by torture. (There couldn't be a good celebration without that, either in their time or ours.) The torture and death were ordinarily just symbolic—an effigy of Herod, representing his soul, was burned at the stake.

The last year these holy orgies took place, an event happened which may have hastened their end. This event does not appear in the written chronicles, but Marie Verdet did not have the slightest doubt that it happened, for her grandfather had heard it from his grandfather, who had heard it from his grandmother. At this particular torture and death, the effigy of Herod had gestured so beautifully that the audience enjoying themselves at the "torture" had filled the valley of the Ecoliers. Suddenly the effigy began to moan and people went into ecstasy. The miracle was believed all the more easily since the people later found charred bones in the ashes of the stake. But, if they found charred bones, they no longer found the handsome singer Nicias Guy; it was he who had been so terribly murdered out of love's vengeance.

Let me add here a few notes on my native region, the Haute-Marne. Plows bring to light the stone coffins of our fathers, the Gauls; the knife for slitting victims' throats; Roman incense. The plowman, accustomed to these finds, turns them aside, sometimes making a watering trough from a coffin, or using the incense to scent the enormous stump which burns beneath his great chimney. He continues to sing to his oxen, while behind him the birds gather worms in the open furrows.

Formerly, near a ruined fortress, the *châté païot,* people used to go to conjure the spirits of the ruins with a silver piece, a lighted candle, a white shirt, and a sharpened knife.

"Why the piece of silver?" I asked Marie Verdet, and lowering her voice, she answered, "For the devil!"

"And the lit candle?" "It's for the good Lord!" "And the white shirt?" "For the dead!" "And the knife with the sharpened blade?" "For the person carrying out the ceremony if he betrays his fealty."

"His fealty to whom?"

"To the unknown, to the Ghost-in-Flames."

Enough of these stories found in the stones that I walked over as a child. Let me return to the events of my own early life. I never learned to write script properly. For a long time as a child I wrote my poems in letters I had invented myself, modeled after those in books. Finally, my family realized it was time to teach me to write like the rest of the world. *The Naughty Deeds of Helen* was the last work I wrote with my own letters instead of writing in proper script. Because no one at the Tomb could write script properly, and also because they thought it would be better if I had less free time in which to occupy myself as I pleased, I was sent to the village school every day.

In spite of the five styles of writing taught at Vroncourt, and the beautiful English script I learned in teacher-training courses at Chaumont, I returned later to the style I used at home. I rolled my letters, disheveled my words, and let my handwriting change as my thought changed. It makes my handwriting very difficult to imitate. People have tried anyway. Two years ago, my poor mother got a fairly well-forged letter—the signature was a masterpiece—saying that I was sick and asking for her at the prison of Saint-Lazare. That was a terrible thing to do. Another time someone sent the authorities a well-counterfeited request asking that I be allowed to see my mother; the forger didn't know that, at that very moment, I had been with my mother for several days.

Anyway, I was sent every day to school at Vroncourt to improve my script and occupy my time. The teacher was named Michel, but he was not related to me.

The school at Vroncourt was a dark house with only two rooms. The larger, which looked out onto the street, was the classroom. The other, which was never brightly lit, was where the teacher and his wife lived. It looked out on a grass-covered slope through a window at ground level which was like a vent in a cave. This window, like the window of the classroom, was made of many tiny panes and bordered by red cotton curtains.

By the light of the classroom window the schoolteacher's wife, Mme Michel, sewed all winter long. Her profile, a little severe under her great white headdress, seemed very beautiful to me. On the days when we recited catechism, my Aunt Victorine used to come in and sit near her, so that she could hear if I had learned it well.

The tables in the classroom were arranged around three sides of the room, the fourth side, where the front door was, being left empty. There were two or three benches for the little ones who couldn't write yet. A few of the older ones who had what was called beautiful hands also sat on those benches writing on their knees. They didn't need to polish their style any more, and they were proud of their status.

I put my mind to figuring out ways to make mischief, and I soon discovered one way. Monsieur the teacher, as we called him, sat on a high wooden chair we called the pulpit. He dictated passages to us, telling us to write down the dictation precisely as he said it. I went to some pains to write down everything he said, not just what he was dictating. It would come out something like this:

> The Romans were the masters of the world (Louise, don't hold your pen like a stick;—semicolon)—but Gaul resisted their domination for a long time (You children from up on Queurot, you're coming in very late;—a period. Ferdinand, blow your nose.—You children from the mill, warm your feet)—Caesar wrote the history of their resistance, etc.

Not losing a minute, I even added, scratching furiously, some things the teacher didn't say. He finally caught me. I would have been as unresponsive to his anger as I was to ordinary reproaches, if he hadn't said to me dispassionately, "If the inspector of schools saw that, you would get me fired."

A great sadness fell over me. I could think of nothing to reply, even when he forbade me to bring him any more rose petals. Those rose petals, dry in winter and fresh in summer, he liked to add to his cherrywood snuff box, which he opened and closed with a little leather thong.

The next day my dictation was irreproachable. For more than a week, under his severe eye, I kept twisting in the pocket of my pinafore a little white paper full of dried roses that I had fixed for him without hope. Finally, seeing that my heart was breaking, he asked me for them, and all was well. After that, even though I played other tricks, they weren't ones the inspector could blame Monsieur the teacher for.

He earned so little that he did all sorts of odd jobs during the long summers when the children in our village didn't have classes, but the old teacher was always cheerful. I never heard him say a bitter word.

Although books for children and even for grown-ups give the illusion that merit is rewarded, merit is rarely recognized in this world. I first realized that truth from observing the teacher, Michel. Like my hatred of force, this perception comes from my earliest years. Since then I have seen a thousand examples, so I was astonished only the first time I saw it.

Any mathematical calculation became easy when M. Michel explained it. By nothing more than the way in which he asked the question, Monsieur the teacher provoked the right answers. He put it under your nose. When a student was at the blackboard working on some problem under the eye of the outstanding old mathematician, the teacher showed the position of the number with the end of his hazel rod. Your mind kept the whole operation in view at the same time, and it seemed to me that the questions he asked had a rhythm to them.

I told my grandfather about that. Monsieur the teacher was a frequent visitor at the Tomb, and one evening I heard my grandfather and Monsieur the teacher chatting about things far removed from my poor, little problems. I could have stood listening to them forever. That evening I discovered that Monsieur the teacher was simply a genius in numbers, as well as a great astronomer and poet. I also found out that algebra is easier than arithmetic.

"Why haven't you written on mathematics?" my grandfather asked M. Michel.

The old schoolteacher laughed sadly and ruefully. They exchanged various remarks that I didn't understand until I was much older, but the teacher's laugh stayed in my memory. Later, when I read in books about merit being recognized and virtue being rewarded, I laughed the same way.

In later years, I found artlessness like M. Michel's in other people of merit many times. I thought about him when the captain of the *Virginie,* on which I was being sent to New Caledonia, told me about his trip to the North Pole. The old seaman, keyed up by the day's storm, the high seas off the Cape, and the spume left after each wave crashed down on the deck, relived for me his voyage to the North Pole and made it come alive.

"Why haven't you written all that down?" I asked.

"I'm not a writer," he answered. "Anyway, scholars have already written about all those things."

How many scholars are as scholarly as the captain of the *Virginie?* Have they seen things for themselves? Knowledge must be presented in a manner that enlarges the horizon instead of restricting it. As long as poverty, which shackles people like my old schoolteacher, is combined with prejudice, which makes the unknown fearful and fetters people like the captain of the *Virginie,* ignorance will continue to imprison the world.

The development of the human race and the development of new sensitivities are thwarted because people take their point of view from the part, not the whole. Only when totality, completeness, is seen can each person rummage in his own little corner in harmony with wisdom and the development of the human race.

Chapter 3

The End of Childhood

As the seed contains the full-grown tree, all life from its very beginning contains whatever it will be—whatever, despite everything, it must become. Thus, I am trying to go back to the sources of the events in my life. One piece of verse I found in my old papers sketched out the pattern my life would take.

The Voyage
At the rim of the desert how immense is the sky.
On your new unknown path, child, where do you go?
What do you hope for, now hid in deep mystery?
—If only I knew. Toward beauty and goodness!

Child, what's your choice? Peace, calm, and surrender?
You could live like a bird and build up your nest.
Hear, while there's time; shun the hard brutal path,
Where your fate will be damned, and your life will be tears.

I don't want to cry, or look backwards too much.
If it weren't for my mother, I would go far indeed
Through chance-controlled life, where the tempest is blowing,
Go, as one follows the faraway horn.

From deepest concealment, I hear a loud fanfare.
Others have gone there whom I would meet.
Heavy steps on the land! I hear them! I hear them!
It's humanity marching. With them I would go.

I look at the sand and the heaped-up grain.
In profoundly blue skies I see endless cloud-worlds.
Does it make any difference? One world's like another.
Where those clouds disappear, it is there I must go.

Those years, the years of the Tomb, when all those so dear to me surrounded my being, those years of my grandfather, of my Aunt Victoire, of Nanette and Josephine, of M. Michel and the schoolroom of Vroncourt—those years live for me still, though the Tomb is now a ruin and those who people these pages died long ago.

Deep down in the wellsprings of my life are the tales of old legends. Today, I see those phantoms still: Corsican sorceresses, mermaids with green eyes, medieval bandits, Jacques Bonhommes, red-haired Teutons, tall, blue-eyed Gallic peasants. From Corsican bandit in his wild gorges to judge of the High Court of Brittany, all of them are in love with the unknown. All of them bequeath to their descendants, bastard or legitimate, the heritage of the bards.

My love lies in these atavistic legends. People are always taunting me for never speaking of love. I have to go back to those hours when young women are just learning to dream. From the pages of old books read in the dawn of life many songs of love escape, and within those pages a young woman can be in love with love as much as she wishes. I mean she can look for an ideal person she could love if she were to meet him in real life. Among the sons of Gaul, among the barbarians, she chooses the bravest of the brave. She can look into the far past at men of the north, the men of the Ghilde who fought for freedom and who used to pour three cups of wine on the flagstones—one for the dead, another for their ancestors, and a third for the brave. The Bagaudes, who died in their flaming tower; the poets; the troubadors; the great leaders of robber bands who stole from the rich bandit in the manor to give to the miserable beggar in his thatched cottage—they are my loves.

I couldn't be faithful to only one of those loves; there were too many of them. From the devil to Mandrin, from Faust to Saint-Just, how many phantoms made me dream when I was a child! I dreamed of the Jacqueries and the peoples' rebellions of the Middle Ages.

Many things float in children's dreams. Some are red like blood and some black like a night of mourning. Such were the banners of the rebels who dwelt deep in my thoughts. The weddings of those who loved each other were the red weddings of martyrs, and they signed their covenants in blood.

I wasn't the only young girl who loved stories of rebels. Often the other girls of the village and I talked of the things which the old songs or legends of the country spoke of. I remember part of one song:

He whom she loved,
Proud he was,
Helmet on head.
Hear the lark
That sings for him.
White she was;
Hands gathering
Mistletoe
From the dark oak,
And verbena
Deep in the woods.

I created poems from these old legends. Even if there hadn't been a little atavism in my blood helping me to write poetry, no one could have escaped being a poet in this country of Champagne and Lorraine, where the very winds sang Germanic war chants and songs of love and rebellion. Through the great snows of winter, past the sunken paths full of hawthorn in the spring, pushing through the deep black woods of enormous oaks and poplars with trunks like columns, you can still follow the paved roads of the conquering Romans, and in many places see where the unconquered, long-haired Gauls ripped up those paving stones.

Everyone is a bit of a poet. Nanette and Josephine, those daughters of the fields, were poets naturally. After many years and across many seas in New Caledonia, one of their songs, "The Black Bird of the Fallow Field," came back to my mind during a cyclone. In my version of it you can hear the same black chord which vibrates in the heart of nature, but their version in dialect is sweeter and more mysterious. In theirs you can smell the wild rosebush of the hedges, and at the same moment hear the bird of the fallow field, who lets his melancholy notes trickle down like someone telling his beads, and a deeper note like a tide grinding against a reef.

In the patois of the Haute-Marne their song goes like this:

L'Agé Na Deu Champ Fauvé

1.

Dans l'champ fanné c'etot
Un bel âgé chantot.
Teut na il étot
Il fo y brâchot.
Ka ki dijot l'âge,
L'âgé deu champ fauvé?

2.

C'étot pa les échos
Sous les âbres du bos,
Li bise pleurut
Deven lu brâchot
Ce que dijot l'âgé
L'âge deu champ fauvé?

My version, translated word for word [from the patois], is:

The Black Bird of the Fallow Field

1.

In the fallow field
A pretty bird sang.
Black, black it was,
And it sobbed strongly.
What was it saying,
The bird of the fallow field?

2.

Through its echoes
From under the trees,
The north wind was crying,
Sobbing with the bird,
What the black bird was saying,
The bird of the fallow field.

How many memories I have. Is it irrelevant to put down all this foolishness? Yesterday, I had trouble getting used to writing about myself; today, searching the days that have disappeared, I can't stop. I see everything again.

I can see the round stones at the far end of the yard near the knoll and the thicket of hazel trees close by. There, thousands of young toads peacefully underwent their metamorphosis, if we didn't kidnap them and throw them against the legs of nasty people. Poor toads!

In the courtyard, behind the well, we children put bunches of twigs, bundles that let us erect a scaffold with steps, a platform, two tall wooden poles, everything. Then we depicted historical epochs and characters we liked. We put the Terror of 1793 into dramatic form, and we climbed one after the other up the steps of the scaffold, where we made ready for our executions, crying out "Long live the Republic!" The public was represented by my cousin Mathilde, and sometimes by chickens and roosters gobbling and pecking and spreading their tails wide. We searched history books for human cruelties. Our scaffold became the stake of John Hus, or still further back in the past, the burning of the rebel Bagaudes in their tower in the year 280.

One day, as we were climbing our scaffold singing, my grandfather suggested to us that it would be better to climb the steps to the platform in silence, and at the top to affirm the principle for which we were dying. Afterwards, we modified our dramas to follow his advice.

Our play wasn't always so serious. Sometimes we had mock hunts. Pigs served as boars, and we lit brooms to serve as torches. We ran with the dogs to the dreadful noise of shepherds' horns, which we called the trumpets of the hunt. An old gamekeeper had taught us how to sound something he called the "hallali."

We observed all the rules of the art of venery in these disheveled chases with our running dogs. They ended with our taking the pigs home, whether they liked it or not, and several times the pigs fell in the kitchen garden waterhole, where their fat supported them while they made desperate "oufs" until someone pulled them out. Pulling them out wasn't easy. Men with ropes took charge of the operation, yelling at us. They looked at me as if I were a runaway horse.

I have never met children who were, at the same time, as wild and as serious, as naughty and as fearful of causing hurt, as lazy and as industrious as my cousin Jules and me. Each year during vacation he came to the Tomb with his mother, Agathe, whom I loved dearly and who spoiled me very much.

The diversity of the questions that Jules and I discussed astonishes me now. Sometimes we would stop to argue in the middle of a performance of a drama by Victor Hugo, which we had arranged for two actors. "They don't respect anything," people said. At other times we would argue from the branches of apple trees, where we had chased our cats. Why did we chat from one tree to another? I really don't know. It was pleasant up in the branches, and, too, we used to throw each other all the apples we could reach, which gave Marie Verdet lots of good, fallen fruit to pick up. Marie Verdet was the old, old woman who told me the story of the Three Washerwomen; she always saw those things, and Jules and I never did.

That we never saw the things she saw didn't keep us from enjoying her stories. Indeed, I enjoyed them so much that I fell in love with all that was fantastic. Among haunted ruins I drew magical circles, and I declared my love to Satan. Satan didn't come, which led me to think he didn't exist.

One day, chatting from tree to tree with Jules, I told him of my declaration of love to Satan and his failure to answer me. Jules confessed to me that he had sent a declaration of love no less tender to the famous woman of letters, George Sand, and she hadn't answered any more than the devil had.

After a performance of Hugo's *Burgraves* or *Hernani* which we had arranged for two actors, I gave Jules a lute, made like mine. In one stormy discussion on the merits of the sexes, Jules maintained that if I learned from the schoolbooks he had brought with him during the vacation, and learned so that I was more or less on his level, it was only because I was an anomaly. Our lutes served as projectiles, and broke our discussion.

While still a child, I started writing a *Universal History* for inclusion in the rows of redbound manuscript books my grandfather kept. I started writing it because Bossuet's *History* bored me and because Jules, one vacation, brought me the history he used in school. I documented the main facts as well as I could, and went about my studying as if I were a male.

A long time ago I recognized the superiority of the course of study in boys' preparatory schools to the education of girls in the provinces. Some years after I studied my cousin's textbook, I had the opportunity to verify the difference in emphasis given the same subject between the two courses of study—one for "the ladies" and the other for the "strong sex"—and to examine the result of that difference.

I'm convinced that my first impressions were correct; adults give girls a pile of nonsense supported by childlike logic, while at the same time they make "our lords and masters" swallow little balls of science until they choke. For both of us, it is a ridiculous education. A few hundred years from now people will see it all as a heap of trash—even the education of men.

The *Universal History* I started to write must have contained some extraordinary mistakes. I consulted enough infallible books to assure their presence. But after I had worked on it for a long time, someone gave me several volumes of Voltaire, and I left my historical masterpiece for a poem.

Then I deserted my poem for a mammoth's tooth, of which even Big Laumont spoke with enthusiasm. At the top of the north tower I set up a small cell full of everything that looked like geological findings. I added modern skeletons of dogs and cats, skulls of horses, crucibles, a stove, and a tripod. The devil, if he exists, knows everything I tried there: alchemy, astrology, the summoning of spirits. Every legend, from the alchemist Nicholas Flamel to Faust, had a home in my tower.

Also in my tower I had a lute, a horrible instrument I made myself out of a fir board and old guitar strings. I wrote verses that I addressed to Victor Hugo, and in them I spoke pompously of my barbaric instrument. He never knew what this poet's lute really looked like, this lyre with which I sent him the sweetest greetings.

In my tower I also had a magnificent barn owl with phosphorescent eyes, whom I called Olympe, and I had some darling bats who drank milk like little cats. I stripped the grills out of the big winnowing basket to make cages for them, because it was safer for them to be confined during the day.

When I was twelve or thirteen I had two grown-up suitors. The memory of those two ridiculous persons who followed each other like geese and who asked my grandparents for my hand would have driven me away from marriage even if I hadn't already decided it was repulsive. The first one, a true comic character, wished to "share his fortune"—he made each word ring like a little bell—with a wife reared according to his principles, that is to say, like Molière's Agnes.

After all that I had read, it was too late to rear me this way. That animal! He must have slept for a century or two, and when he woke up he came to my grandparents to recite this nonsense.

My grandparents let me make up my own mind and answer for myself. The very day that fool appeared my grandfather and I had just been reading from an old edition of Molière. The suitor looked to me so much like Agnes's guardian in *L'Ecole des femmes* that I found a way to slip into my answer a great part of the scene beginning, "The little cat is dead," when her guardian questions her about an unknown male visitor. I gave him Agnes's speech as an answer, word for word, and naturally he didn't understand. Then, driven to despair, I looked straight in his face, and with the ingenuousness of Agnes, I said to him boldly, knowing he had one glass eye, "Monsieur, is your other eye glass, too?" That seemed to embarrass my relatives a little, and as for my suitor, he gave me a venomous look from the eye that wasn't glass, and made it clear he no longer wanted to make me his fiancée.

At this time, I had been growing a lot, and my dress was very short. My pinafore was torn, and in my pocket I had my net for catching toads. I was only sorry that I hadn't already caught a few so that I could slip them into his pocket, but I didn't need to. He never returned.

Molière inspired me just as much when I dealt with the second of my two suitors. I don't think they knew each other, and yet they made a good pair. So many persons seem to go in pairs or threesomes, like stars that orbit around each other. They both had the idea of choosing a very young fiancée and having her molded like soft wax for a few years before offering her up to themselves as a sacrifice.

To my second suitor, I said, more or less: "You see plainly what's hanging on the wall over there." It was a pair of stag antlers. "Well, I don't love you. I will never love you, and if I marry you I won't restrain myself any more than Mme Dandin did. If I marry you, you will wear horns on your head a hundred thousand feet higher than those antlers."

I suppose I convinced him I was telling him the truth, for he never came back. My relatives advised me, however, to be a little more reserved in quoting old authors in the future.

There have been unfortunate children who were forced to marry old crocodiles like those. If it had been done to me, either he or I would have had to jump out the window.

Not too long after that affair, my grandfather was returning from Bourmont on the stagecoach. Seated next to him was a third maniac who pointed out Vroncourt and the Tomb and said to him:

"You see that old rats' nest."

"Yes," grandfather replied.

"An old fellow lives there who is raising his grandchildren for prison and the scaffold."

"Oh, really?" said grandfather.

"Yes, monsieur. My friend X—— recently proposed marrying one of them, a little smart-aleck, in a few years, if her education were directed as he wished."

"Well?"

"The old fellow let her give her own answer. Whatever she wished. She said such horrible things that my friend doesn't even want to repeat them. If I had a daughter like that, I'd put her in a reform school. And her a little wench who doesn't have a sou to her name. Hey, where are you going?"

"I'm getting off at Vroncourt," grandfather said. "I'm the old fellow you've been discussing."

....

So these were the days of my childhood. Now they are sketched out, laid out on the table, the cadaver of my life. These days of former times were so calm in events and so full of tormented dreams. Even then I sensed my destiny. People do sense their destinies, as dogs sense a wolf, and sometimes it comes true with a strange precision. If everybody told of their prescient thoughts in minute detail, it would be like reading the *Tales* of Edgar Allan Poe.

I must write things as they come to me. They are like pictures passing from sight and going away endlessly into the shadows. Of my old relatives, of my young and old friends, of my mother, nothing remains today but the dreams of my childhood. I see those who disappeared yesterday or a long time ago, just as they were, and I see all that surrounded their lives, and the wound of their absence bleeds just as much now as it did in the first few days. I have no real homesickness for a country, but I am homesick for the dead. And the further along I get in these memoirs, the more numerous are the images that press close to me of those whom I shall never see again.

At the Tomb, near the hazel tree in a bastion of the wall, was a bench where my mother and grandmother used to come during the summer after the heat of the day. My mother, to make Grandmother happy, had filled this corner of the garden with all kinds of rosebushes. While the two women talked I leaned on the wall. The garden was cool in the dew of the evening. The perfumes of all the flowers mingled and climbed up to the sky. The honeysuckle, the reseda, the roses, all exhaled sweet perfumes which joined each other. Bats flew gently in the twilight, and their shadows soothed my thoughts. I used to recite the ballads that I loved, without ever thinking that death was going to pass over us.

When these days of my dawning ended, so ended my songs that were sad and dreamy. Death swooped down on the Tomb. The foyer was empty and those old people who had reared me were laid to rest under the pines in the cemetery.

I inherited a small tract of land. I can only picture one piece of it now, a small copse my mother planted on the hill near her little vineyard.

From the hill I could see the woods of Suzerin and the red roof of the farm, the blue mountains of Bourmont, Vroncourt, the mill, and the entire hill of wheat waving in the wind. In my mind I imagined that the sea would look like that waving wheat, and I found out later I was right. My mother took care of the copse during her long stay in the Haute-Marne while I was an assistant schoolmistress in Paris.

There was so little time for living together. "Things have tears," Virgil wrote. I feel them when I think of the little woods and the vineyard watered by Mother's sweat. Years later, her own mother Marguerite wanted to see the vineyard one last time before she died, and my uncle carried here there in his arms.

During the Franco-Prussian War, Prussian soldiers went through like victors. They cut down the woods and destroyed the vineyard. There was a little hut in the middle, and I believe they burned it down while making a fire to warm themselves out of the trees they cut down. When I was sent to New Caledonia, people claimed payment for various debts I had incurred during the Siege of Paris, and my mother had to sell the land.

When my paternal grandparents died, I had to leave my calm retreat in the Tomb. From this time until her own mother died, my mother lived in Vroncourt near the cemetery. From there she could hear the wind in the pines that shadowed the family's cherished graves. I can still see the tops of the pines, heavy with snow during the winter. Never have I seen winters so long as in the Haute-Marne, and never have I felt such cold, except in polar oceans.

Before I left the Tomb, I wrote a farewell verse and carved it in the wall of the tower. The old ruins did not take good care of my farewell very long, for not a stone of it remains today.

Farewell, my dreaming retreat in the manor.
Goodbye, my high and windy tower.
Only your old moss remains,
And I, a frail, storm-broken branch,
Shall follow the currents on.

Your swallows will circle without me
And sing summer days on the rooftop,
While I drift on, an outcast.
Won't your turret be missing its mistress
When my voice is no longer its echo?

Chapter 4

The Making of a Revolutionary

Above everything else I am taken by the Revolution. It had to be that way. The wind that blew through the ruin where I was born, the old people who brought me up, the solitude and freedom of my childhood, the legends of the Haute-Marne, the scraps of knowledge gleaned from here and there—all that opened my ear to every harmony, my spirit to every illumination, my heart to both love and hate. Everything intermingled in a single song, a single dream, a single love: the Revolution.

As far back as I can remember, the origin of my revolt against the powerful was my horror at the tortures inflicted on animals. I used to wish animals could get revenge, that the dog could bite the man who was mercilessly beating him, that the horse bleeding under the whip could throw off the man tormenting him. But mute animals always submit to their fate.

In the Haute-Marne, the brooks and the lush fields shaded with willows are filled with frogs during summer. You can hear them in the beautiful evenings, sometimes an entire choir.

The peasants cut frogs in two, leaving the front part to creep along in the sun, eyes horribly popping out, front legs trembling as they try to flee under the ground. Able neither to live nor to die, the poor beasts try to bury themselves beneath the dust or mud. In the bright sunlight their soft, enormous eyes shine with reproach.

And geese being fattened: The peasants nail a goose's webbed feet to the floor to keep it from moving around. Or horses, which men gore with bulls' horns. Animals always submit, and the more ferocious a man is toward animals, the more that man cringes before the people who dominate him.

The peasants give little animals and birds to their children for playthings. In spring on the thresholds of peasants' cottages you can see poor little birds opening their beaks to two or three-year-old urchins who stuff them innocently with dirt. They hold up fledglings by a foot to watch them flap little featherless wings trying to fly, or they drag puppies or kittens like wagons over stones and through brooks. When the beast bites the child, the father crushes it under his shoe.

When I was a child I saved many an animal. They filled up the crumbling Tomb, but it didn't matter if I added another to the menagerie. At first I traded things with other children to get the nests of nightingales or linnets, but then the children came to understand that I raised the little creatures. Children are less cruel than people think; people just don't bother to make them understand.

And then there are dogs and cats that have grown too old: I have seen them thrown live into crayfish holes. If the woman who was throwing the beasts in had fallen into the hole herself, I wouldn't have reached out my hand to pull her out.

All of this happens without anyone really thinking about it. Labor crushes the parents; their fate grips them the way their child grips an animal. All around the globe people moan at the machine they are caught in, and everywhere the strong overwhelm the weak.

The dominant idea of an entire life can come from some random impression. When I was very small, I saw a decapitated goose. I was very little, I know, because I remember Nanette holding me by the hand to cross the hall. The goose was walking about stiffly, and where its head had been its neck was a bruised and bloody wound. It was a white goose with its feathers spattered with blood, and it walked like a drunkard while its head, thrown into a corner, lay on the floor with its eyes closed.

The sight of the headless goose had many consequences. One result was that the sight of meat thereafter nauseated me until I was eight or ten, and I needed a strong will and my grandmother's arguments to overcome that nausea. The impression of the headless goose lies at the base of my pity for animals, and it also lies at the base of my horror at the death penalty. Some years after I saw the headless goose, a parricide was guillotined in a neighboring village, and at the time he was to die, the sensation of horror I felt for the man's anguish was mixed with my remembrance of the goose's torment.

The impression I had gotten from seeing the decapitated goose was kept vivid by stories of sufferings I heard at *écrègnes*. During the long winter evenings of the Haute-Marne, the women of each village met in a special house set aside for them known as the *écrègne*. In their sessions, also called *écrègnes,* they would spin and knit and tell old stories like those about the Ghost-in-Flames, who dances through the fields in his fiery robe, and gossip about what was going on in various peoples' homes.

I liked to hear those stories told against the whir of spinning wheels at the *écrègne* on evenings when Nanette and I received permission to go there. The clack of knitting needles cut through the drone with a little dry noise. And outside, the snow, the great white snow falling, stretched out over the ground like a shroud. We were supposed to return home at ten o'clock, but we always stayed late. It was a beautiful time. Old Marie

Verdet rested her knitting on her knees, and her eyes grew wide under her headdress, which came forward over her face like a roof. In her broken voice she told story after story about apparitions: about the Ghost-in-Flames, the Three Washerwomen, and the Valley of the Sorcerers. Her sister Franchette had seen it all, too, and she nodded her head approvingly. When Nanette and I had to leave, we left regretfully, skirting the walls of the cemetery, where we always saw, alas, only the snow and heard only the north wind of winter.

My evenings at the village *écrègnes* added to the feeling of revolt that I have felt time and time again. The peasants sow and harvest the grain, but they do not always have bread. One woman told me how during a bad year—that is what they call a year when the monopolists starve the country—neither she, nor her husband, nor their four children were able to eat every day. Owning only the clothes on their backs, they had nothing more to sell. Merchants who had grain gave them no more credit, not even a few oats to make a little bread, and two of their children died—from hunger, they thought.

"You have to submit," she said to me. "Everybody can't eat bread every day."

Her husband had wanted to kill the man who had refused them credit at 100 percent interest while their children were dying, but she stopped him. The two children who managed to survive went to work ultimately for the man whom her husband wanted to kill. The usurer hardly gave them any wages, but poor people, she said, "should submit to that which they cannot prevent."

Her manner was calm when she told me that story. I had gone hot-eyed with rage, and I said to her, "You should have let your husband do what he wanted to do. He was right."

I could imagine the poor little ones dying of hunger. She had made that picture of misery so distressing that I could feel it myself. I saw the husband in his torn shirt, his wooden shoes chafing his bare feet, going to beg at the evil usurer's and returning sadly over the frozen roads with nothing. I saw him shaking his fists threateningly when his little ones were lying dead on a handful of straw. I saw his wife stopping him from avenging his own children and others. I saw the two surviving children growing up with this memory, and then going off to work for that man: the cowards.

I thought that if that usurer had come into the *écrègne* at that moment I would have leaped at his throat to bite it, and I told her that. I was indignant at her believing everybody couldn't have food every day. Such stupidity bewildered me.

"You mustn't talk like that, little one," the woman said. "It makes God cry."

Have you ever seen sheep lift their throats to the knife? That woman had the mind of a ewe.

I was thinking about that little story one day at catechism, and it caused me to argue energetically for the opposite of the old proverb, Charity begins at home. The old curé (a real believer, that one) had placed a book, bound like the encyclopedia I had stolen from Big Laumont, near his hand. I confess that from the instant the curé put it down I was preoccupied by what could be inside its brown leather covers. It couldn't be a child's book. I was afraid the old curé would notice my preoccupation, and when he called on me, I was fearful of being punished, but he was calling on me only to give me the book.

It contained meditations on the Psalms of Exile, and was all I needed to give me a horror of conquerors to add to my horror of other human vampires. Reading the book, I cursed those who crush peoples as much as I cursed those who starve them, never suspecting how many times later I would see that very crime in high places.

Meanwhile, the family property was bringing in so little that neither we nor my uncle, who cultivated half of it, was succeeding in making ends meet. Many similar years would follow, I felt. People couldn't always help others, and indeed something more than charity was necessary if each person was always to have something to eat. As for the rich, I had little respect for them.

I know the full reality of heavy work on the land. I know the woes of the peasant. He is incessantly bent over land that is as harsh as a stepmother. For his labor all he gets is leftovers from his master, and he can get even less comfort from thought and dreams than we can. Heavy work bends both men and oxen over the furrows, keeping the slaughter-house for worn-out beasts and the beggar's sack for worn-out humans.

The *land*. That word is at the very bottom of my life. It was in the thick, illustrated Roman history from which my whole family on both sides had learned how to read. My grandmother had taught me to read from it, pointing out the letters with her large knitting needle. Reared in the country, I understood the agrarian revolts of old Rome, and I shed many tears on the pages of that book. The death of the Greeks oppressed me then as much as the gallows of Russia did later.

How misleading are the *Georgics* and *Eclogues* about the happiness of the fields. The descriptions of nature are true, but the description of the happiness of workers in the fields is a lie. People who know no better gaze at the flowers of the fields and the beautiful fresh grass and believe that the children who watch over the livestock play there. The little ones want grass only to stretch out in and sleep a little at noon. The shadow of the woods, the yellowing crops that the wind moves like waves—the peasant is too tired to find them beautiful. His work is heavy, his day is long, but he resigns himself, he always resigns himself, for his will is broken. Man is overworked like a beast. He is half dead and works for his exploiter without thinking. No peasants get rich by working the land; they only make money for people who already have too much.

Many men have told me, in words that echoed what the woman told me at the *écrègne:* "You must not say that, little one. It offends God." That's what they said to me when I told them that everyone has a right to everything there is on earth.

My pity for everything that suffers—more perhaps for the silent beast than for man—went far, and my revolt against social inequalities went still further. It grew, and it has continued to grow, through the battles and across the carnage. It dominates my grief, and it dominates my life. There was no way that I could have stopped myself from throwing my life to the Revolution.

I have often been accused of having more solicitude for animals than for people. It is certainly true that a sadness takes hold of me when men must destroy a beast to whom mercy cannot be shown without endangering others. You hold in your hands a being that wishes to live.

Once, near where I lived, on the hill down which vineyards sloped, men had surrounded a poor she-wolf that howled as she tried to hide her little ones within her paws. I begged mercy for her, but naturally it wasn't granted.

The mercy that as a child I asked for the wolf, I wouldn't ask now for the men who behave worse than wolves toward the human race. Whatever the pity that wrings the heart, harmful beings must disappear. At the death of those who, like the Russian czars, represent the slavery and death of a nation, I would now have no more emotion than I would have about removing a dangerous trap from the road. Such persons can be struck down without remorse. If the opportunity arose, I would always feel that way, as I did yesterday, as I will tomorrow.

I was accused of allowing my concern for animals to outweigh the problems of humans at the Perronnet barricade at Neuilly during the Commune, when I ran to help a cat in peril. I did that, yes, but I did not abandon my duty. The unfortunate beast was crouched in a corner that was being scoured by shells, and it was crying out like a human being. I went to find him, and it didn't take a minute. I put him more or less in safety, and later someone even picked him up.

Another incident happened more recently. Some mice had appeared in my cell at Clermont. I had a pile of wool coverings my mother and friends had sent me, and I immediately used them to stuff up all the mouseholes. From behind one of my makeshift plugs during the night, however, I heard a poor little cry, a cry so plaintive that it would have taken a heart of stone not to open up the blocked hole. So I did, and the beast came out.

The mouse was either imprudent or a genius in knowing how to judge her world. From that moment on she came boldly up on my bed, carrying morsels of bread. She made fun of the gestures I made to get her to leave, and she used the underside of my pillow as a pantry and even worse.

She wasn't in my cell when I was taken away, so I wasn't able to put her in my pocket. I asked my neighbors in nearby cells to care for her, but I don't know what happened to the poor beast.

Why should I be so sad over brutes, when reasoning beings are so unhappy? The answer is that everything fits together, from the bird whose brood is crushed to the humans whose nests are destroyed by war. The beast dies of hunger in his hole; man dies of it far away from his home. A beast's heart is like a human heart, its brain like a human brain. It feels and understands. The heat and spark will always rise up. It can't be crushed out.

Even in a gutter like a laboratory, a beast is sensitive both to caresses and to brutalities. More often it feels brutalities. People find it interesting to torture a poor animal to study mechanisms which are already well known and which fresh tortures cannot make known any better, because the pain being inflicted causes the animal's organs to function abnormally. When one of its sides is dug into, someone turns it over to dig into the other. Sometimes, in spite of the bonds that immobilize it, the animal in its pain moves the delicate flesh on which someone is working. Then a threat or a blow teaches it that man is the king of animals. I have heard that during an eloquent demonstration a professor stuck his scalpel into the living animal as he would have into a pincushion, because he couldn't gesture holding the scalpel in his hand. The animal was already being sacrificed, so additional pain made little difference. At Alfort, people did sixty-some operations on the same horse, operations that did no good, but made the beast suffer as it stood there trembling on its bloody hooves with their torn-off shoes.

All this useless suffering perpetrated in the name of science must end. It is as barren as the blood of the little children whose throats were cut by Gilles de Retz and other madmen at the beginning of modern chemistry. Ultimately, a science, not gold, came out of their crucibles and their search for the philosopher's stone, but science came from the nature of the elements and not from the cruelties of experimenters.

New wonders will come from science, and change must come. Time raises up volcanoes under old continents, and time allows new feelings to grow. Soon there will be neither cruelty nor exploitation, and science will provide all humanity with enough food, with nourishing food.

I dream of the time when science will give everyone enough to eat. Instead of the putrefied flesh which we are accustomed to eating, perhaps science will give us chemical mixtures containing more iron and nutrients than the blood and meat we now absorb. The first bite might not flatter the palate as much as the food we now eat, but it will not be trichinated or rotten, and it will build stronger and purer bodies for men weakened by generations of famine or the excesses of their ancestors.

With the abundance of nourishing food in that future world, there must be art, too. In that coming era, the arts will be for everyone. The power of harmonious colors, the grandeur of sculpted marble—they will belong to the entire human race. Genius will be developed, not snuffed out. Ignorance has done enough harm. The privilege of knowledge is worse than the privilege of wealth. The arts are a part of human rights, and everybody needs them.

Neither music, nor marble, nor color, can by itself proclaim the Marseillaise of the new world. Who will sing out the Marseillaise of art? Who will tell of the thirst for knowledge, of the ecstasy of musical harmonies, of marble made flesh, of canvas palpitating like life? Art, like science and liberty, must be no less available than food.

Everyone must take up a torch to let the coming era walk in light. Art for all! Science for all! Bread for all!

Chapter 5

Schoolmistress in the Haute-Marne

When my grandparents died and I had to leave the Tomb, I began to prepare for my examinations as a schoolmistress because I wanted to make my mother happy. There was little money, but the arrangements for my legal protection were complex. My mother served as one guardian and M. Voisin, a former magistrate, was another, just as if they were administering a fortune. The attorney, Maître Girault, notary at Bourmont, served as surrogate of the court. People said that all this wasn't enough to keep me from immediately wasting the eight or ten thousand francs in land that I had inherited.

For the moment, however, I devoted myself to my education. Except for three months at Lagny in 1851, my whole higher education came from the teacher-training course under Mmes Beths and Royer at Chaumont.

I see Chaumont now as it was then. I see the Boulingrin, the street of Choignes with its sinister memories, for that was where the executioner lived. I see the viaduct crossing the whole valley of the Ecoliers. Most of all, I see Sucot's bookstore, where first as a student and then as a schoolmistress I always had debts. I see the large curly head of M. Sucot looking out of the window in which he displayed his fanciest stationery, newest books, and latest musical scores from Paris. As a child I had been dazzled when I looked at the bookstore in Bourmont, and certain displays of books still affect me.

I see Chaumont, and the old boarding house where I lodged, and my teachers, and my friends, with whom I played practical jokes on nasty people. With Clara, one of my friends, I remember causing a great commotion at the homes of people who were bullying republicans. On the doors of their houses, we made a mark—a mysterious mark, they said—with red chalk. Some people saw the mark as an egalitarian triangle (a little elongated); others saw an unknown instrument of torture; those who were disinterested in the affair saw a big donkey's ear. The last were right.

The three months at Lagny came when my mother and I visited relatives in the area. We stayed with my uncle, who was disturbed by my constant writing, for he feared I would desert the teacher's examination to write poetry. To forestall this, he put me in Mme Duval's private boarding school at Lagny, where his own daughter had been educated, and I stayed there about three months.

At Mme Duval's, as at my school in Chaumont, everybody lived for books. The outside world stopped at the threshold, and I concentrated all my enthusiasm on the crumbs and bits of science I was reading about.

The lack of time! You learn just enough to make you thirsty for the rest, and there is never time for the rest. Before 1871 that was the torture of every schoolmistress's life. Before getting her diploma she was faced with a program of study that kept growing boundlessly, and after getting her diploma she saw that she knew nothing. To be sure, that predicament was nothing new, and it was shared. All of us schoolmistresses were in the same position. The living springs where you could quench your thirst for knowledge were not for those who had to fight for existence.

At my boarding house at Chaumont I met my friend Julie. Sometimes the destinies of different persons intertwine for a time and then take opposite courses. Julie and I were both schoolmistresses, first in the Haute-Marne and then in Paris, where we stayed together while we were assistant schoolmistresses at Mme Vollier's.

In Paris Julie kept busy at her studies, and the hatred I felt for Napoleon's Empire left her cold. It was music and poetry that swept her away. Then the great events of 1870–71 came and Julie remained a stranger to them. Our paths diverged completely. But before those events, during our vacation, we had gone into the deep woods, and under the oak tree traditional for such oaths we had sworn eternal friendship for each other. Neither of us really broke that oath. Events pulled us apart.

When I took my diploma at the end of 1852, I would have liked to have taught in Paris and worked as a schoolmistress while I continued my studies. Many people did just that. But at the time I did not want to be separated from my mother, and I taught in the Haute-Marne so I could live near her and my grandmother Marguerite. That is why I began my career, in January 1853, as a schoolmistress at Audeloncourt.

The road from Chaumont to Audeloncourt is long. It turns and spirals around Mont Chauve, comes down the slopes by the easiest descents possible, and then shoots forward, straightening out its bends through villages whose houses still have thatched roofs. Then the road comes to the Sueur Woods, where, under the low branches of twisted apple trees, sits the collapsed ruin of a little inn. The old people of the area claim that the throats of travelers used to be slit in that inn. Only a little over a century ago those who entered that inn rarely left it.

Travelers got on and off the coach that stopped at each relay station from Chaumont to Audeloncourt. Some were dressed in ordinary blue work shirts with cherrywood snuff boxes in their pockets, and they carried sticks hanging from their wrists by little leather straps. Others were dressed in their very best, clothes worn so rarely that folds from the cupboards where they had been packed were traced on them as if a pressing iron had done it.

Part of my maternal family lived in Audeloncourt. My maternal great-uncles—Simon, Michel, and Francis, who was called Uncle Franc-fort—lived there. They were tall, handsome old men, with strong shoulders, powerful judgments, and simple hearts. They all had red hair with no silver threads in it, even as old as they were when I began teaching. They had quick minds and, like my mother's brothers, they had somehow learned a great mass of information and spoke well.

Many years ago some ancestor had bought an entire library by the kilogram. There were old texts illustrated with Homer calling down the clouds on his characters; old chronicles from which legends flew so strongly that my great-uncles had adopted some of them; volumes of out-of-date science; novels of by-gone days—all published under the king's censorship. I heard all of those books spoken of so enthusiastically that I deeply regretted the pages that were missing from some books, and the other books that had been lost completely.

The women of Audeloncourt used to read my great-uncles' novels in their late-night *écrègnes*. The reader of the evening would lick her thumb to turn the pages while her gentle eyes dropped tears over the misfortunes of the heroes. Some people read aloud so well that they charmed their listeners, and the *écrègne* lasted until midnight. Then, still trembling from the emotional impact of the story, some of the women would walk the others back to their homes. The snow spread over everything. The hoarfrost, like flowers in May, covered the branches. The last women, the ones who lived farthest away, ran through the snow to their houses while their friends yelled after them to reassure them.

Perhaps my uncles' library also gave my maternal family the habit of studying alone, for none of them was rich enough to afford any formal education. My mother's brother, Uncle Georges, had an astounding historical erudition. Uncle Michael had a passion for mechanical things, which I abused when I was a child, making him descend to the construction of a little chariot and a thousand other devices.

I loved my mother's brothers a great deal, and I imprudently called them Georges and Fanfan until one day when my grandmother told me it was bad to treat one's elders with so little respect. I had a third uncle who died in Africa many years ago. He had been in military service and either from that experience or from books had gotten a taste for travel. He also had a sound appreciation of many things—above all, discipline, which provided him with many reflections that he didn't think I was capable of understanding. Anarchy, I believe, germinates in the heart of all discipline.

My school in Audeloncourt, which I opened in January 1853, was classed as a Free School, because for it to become a communal school I would have had to have taken an oath to support the Empire. I was optimistic; I even nourished the illusion of making a happy future for my mother. But a month's charge for a student could only be one franc, which was a relatively large sum for farm-workers. Because I wasn't old enough to meet the age requirement for keeping boarders, I was obliged to put my students from other villages into the homes of my Audeloncourt pupils. Still, in spite of accusations some idiots made about that and about my political opinions, my class went very well because I taught with passion. I had the zeal of the very young.

When we were in my classroom at Audeloncourt we could hear the incessant noise of water. During the summer a brook flowed downhill murmuring to the listener. In the winter, the brook became a furious torrent. Who listens to it now? Who listens from the dark school where I was surrounded by attentive students? Students are always attentive in the villages, where no harsh distractions come from outside.

I can still call all my students by name, from Little Rose, whom we called Little Mole because of her lustrous black hair, to Big Rose, who is a schoolmistress herself now. Claire also became a schoolmistress. Eudoxie died in my arms during an epidemic. There was Tall Estelle who looked like a vivacious shepherdess of Floridan, and poor Aricie, thin, lame, weak, who could absorb a whole textbook in a few days. And Zélie, the sister of the public courier of Clefmont, I loved doubly because of her vivid imagination and because she had the same name as a friend of mine at Vroncourt, whom I mourned for a long time. The public courier and his sister were orphans. He was the eldest of the family, and although he was very young, he filled the place of their dead parents and had wanted his sister to attend my school. In my trips between Audeloncourt and Chaumont, he and I used to talk of all sorts of things, the way people do who read a great deal.

In my class at Audeloncourt, we sang the Marseillaise before the morning's study began and after study ended in the evening. The stanza especially for children:

> We'll take over this course
> When our elders are no longer here

was sung kneeling; one of the youngest, the little brunette Rose, sang it solo. When we picked up the chorus again, the children and I often had tears flooding from our eyes.

I found that same feeling again at Nouméa during the last year of my exile in New Caledonia. It was July 14, Bastille Day. At this period I was in charge of teaching drawing and singing in the girls' schools in the city. M. Simon, who was the interim mayor, wanted the children to stand in the open bandstand in the Place des Cocotiers and sing the Marseillaise between the two customary evening cannon shots. Night had fallen suddenly. In tropical areas like New Caledonia there is neither dusk nor dawn. The palm trees were rustling gently, swayed by the evening breeze. The lanterns lit the bandstand a little, but left the square in shadow. We felt the pressure of the crowd—a black and white crowd. In front of the bandstand was the military band. Mme Penand, the first lay schoolmistress who had come to the colony, was standing near me, as was an artilleryman who was going to sing with us. Arranged in a circle the children surrounded us.

After the first cannon shot such a silence fell that our hearts stopped beating. I felt our voices soaring into this silence, and it seemed as if we were being carried off on wings. The penetrating voices of the children's choir and the thunder of the brass instruments between the stanzas thrilled us beyond belief. That song had led our fathers; it was the living Marseillaise and we loved it.

Upon my return from New Caledonia, I found the sacred hymn was being used in all sorts of public spectacles. It had not really recovered from the mire through which the last days of the Empire had dragged it, and wounded once again, the Marseillaise was dead for us.

At Audeloncourt on Sundays, small black wooden shoes clicked hurriedly toward the door of the church, in order to get out by the time the priest intoned "Domine, salvum fac Napoleonem." I had told the children that it was sacrilegious to take part in a prayer for that man. The little black wooden shoes ran hurriedly out of the church, making a gentle, dry noise like hail, the same little dry noise that the bullets made on 22 January 1871, raining down from the windows of the Hôtel de Ville upon the unarmed crowd. Later, I heard the sound of wooden shoes again. Those were on the tired feet of the women prisoners at Auberive, and they clumped sadly as the woman shuffled around the prison.

In those years when I was teaching in the Haute-Marne, I often thought of going to Paris. Paris, of which I had only an imperfect notion and of which I had only glimpsed the marvels that people spoke about, attracted me. Only there could people fight the Empire, and Paris called so strongly that a person could feel its magnetism.

The self-proclaimed defenders of law and order around Audeloncourt who deigned to bother about me at all, called me a "red," meaning a republican, and they accused me of wanting to go to Paris. I still don't see why my wanting to go there should have upset them. If my opinions bothered them so much, they should have been happy to see me go.

Those denunciations did trouble my mother. They also got me a good trip to Chaumont, the capital of the Haute-Marne. The business there was supposed to occupy me for two days, but it ended as soon as I arrived. I went to the home of the rector of the departmental academy, M. Fayet, and there I sat on his hearth as I used to sit talking to my grandparents at the Tomb. I explained my actions in the light of the accusations made against me. I said people claimed that I wanted to go to Paris and that I was a republican. Both claims, I admitted, were perfectly true. In speaking of my studies, of the passion that called me to Paris, and of the Republic, I opened my heart.

The rector looked at me in silence a long time before answering. His wife, who took my side, smiled, while their pet doves flew around the room, which was full of sunlight and smelled like spring and like morning the entire day. The rector ended the interview by chiding me gently.

I drove back from Chaumont with the public courier, who was the brother of my student Zélie. Never did we have a more serious conversation than we had on that drive. In my pocket I had a piece of red chalk similar to that with which Clara and I had drawn donkeys' ears on the doors of Bonapartists in Chaumont. On the trip I used it to make the same drawing on the back of a traveler who was trying to praise Bonaparte. I also made him tremble when I said: "The Republic must come. We are many, and we are strong."

Another time, the accusations against me were of a different nature. From Audeloncourt I sent verses to Victor Hugo. My mother and I had seen him in the summer of 1851. Later, he answered the letters I wrote to him from my exile, as he had sent letters from Paris to my nest in Vroncourt and to my boarding house at Chaumont. I also sent a few articles to the Chaumont newspaper. I still have a few fragments of those articles, which are less fragile than the cherished hands that saved them for me. One of my articles contained a passage that got me accused of insulting His Majesty, the Emperor. That accusation was correct, of course, and could have been made on the basis of other pieces I wrote at the time.

The article was a history of the martyrs and began:

> Domitian was ruling. He had banished . . . philosophers and scholars from Rome, increased the salary of the praetorians, reestablished the Capitoline games, and everybody therefore adored the merciful emperor while they waited for others to stab him. . . .
> We are in Rome in the year 97 A.D.

The prefect summoned me to his office. There he told me I had insulted His Majesty, the Emperor, by comparing him to Domitian and that if I were not so young he would have the right to send me to the prison colony at Cayenne.

I answered that anyone who saw M. Bonaparte in the portrait I had painted insulted him just as much as I was accused of doing, but that it was indeed M. Bonaparte that I had in mind. I added that, as for

Cayenne, I would be perfectly happy to set up an educational establishment there, and since I could not afford to pay for the expense of the trip myself, it would be very nice if the state sent me there. Things went no further.

Some time after this interview a credulous man wanted to ask the prefect for some favor; what, I'm not sure. He came to me saying that since I had been at the prefect's, I could recommend him there. In vain I tried to tell him I had been called to the prefecture only to be accused and threatened with Cayenne, and that my recommendation would be worth very little. The good man wouldn't give up, so in the end I wrote him a letter of recommendation that read, more or less:

> Monsieur le préfet,
>   The person to whom you were kind enough to promise a trip to Cayenne is being tormented to give a letter of recommendation to you.
>   I have not been able to make this man understand that this would be the way to have him kicked out of your office. He is as stubborn as a donkey.
>   Let him not learn to his sorrow that I was correct in my reluctance to write a letter for him.
>   I beg you, dear sir, not to forget the trip you spoke to me about.

After he had made his expedition to Chaumont, the man came up to me. I confess I was already laughing at the tale of woe he was going to tell me, when to my great surprise he said: "I knew it. You're lucky for me. I got what I requested." He, not I, was lucky.

My dear friend Julie taught nearby at Millières, and two institutions with no resources were barely able to subsist near each other. The obvious thing was for us to get together, which we did at Millières. Julie and I used to sing together in the spring evenings with a piano serving as an organ. At that time she had a voice like the forest nightingales.

But always I dreamed of Paris. Throughout these years in the Haute-Marne, Paris called me ever more strongly, for in Paris I would be at the heart of affairs. In 1855 or 1856 I finally decided that there was no alternative to my going there.

Chapter 6

Schoolmistress in Paris

When I left the Haute-Marne to become a schoolmistress in Paris, I had to leave my mother and grandmother behind. Being separated from them made me suffer deeply, but I hadn't yet given up the hope of making a happy future for them, and I held tightly to that illusion.

I became a teacher in Mme Vollier's school at 14, rue du Château-d'Eau in Montmartre. From the time I went to Paris until Mme Vollier died in my own school four years before the Siege, we never left each other. Her portrait is among my most precious souvenirs that my mother preserved carefully for me—half-faded portraits, worm-eaten books, bunches of yew and pine, and withered red carnations and white lilies. Today those souvenirs also include the white roses with drops of blood on the petals which I sent my mother from Clermont.

I see the pupils at the rue du Château-d'Eau again in groups. There were the seniors, two or three of whom were very tall—Léonie, Aline, Léopoldine. There were the blondes, two of whom had wide foreheads and steel-blue eyes—Héloïse and Gabrielle. There was a group of pale children: Josephine, little Noël, Marie. And others so brown they were black: Elisa, who had the sharp features of someone from the Midi; little Julie, whose voice was loud even though it wasn't beautiful yet; Elisa, who played her little piece in a prize competition at a younger age than even Mozart had done. And so many more. What has become of them?

Julie joined me as a teacher at the school, and Mme Vollier was as affectionate as a mother. She even found ways to dress Julie and me stylishly. I remember hats made of white crepe with bouquets of daisies, a dress of black silk, and mantelets of lace. Pawn shops and secondhand stores helped, and we were fitted out for much less money than people would have believed.

While Julie and I were at Mme Vollier's we always dressed alike and because both of us were tall and brunette, people used to think we were sisters. In 1871, when the police took down detailed information about me, I had to explain that misconception.

At this time, two of my cousins were also assistant schoolmistresses, one in the Puteaux suburb of Paris, the other at La Chapelle. We all had about the same income, the little that teaching earned in this period. That lack of money didn't depress us, for we realized that this poor income would continue under the regime of His Majesty Napoleon III as it had under his predecessors. There is no profession in which people have less money, and no trade in which people know so well how to do without it. Some women of letters among our friends suffered far more. We were all a little bohemian, even Mme Vollier. As much as any woman who lives on her wages, and in spite of her age, she knew how to laugh at the situation.

We used to joke about our troubles when we gathered every Thursday evening and drank cups of steaming coffee. I kept from telling my mother that I had great difficulty making my income equal my expenditures, however restrained they were.

Recognizing that we wouldn't earn anything from teaching, but not wishing to publicize that fact, Mme Vollier, Julie, and I drew up a formal partnership. I was able to send my mother the act of partnership, executed in good and proper form, which stopped people from saying things to her like: "Your daughter will never earn anything"; or, "She spends everything and you shouldn't send her any more"; or, "A cook earns ten times more than your daughter does." We knew quite well that teaching paid almost nothing, but any other trade open to women offered less fulfillment when money wasn't the only objective. Are women's professions any better today? Men's aren't.

My own dear mother found a way to send me a little money occasionally, which unhappily for my wardrobe I spent on books and music. Because of the act of partnership, she was entirely at ease about my financial position. The lamentations that imbeciles made about how wrong she had been in not forcing me to marry had ceased.

I continued to reject all thought of marriage. There are enough tortured women in the world without my becoming another one. True, I can think like this since those people who asked to marry me, although they are as dear to me as brothers, would be equally impossible as husbands. Why I feel this I truthfully don't know. Like all women, I set my sights very high, and I believed in remaining free for the coming Revolution. Anyway, I have always looked upon marriage without love as a kind of prostitution.

After the partnership there was nothing those who had been taunting my mother could say. I was a partner in a day school in Paris, even if it was less grand than they assumed. None of us was lazy, but educational establishments crowded the neighborhood, and our rent was very high. In the evening after classes we gave lessons to supplement our income. Even Mme Vollier, although she was very old, gave some. And to a lesser degree she told her sons the same lies I had told my mother.

"If your daughter earns so much money," people asked my mother, "why doesn't she ever send you any presents?" Moreover, I hadn't been able to go see her during our vacation. We had only a week's vacation a year in our day schools, because otherwise we would have lost our students. Parents who had to look after their children only when they weren't in class couldn't or wouldn't take complete charge of them for a vacation of more than eight or ten days each year. Then, too, because we were giving private lessons, we couldn't get away for long. Besides, how could we have made enough money to pay the terrible rent if there had been no income for a month?

My mother came to Paris to see the situation for herself. A warm friendship sprang up between her and Mme Vollier, who resembled my grandmother. The two of them used to say bad things about me, but what a good two weeks we spent during my mother's first visit, with one exception.

It was the evening of my mother's arrival, and the three of us were dining together. I was so happy that it seemed inevitable that this happiness would be disturbed. I was right. A great lout of a man with shifty eyes came to the door unexpectedly and demanded payment for a promissory note I had completely forgotten about. He came just at the moment when I was speaking warmly to my mother—not to deceive her but to reassure her—about a resolution I had made not to spend everything I had for books. The obvious silence of Mme Vollier while I was saying this didn't presage anything good, and the intrusion of that jackass showed in the most absolute possible way that I was lying. Mme Vollier, then, to put my mother at ease, took part of the rent money that her sons had just finished getting together and gave it to the man. It was just enough to pay off the note. My mother sent me the sum when she returned to Vroncourt, and she gently drew my attention to how many deprivations my purchasing books had already caused her. I didn't buy any more books for a long time, but it was hard to resist, for there were so many that tempted me and to me books were everything.

Except for being unhappy over the struggle for existence, I have never been unhappy as a teacher. When we played games during recess, I had a magnificent time with the older students. We extemporized dramas that we performed for the younger children. Through everything I stayed young.

One Sunday, alone at Mme Vollier's, I was sitting at the piano trying to write some music that I knew would never see the light of day. It was no less than an opera, *The Dream of the Witches' Sabbath*. I knew it would never be presented, and I had resigned myself to that fact bravely. It is impossible to find publishers when you're unknown, and you can't be known until you find a publisher. You don't waste your time dragging your manuscripts into waiting rooms. You continue your regular trade, whatever it is. If you don't have a trade, I, at least, would rather become a ragpicker than go looking for recommendations to influence publishers. I even feel a kind of pleasure in throwing stanzas and motifs and sketches into the wind.

The plot I had written for *The Dream of the Witches' Sabbath* was a simple one. After the destruction of all life on our planet, hell was established here, where things were very suitable. In the first act, the end of life has already been caused by a geological revolution. The stage looks like a lunar landscape. Satan is seated on top of a Parisian building whose base rests in molten lava.

The basis of all the action is the love that Satan and the other main character, Don Juan, have for a druidess. Their love for her kindles an infernal war. Every person in history, poetry, or legend who ever inspired me had a role to suit his character in my drama.

The end comes when the globe itself crumbles. All the spirits are absorbed in the forces of nature, whose chorus is heard in a night crossed by flashes of lightning. The general clamor of the orchestra diminishes little by little. First one instrument, then another, becomes silent. Finally nothing is left but a chorus of harps, and one after the other they too fall silent. Then only one remains, and it fades in a pianissimo sweeter than water falling on leaves. At last these final notes also fade away, and all is silent.

I scored this work for every instrument possible, from cannon to harmonicas, lyres, flutes, bugles, and guitars. A choir of devils speaks wordlessly onstage with violins, twenty of them. To hold this monstrous orchestra you'd need a valley in the mountains or some bay in the New World.

As I was working at the piano that Sunday on the music for the scene of the infernal hunt, someone rang the doorbell. It was an old Jewess, the grandmother of one of my pupils. She stood as straight as the ghost of Don Juan's commander, and she was very beautiful. Her face looked as if it had been carved from marble. She must have been listening to me outside.

"Is it really you," she asked, "who is responsible for that savagery I have been hearing?"

"Yes," I answered. "It is I."

"I'm sure you wouldn't dare to continue those horrors in front of me," she said. "To punish you, I want to hear the rest."

Because of that challenge I started *The Dream of the Witches' Sabbath* over. The wild motifs made her indignant, but I kept going. She wasn't so hard on several parts, and she liked the love songs. She liked the "Ballad of the Skeleton."

Lady of the green turrets
Who sings to the evening stars,
Come down and open up my heart.
White are my hands before you
And faithful my love. Come:
Then I will have light
In my eyeless sockets
And I will see
The tournament's queen of beauty.

At the end of the ballad the girl, of course, has fallen in love with the skeleton, and she follows him off into the unknown. They go off into a valley of solitude to the accompaniment of only a lute solo.

The old lady also deigned to approve my "Lay of the Troubadour":

The bird was singing
As it shivered
Beneath the falling leaves.
And in the wind,
The soul took wing,
And was crying,
Crying.

I went on through the finale, and after my grotesque imitation on the piano of the last fading notes of the last harp, the Jewess looked at me with amazament.

"Poor girl," she said. "Those monstrosities really are yours."

I didn't answer.

"The most unfortunate thing about it is that there are some good parts there."

"If there weren't any good parts," I said, "I wouldn't be stupid enough to work on it."

"You know very well," she said, "that you have to be either rich or famous to indulge in things like that."

"I'm not simply indulging myself. I intend to stay on here as a teacher, and as proof I shall leave this unproducible piece just the way it is now. It really is a dream, you know, whether it is about covens or real life, and I will throw it away as I have thrown away other dreams."

She took my hand. Hers was cold.

"Your heart," she said. "Where will you throw it?"

"To the Revolution," I said.

She sat down at the piano and her icy hands glided over the keys. She began to play some invocation to the God of Israel. In it you could feel the desert and the calm of death, and this calm went straight to my heart. Sometime later this lady took me to a synagogue, where the strangeness of the rites and rhythms, a sort of Kyrie in a majestic place, took hold of me. Seeing the tears in my eyes, she believed I had been touched by the grace of Jehovah.

"No," I told her. "It's just that an impression has taken hold of me. Perhaps everything is that way."

I wrote out part of the score for *The Dream of the Witches' Sabbath* to give to my friend Charles de Sivry. From laziness I substituted a gradual diminuendo for the final catastrophe, which saved me about ten leaves. It's so boring to write out a fair copy.

None of the part where the orchestra fades out and ends on the last harp note appeared worth any great effort. The Revolution was rising, so what good were dramas? The true drama was in the streets, so what good were orchestras? We had cannon.

Today the room where I lived in Montmartre is inhabited by people whom I do not know, but like the house near the cemetery at Vroncourt, I like to let my memory rest on it for an instant. It has been so very long.

The last time I saw Vroncourt was during the vacation of 1865. I went there with Mme Eudes, then Victorine Louvet. She was very young then, perhaps sixteen or seventeen years old, and she was preparing for her teacher's examination.

During the illness from which she died so young, after her return from exile, Victorine still talked to me about that autumn vacation in Vroncourt. We had gone together into the woods, and I had shown her the oak tree where oaths were exchanged. The Tomb was still standing then, and I took her to see that, too. She went with my mother into the vineyard, which was full of young trees my mother had planted. One evening, as we went through the forest from Thol to Clefmont, going to the home of "Uncle" Marchal, an old forester who had just married off his daughter, the regular steps and luminous eyes of a wolf followed us the whole way. That gave me the setting for "The Legend of the Oak."

The Legend of the Oak

1.

Beneath the oak the priestess stands,
Vines of verbena entwining her hair,
Silence seizes the shadowed forest,
Except for the bards and the mystical priests,
   Spreading their tools for the rite.

The great songs end; the air holds their echo.
Wind-blown branches strum the strings of a lute.
From goblets of oak the white bull's blood pours,
But the sacrificed beast cries out in his pain,
   A sinister omen.

The priestess beseeches the fates and hears
The rumbling storm demand she give
A human sacrifice. He comes
To let his blood be poured on the earth,
   Let out of his heart with a golden scythe.

His death-glow lighting the purpling sky,
He waits the ennobling martyr's death.
She strikes his heart with her golden scythe
And trembling, strikes herself, to fall
   Piercing her heart again.

2.

Fierce, proud men of Gaul long past
Wore over their hearts a talisman.
The furze that blooms above their bones
Allows them to wear their symbol still.

That was the time when every slave
Rose against bloody Caesar's Rome.
That was the time when Gaul was brave
And gathered home her scattered sons.

Proud and ferocious great grand-sires,
How long and heavy is your sleep!
O Fathers, omens still occur today,
And your red blood flows in our veins.

You who arm yourselves, why live?
Liberty's love is stronger than death.
A person must seek for freedom's joy.
Happy are those who seize the chance!

Marriage fetters a hundredfold;
It gives new slaves to the tyranny
Of Tiberius with bloody eyes.
No, we'll not be slaves in his games.

3.

My friends, beneath the oak is good.
Regardless, oaks keep oaths once sworn,
An oath of love, an oath of hate,
Sealed with blood on the mistletoe.

That vacation in the autumn of 1865 should have lasted forever. My
mother's and grandmother's joy in seeing me again was as great as my
own, but it was over far too soon. When Victorine and I left Vroncourt
and those two women, I didn't dare to turn my head, for my heart was
breaking. I was never to see my grandmother Marguerite again. But it
was the moment when the struggle against the Empire was intensifying
and each person kept his place, as small as it was.

I am afraid to dwell too long on this first period of my life, the days of
calm with tormenting dreams. I have described puerile and childish
things; that is the way of every person's earlier years, and sometimes it
lasts throughout whole lives. As I continue the narrative I will return to
moments and events from these early times, drawn by some association
or other; sometimes the pen, like spoken words, rushes off pursuing its
own goal.

Chapter 7

The Decaying Empire

The city of Paris condemned our school building on the rue du Château-d'Eau. Mme Vollier hoped in vain that after its demolition we would get an indemnity which would let us establish a day school in the suburbs. Julie had received a small sum from her family, and she struck out on her own. Relinquishing her share in the partnership to us, she bought a day school in faubourg St. Antoine; I chose not to go with her, but on holidays we got together, and on Thursday evenings I gave music lessons at her school.

My mother sold all her remaining land except the vineyard to give me enough money to buy a day school in Montmartre. The poor woman, how little she got back for that money, and what sacrifices she and Grandmother imposed on themselves to raise it! Mme Vollier and I lived in the day school. Her sons gave her an annuity, and gradually the number of our pupils increased, so that for schoolmistresses we were nearly comfortable. What plans we made. Those were good times, when my grandmother was still living, and I continually got good news about her and my mother. For a few brief years, joy filled my heart.

But then Mme Vollier died. One evening Julie and Adèle Esquiros had come over to dine with us. It was a holiday, and all four of us were very warm in our little room high up. We spoke gaily, especially Mme Vollier. I had never seen her so cheerful. She had just received her pension, so we were momentarily rich, and we were even talking about sending a little gift to the Haute-Marne. Julie had brought something to eat from the country, and Adèle was responsible for some dainties.

On the open piano, the fat, black cat paced back and forth on the keys, listening to the tune which his paws produced. His head was raised, and earlier he had lapped up a whole bowl of coffee cream.

I told the others how, the day before, I had pasted a republican poster on the back of a policeman. I had been holding the poster, and there was nowhere else to put it.

Mme Vollier told us that, in the best interests of the household, she had collected all the keys and put them in her pocket. She made them clink in her pocket with the same smile in her eyes I used to see in my grandmother's and that I had seen so many times in my mother's when she snatched something back from my little larcenies.

Our friends applauded Mme Vollier, and we laughed still more when, full of remorse, I gave her back the purse I had stolen from the chest of drawers that morning. Almost nothing was missing from it. In the midst of all this happiness some kind of terrible grief took hold of me. We were so happy it couldn't last, but I did my best to try to ignore that foreboding.

Our friends left fairly late, and I walked with them as far as the omnibus on the rue Marcadet. The night was black and sad, and in this darkness a dog was howling. As I was returning, he began to follow me. It was chance that put this sinister beast on my track; he was an evil portent.

When I got back to school I was careful to avoid letting Mme Vollier see the sadness sweeping over me. She was still gay, but not for long. That night she had her second stroke.

Her portrait is near my bed, opposite a bouquet of red carnations. Her sons gave me a share of memorabilia as if I were their sister. After her death a great sadness forced its way into my heart, but there was no time to indulge my suffering. The Empire became more threatening as it neared its end, and we became more determined.

I kept my school going. Mlle Caroline L'Homme, the first schoolmistress who had established herself in Montmartre, and who had, she rightly claimed, taught the whole neighborhood to read, had become sick and old. She still had a few pupils, and one day she brought them to me and established herself in my school. She was exhausted.

She was like one of the legends of the North. She appeared to be one of the Norns, so quietly did she walk. Pale, her long white hair fastened by a large needle, she exhaled a spirit of something prophetic and fateful. There was no person more charming than Mlle L'Homme. She was so sweet and at the same time so proud, and now she too is dead.

Then my grandmother died. My poor mother had so few peaceful days. Broken by the death of her mother, she came to Montmartre, but when she came the Revolution was imminent, so I left her alone during many long evenings. Afterwards it was days, then months, then years. Can the mothers of revolutionaries be happy? I loved her so much that I will be happy only when I go to meet her in the earth where we shall sleep.

Of all the schoolmistresses I have known, one of the most keen to collect all of the details of science was Mlle Poulin in Montmartre. Although her health had been undermined by consumption for a long time, she no longer felt it. She kept busy piling up the greatest amount of knowledge possible so that she could take it with her to her grave. At the very end of the Empire, Mlle Poulin and I united our two schools into a new school at 24, rue Houdon. Mlle Poulin lived for only a brief time, and by coincidence I saw her tomb one last time at the climax of the fighting in May 1871.

I had met Mlle Poulin at the rue Hautefeuille. Many of us schoolmistresses continued our educations at the center where various activities took place. We had free courses in elementary teaching, professional courses, readings to mothers of families, and a night course for young people who had to work. I taught a great number of those poor children there. Young as they were they had to work all day, and if it hadn't been for the center on the rue Hautefeuille, they would never have been in a class. Instruction continued up to ten o'clock at night, and when I got out even the bookstores were closed. Under the Empire those women who were either young teachers or were preparing themselves to become teachers were eager for this learning. They had only what they had been able to snatch here and there, and at the rue Hautefeuille they became even more thirsty for knowledge and liberty. Many good friendships were born there.

It was comfortable there in the evenings, both in our little groups and when a large meeting occurred. When big meetings took place, we left the floor of the hall to the strangers, and our little group of enthusiasts gathered near the instructor's desk, where a skeleton and other things we liked were kept. From that spot near the desk we could see and hear much better than if we had tried to join the mob in the room.

The rue Hautefeuille overflowed with life and youth. We lived in the future, in the time when people would be more than beasts of burden whose work and blood other people made use of. At the rue Hautefeuille in the long night of the Empire we had glimpses of a better world. Five or six years before the Siege, it provided an untainted refuge in the middle of imperial Paris, a place impervious to the stench of the charnel house, although sometimes our history courses roared out the Marseillaise and smelled of gunpowder.

Somehow we were always able to find the time to attend courses several days a week. There were lectures on physics, chemistry, and even law. People tried out new methods of teaching, too. In addition to listening to others, we found time to give lectures ourselves. I had never understood how time could be so elastic. We didn't waste a minute, and our days were stretched to fit so that midnight seemed early.

I remember a tall old man with white hair explaining how useful stenography could be in teaching. Using stenographic techniques would allow many things to be abbreviated. People have so little time for study, and they waste so much of it.

Several of us began spasmodic studies for the baccalaureate again. My former passion for algebra engrossed me once more. I was able to verify, and this time with certainty, that if a person isn't an idiot (at least all the time), he can get along in mathematics without a teacher. The trick is to leave no formula behind without knowing it and no problem behind without finding its answer.

A frenzy for knowledge possessed us. It was refreshing to sit two or three times a week on student benches ourselves, side by side with our own most advanced pupils, whom we sometimes brought with us. They listened happily and proudly beside us, scarcely thinking about the time.

The more excited we got about all these things, the more we lapsed into the high spirits of schoolchildren. We had good times, and often we resembled students more than teachers.

When we were sad, we played jokes, for laughter cuts the shadows. One vacation day, I went to an employment agency to get a job as a cook at the home of some bourgeois family. After the first dinner I planned to cook for them, they would have fired me pretty rapidly. The employment agency was next to the Bastille on a fourth floor. Of course I had no papers, so I told the employment agent I had forgotten them. When I gave him the names of the imperial gangsters I claimed to have worked for, he got giddy. He ended up making me feel sorry for him, and I gave up the project; I flung it all in his face, laughing till my sides hurt.

Why are people so entranced with name-dropping? That was the lesson I gave that poor devil, and it would have been worth the trouble to go put pepper in the sugared dishes of some bourgeois soul used to cordon bleu cooks. Once the employment agent understood what was happening, he began to rail at me. Still laughing at him I left, after I warned him against being too easily "bonaparted" with name-dropping.

I recall another incident. One evening at the rue Hautefeuille we had been learning Danel's method of musical notation. As in England and Germany the notes in Danel's method are represented by letters of the alphabet, but with the difference that they are written without a staff. We left the rue Hautefeuille late, and because there were no more buses, we were returning to our homes on foot. Some idiot began to follow me, walking up on his toes with long heronlike legs. At first it amused me to watch this shadow of a bird glide along under the streetlights.

He kept repeating the foolish remarks people use when they don't know if you will answer them. I became impatient, and that spoiled the impression I got of his being some kind of fantastic bird running around on his long legs. I looked him straight in the face, and in my loudest voice I began to descend the Danel scale: D, B, L, S, F, M, R, D!

The effect was overwhelming.

Perhaps it was the somewhat masculine accent, or perhaps it was the strange syllables formed by the letters. I never found out. The bird disappeared.

Another time I was returning home on foot fairly late, and I had on a long cloak which enveloped me completely. I was wearing a sort of wide hat made out of shaggy cloth which cast a lot of shadows on my face, and brand-new ankle boots from the pawnshop. For some reason the heels made a lot of noise. The newspapers recently had been writing a lot about nocturnal attacks. Some good bourgeois heard my boots ringing, and being unable to make out my exact form because of my cloak and hat, he began to run with such fear that it gave me the idea of following him for a bit to scare him properly.

He went along, looking around to see if anyone would come to help him. With the black night and the deserted streets, the bourgeois was scared witless, and I was having a really good time. He lengthened his stride as much as he could. I kept to the shadows and made my heels strike even louder, because that noise was what kept up his fright. I don't know what district we had come to when I let the bourgeois go, yelling at him: "Must you be so stupid?"

That night I returned home very late, or rather very early in the morning, and I was no longer laughing. In the same night, after I had scared the bourgeois idiot, I had seen the people who live off victims, and people who are the victims themselves. It was an ordinary night of what people call civilized society.

Mme Vollier was still living then, and when I got home she scolded me for my lateness, in spite of my daily precaution of setting back the clock. The poor woman had been worrying about me as my mother would have done, and she told me how tired I would feel the next day.

As she was talking to me I composed in my mind a few verses about the bandits and girls I had spoken with that night, and with whom I have often spoken since.

Criminals and Whores

Discerned in the dark of ill-lit streets,
The sublimely wretched shamble through the night,
Namelessly slide past and cast no shadow,
Past obscured doorways at the edge of light
   For other phantoms to erase.
....

I have seen criminals and whores
And spoken with them. Now I inquire
If you believe them made as now they are
To drag their rags in blood and mire,
   Preordained, an evil race?

You, to whom all men are prey,
Have made them what they are today.

No one comes into the world with a knife in his hand to stab others, or with a card in her hand to sell herself. No one comes into the world with a club ready to be a cop, and no one comes into the world carrying a minister's portfolio, so that he may be captured by the dizziness of power and drag nations down.

No bandit who could not have been an honest man. No honorable man who is not capable of committing crimes.

Among the people associated with the rue Hautefeuille was Jules Favre. At this time he was a true republican leader, but after the fall of Napoleon III he became one of those who murdered Paris. Power would poison him as it poisons all those who are clothed in that cloak of Nessus.

In those years during the twilight of the Empire that same Jules Favre was like a father, and he treated us with a father's kindness. Many times I used his being a chairman of our association as a pretext for taking people to him who needed a lawyer's opinion and couldn't pay for it.

One day, I remember I took him an old woman who thought she was being persecuted, and he had to try to reassure her. Dealing with her cost him a lot of time. I was with her in his office, and Favre came over to tell me how annoyed he was with me. The obtuse angle made by his forehead and his chin closed into a right angle, a bad sign.

"This is too much," he muttered to me while the old woman kept curtseying to him and telling him how she had been persecuted for twenty years.

I can still see the spot where that took place; Favre and I were whispering near a large vase his voters had given him. An uncontrollable desire to laugh took hold of me, and I did. I laughed so heartily that the right angle of Favre's profile was transformed into its usual obtuse angle again, and his eyes shone. He couldn't stop himself from laughing, too.

Still curtseying, the old woman left saying, "Thank you very much. Till another time. See you soon."

Another chairman of our association was Eugène Pelletan, a republican member of Bonaparte's assembly. His eyes, sunk under thick, gray eyebrows, glowed like coals and gave him a strange appearance. He reminded me of Nicolas Flamel or Cagliostro or some other alchemist out of the legends. It was when he was speaking from the desk at the rue Hautefeuille that we especially liked to huddle near the skeleton and observe events from there, listening, caught up in the poetry of science, caught up in his words on liberty, his love of the Republic, and his hatred for the Caesars.

Under this inspiration we began to write many works that are lost today. I wrote an enormous manuscript that I entitled *The Wisdom of a Madman*. Pelletan was then our chairman, and I carried it to him so that he could read it and give me his opinion. Since then I have come to understand how patient he must have been to read that enormous, unintelligible book and to annotate a few passages in it.

"This is not the wisdom of a madman," he wrote. "One day it will be the wisdom of peoples."

Bringing that manuscript home, I seemed to walk on air. I reread much of it carefully, but I didn't have time to revise it. I had to give more and more lessons after class, and *The Wisdom of a Madman* was laid aside with my other unpublished works. Perhaps I would have looked for a publisher if I hadn't been so busy.

The last two years before 1871, the rue Hautefeuille was a hotbed of intellectual women. My friend Marie L—— wrote page after page, and Jeanne B—— and possibly her sister were assumed to have manuscripts in progress. Julie L—— and Mlle Poulin threw poems to the winds. But prose and verse and music disappeared because we felt so near the drama coming from the street, the true drama, the drama of humanity. The songs of the new epoch were war songs, and there was no room for anything else.

The professional schools, for which we had Jules Simon, an opposition member of the Assembly, to thank, captured all-out enthusiasm. Those schools saved a few handfuls of girls from apprenticeship, and provided them with trades or diplomas.

In the last years of the Empire there was a free professional school on the rue Thévenot. Each of us gave three evenings a week there. The Society for Elementary Education took care of the rent, and it all worked out. One of our professors, a man whom we called Doctor Francolinus, displayed fiendish activity there. Sometimes the police of the Empire gave us the pleasure of attending our classes, and then an hour of lessons would go by quickly, because we put in occasional comments that gave a good clawed swat at Napoleon III's ugly hyena's moustache.

I taught the literature and ancient geography courses twice a week and Charles de Sivry taught them two other days. We taught them exactly the same way, for Charles and I often had the same ideas. The last idea we had was for a piano whose hammers had been replaced by little bows to give a piano something of the passion that violins have. I wrote an article about this, and it was published in the *Progrès musical* under the name of Louis Michel. I have often noticed that when I sent a periodical material signed Louise Michel it was a hundred to one it wouldn't be printed, but if I signed it Louis Michel or Enjolras, a pseudonym I used, the chances of publication were greater.

What Charles and I taught in the courses on literature was the utility of examining cities and peoples in terms of childhood, youth, and decay. That is the real way it happens, although people think it is a romanesque approach. The lives of individuals and the history of humanity show a parallel progression. In every individual's life you can see the same transformations that you can see in our history, in the story of our collective existence that spans the centuries.

Nevertheless, however aware a person is of those centuries-long rhythms of change, he still lives inside his own epoch. It is inside his own epoch that he feels, suffers, and is happy; and all the love, all the hate, all the harmony, all the power that he possesses—he must throw all this into his surroundings. One person is nothing and yet part of that which is everything—the Revolution.

And so here is Louise Michel. She is a menace to society, for she has declared a hundred times that everyone should take part in the banquet of life. What would be the pleasure of riches if one were unable to compare one's own well-fed condition to that of people dying of hunger? Where would the feeling of security come from if one were unable to compare one's good, solid position to that of people who must work in poverty?

What is more, Louise Michel is a woman. If she could only be fooled by the idea that women can get their rights by asking men for them. But she has the villainy to insist that the strong sex is just as much a slave as the weak sex, that it is unable to give what it does not have itself. All inequalities, she claims, will collapse when men and women engage in the common battle together.

Louise Michel is a monster who maintains that men and women are not responsible for their situations and claims it is stupidity which causes the evils around us. She claims that politics is a form of that stupidity and is incapable of ennobling the race.

If Louise Michel were the only person saying all this, people could say she is a pathological case. But there are thousands like her, millions, none of whom gives a damn about authority. They all repeat the battle cry of the Russian revolutionaries: land and freedom!

Yes, there are millions of us who don't give a damn for any authority because we have seen how little the many-edged tool of power accomplishes. We have watched throats cut to gain it. It is supposed to be as precious as the jade axe that travels from island to island in Oceania. No. Power monopolized is evil.

Who would have thought that those men at the rue Hautefeuille who spoke so forcefully of liberty and who denounced the tyrant Napoleon so loudly would be among those in May 1871 who wanted to drown liberty in blood? Power makes people dizzy and will always do so until power belongs to all mankind.

During the twilight of the Empire the type of things I wrote changed. When I was at Mme Vollier's I sent some poems to the newspapers, *L'Union des poètes, La Jeunesse,* and others. I just threw things out and I barely paid any attention to them; I don't even know which ones were printed. I did send some of the best poems to Victor Hugo when I was in exile.

The time was far removed from those days at Vroncourt when I had sent him verses that the indulgent master had said were as sweet as my youth.

Me, I am the white dove
Of the black arch.

I had sent him that one from Vroncourt. Now, the verses I sent him smelled of gunpowder:

Do you hear the brazen thunder
Behind the man who takes no side?
A reluctant man betrays tomorrow.
Up the mountains and over the cliffs
We go together to sow freedom.

That poem, "The Black Marseillaise," I threw one July 14 into the wicket at the Echelle along with some others addressed to Mme Bonaparte. These later poems, begun in collaboration with Vermorel, had been reviewed and augmented by friends who had the same disdain for rhyme; they added other phrases that were more appropriate to the circumstances.

Under the Empire, literature was strange, as it always is when nations are slaughterhouses. Books were filled with foolishness, but there were forgotten corpses behind each page. All published writing smelled stale.

Adèle Esquiros, the author of captivating works, remained silent during those years as she waited for more propitious times. She continued to write, but submitted nothing to a publisher. From time to time, however, she would read us a few pages full of fresh lines and gracious images that gave us the impression of spring mornings when dew covers the flowers and the sun shines in the branches. There were also bitter passages in her work, but she covered their sadness with some seeming pleasantry. I wonder what has become of her manuscripts; I have never seen any of them appear in print. Because of deportation and prison, I haven't had enough time to visit my old friends. Adèle Esquiros has been paralyzed for several years now, but she is submitting to her fate with the same smile on her lips that she wore before.

At the end of the Empire our revolutionary meetings became more numerous, and many of them were even held in daylight. Evening meetings were more common, however, and one evening while my mother was living with me, I had planned to go to a meeting. To keep her from worrying, I had been claiming that I wasn't actively involved in anything. Two of our friends came by to take me to the meeting, but stayed outside so she wouldn't suspect what was going on. I told her I was going out to give some lessons.

"Impossible," said the poor woman. "You can't be going out to give lessons at this hour."

"Julie sent for me," I said.

She went to the window.

"I knew it," she said. "It is one of your meetings."

And she laughed in spite of herself, as my friends and I left laughing, too.

Most of our meetings took place outside Paris. Often as we were returning to Paris by little paths through fields, we talked about many things. At other times we were silent, dazzled by the idea of sweeping away the shame of twenty years. We were all poets, a little. We have suffered, but we have seen some beautiful things.

One holiday I was going to Julie's when I encountered a vast multitude of people on the boulevard. With the hopes I held, I believed the hour had come, but it was a carnival, in the midst of which the old republican Miot was being taken to prison. Some people in the crowd who were following the carnival performers left them to see the old man dragged off by the varlets of the Empire. It was a joyous crowd on a day of mourning, but they weren't really the people. They were the same crowd you see at public executions, but which you can never find when you need to rip up paving stones to build barricades. They are the same unthinking crowd that bolsters up tyrannies and cuts the throats of people trying to save them. They are the great herd that bares its back for the whip and holds out its neck to the knife.

For five years, from 1865 to 1870, we had believed that the end of the Empire was imminent. For the cup to overflow, however, the defeat at Sedan had to be added to the other crimes. People always wait for the cup to overflow for the same reason that keeps them from ever being upset by the approach of misfortunes they think they can prevent.

How strongly toward the end of the Empire the fearful stanza of Victor Hugo came back to me. "Harmodius, it's time! / You can strike down this man without remorse," Hugo wrote. Hugo's words went into my heart like a knife, and each syllable rang in my ears like the tolling of a bell. Vengeance finally reached Harmodius, the Athenian murderer, when the younger brother of his innocent victim cut him down.

I would have killed my tyrant without feeling any distress. Millions would have been spared if he had died. Someone promised me an entrée to him; even to kill him I wouldn't have requested a formal audience. But I got that entrée only after Bonaparte had left for the war and was no longer in Paris.

Sedan could have been avoided if Bonaparte had been dead. People are used to waiting for the annihilation of multitudes, and to stop bandits like Bonaparte they will accept the annihilation of a nation willingly. Perhaps Sedan will make things understood more quickly, and the destruction of those legions will keep the human race from surrendering itself any longer to those woodcutters of men who chop people down like a forest for their own convenience.

Far away in the forests of New Caledonia, I once saw a rotten tree collapse suddenly. When the cloud of dust dispersed, there was only a heap of trash, over which, like headstones in a graveyard, a few green boughs stretched out, the last effort of the old tree dragged down by the dead trunk. In that tree, myriads of insects had lived for centuries, and they, too, were engulfed in the collapse. Some of them stirred painfully in the dust, and startled and upset they stared at the daylight which was going to kill them, for their kind, born in the shade, could not stand light.

Like those insects, we live in an old tree, and we stubbornly believe it still lives, but the least breath of wind will destroy it, and its debris will blow across the earth. No one can escape change.

Chapter 8

The Siege of Paris

Despite overwhelming support given Napoleon III in a plebiscite held in May 1870, the emperor was coming under increasing political pressure, and his government tried to win public support through an adventurous foreign policy. Conflict with Prussia over the nomination of a German princeling to the empty throne of Spain led the French government to decide for war against Germany on 14 July 1870. Two weeks later Napoleon left Paris to join the French military forces. The Germans defeated the French army decisively at Sedan on 1 September 1870, and captured the emperor.

Crowds in Paris began to demonstrate two days later, and on September 4, amidst severe disorder, the Paris mob proclaimed the Republic. A Government of National Defense headed by Napoleon's military governor of Paris, General Trochu, took power in the name of the Republic. Two weeks later German forces surrounded Paris.

During the terrible year of the war and the Siege, when I saw our people die while they were so full of life, I suddenly recalled an impression from my childhood. I saw an oak standing tall and solid with its shadow falling over the long grass full of white daisies and buttercups. It was the oak of my legend, and it had an axe embedded in its heart; in its trunk was a wide gash, and the iron of the axe was damp with sap. These impressions come back like dead leaves driven by the wind.

Paris was quivering from the Empire's crimes. In spite of the blandishments of the imperial gang, we true republicans were not eager for the war with Prussia. To befuddle the people, the Bonapartists had torn the wings off the Marseillaise, and when we cheered for the Republic in August, Paris should have risen in remembrance of its proud and heroic tradition. The city should have cleansed itself by bathing in the blood of the Empire. Instead, revolutionary Paris stood silent. I can still see the city amid a quiet haze: Every shutter was closed, leaving the boulevard La Villette deserted. Around the carriage in which Eudes and Brideau were prisoners, people cried out: "Attack the Prussians!"

After September 4 there was too little change, for the people didn't insist on it. Some wanted to undertake desperate sorties to drive back the Prussians, but they were forbidden to try. Even after the encirclement of Paris, people waited for an army to liberate the city, for they claimed that a city had never raised a siege without outside help. That something has never happened before certainly does not mean it is impossible.

When several of our friends were condemned to death for having tried to proclaim the Republic in August before Bonaparte was overthrown, André Léo, Adèle Esquiros, and I were appointed to carry to General Trochu a protest against their sentences signed by thousands of people. Some people had signed that protest from momentary indignation and then had become timid, and wanted their names taken off the lists because of second thoughts. Our friends' lives were at stake, and I certainly did not want to erase a single name.

To get our protest to General Trochu was not easy. It took all my feminine stubbornness to get into his office. By almost a direct assault, we got to some kind of antechamber. The people there wanted us to leave before we had seen the governor of Paris.

"We come on behalf of the people," we said, and the words sounded ominous to them in those surroundings. There was only one red sash of the Revolution being worn at the Hôtel de Ville, and that was worn by Henri Rochefort. And yet the Parisians were saying to themselves, "The people are now ruling." We were invited to leave Trochu's office, but we went over and sat on a bench against the wall, declaring that we should not leave without an answer.

Tired of seeing us wait, a secretary went to look for some personage who was said to represent Trochu. That person came over to us, and when we decided it was impossible to see the general personally, we presented our protest to this aide. He weighed the voluminous petition covered with thousands of signatures (which seemed to upset him) in his hand, and he declared that the petition would be taken under consideration because of the number of signatures. That promise would have meant little if the Empire hadn't been collapsing. Rotten as the Empire was, the hammer blow of Sedan killed it.

Shortly after the encirclement of Paris, I was arrested for the first time. Because the city of Strasbourg was in great danger from the Prussian armies, Mme André Léo and I had rounded up a large number of volunteers, determined to make one last great effort or die with Strasbourg. We were crossing Paris in long columns, crying out, "To Strasbourg, to Strasbourg." We were going to sign our names in the register placed on the lap of the statue of Our Lady of Strasbourg in the Place de la Concorde, and from there go to the Hôtel de Ville and demand arms. There we were arrested, Mme Léo, me, and a poor, little old woman who had been crossing the square to get some kerosene while the demonstration was going on. She kept clutching her oil can while she was being accused of intending to commit arson. We testified in her behalf, but the most eloquent witness for her innocence was the way she continued to grip her can, and the authorities let her go. As she left, her oil can dribbled oil on her dress because her hands were trembling so badly.

A fat old jackass came in later, egged on by his curiosity. I tried to tell him what was going on. "What does Strasbourg matter to you?" this insensitive, bedecked functionary asked. "Do you think that Strasbourg will perish simply because you aren't there?"

Finally a member of the Provisional Government got us released, but at that very moment, September 27, Strasbourg surrendered to the Prussians.

In Montmartre, in the Eighteenth Arrondissement, we organized the Montmartre Vigilance Committee. Few of its members still survive, but during the Siege the committee made the reactionaries tremble. Every evening, we would burst out onto the streets from our headquarters at 41, chaussée Clignancourt, sometimes simply to talk up the Revolution, because the time for duplicity had passed. We knew how little the reactionary regime, in its death throes, valued its promises and the lives of its citizens, and the people had to be warned.

Actually there were two vigilance committees in Montmartre, the men's and the women's. Although I presided over the women's committee, I was always at the men's, because its members included some Russian revolutionaries. I still have an old map of Paris that hung on the wall of our meeting room; I carried it back and forth across the ocean with me as a souvenir. With ink we had blotted out the Empire's coat of arms, which desecrated it and which would have dirtied our headquarters.

The members of the men's Montmartre Vigilance Committee were remarkable persons. Never have I seen minds so direct, so unpretentious, and so elevated. Never have I seen individuals so clearheaded. I don't know how this group managed to do it. There were no weaknesses. Something good and strong supported people.

The women were courageous also, and among them, too, there were some remarkable minds. I belonged to both committees, and the leanings of the two groups were the same. Sometime in the future the women's committee should have its own history told. Or perhaps the two should be mingled, because people didn't worry about which sex they were before they did their duty. That stupid question was settled.

In the evenings I often was able to be at meetings of both groups, since the women's, which met at the office of the Justice of the Peace on the rue de la Chapelle, began an hour earlier than the men's. Thus after the women's meeting was over I could go to the last half of the men's meeting, and sometimes other women and I could go to the entire men's meeting.

The Montmartre Vigilance Committees left no one without shelter and no one without food. Anyone could eat at the meeting halls, although as the Siege continued and food supplies became shorter, it might only be one herring divided between five or six people. For people who were really in need we didn't hesitate to dip into our resources or to use revolutionary requisitioning. The Eighteenth Arrondissement was the terror of profiteers. When the reactionaries heard the phrase, "Montmartre is going to come down on you," they hid in their holes; we chased them down anyway, and like hunted beasts they fled, leaving behind the hiding places where provisions were rotting while Paris starved.

Ultimately the Montmartre Vigilance Committees were mowed down, like all revolutionary groups. The rare members still alive know how proud we were there and how fervently we flew the flag of the Revolution. Little did it matter to those who were there whether they were beaten to the ground unnoticed in battle or died alone in the sunlight. It makes no difference how the millstone moves so long as the bread is made.

Everything was beginning, or rather, beginning again, after the long lethargy of the Empire. The first organization of the Rights of Women had begun to meet on the rue Thévenot with Mmes Jules Simon, André Léo, and Maria Deraismes. At the meetings of the Rights of Women group, and at other meetings, the most advanced men applauded the idea of equality. I noticed—I had seen it before, and I saw it later—that men, their declarations notwithstanding, although they appeared to help us, were always content with just the appearance. This was the result of custom and the force of old prejudices, and it convinced me that we women must simply take our place without begging for it. The issue of political rights is dead. Equal education, equal trades, so that prostitution would not be the only lucrative profession open to a woman—that is what was real in our program. The Russian revolutionaries are right; evolution is ended and now revolution is necessary or the butterfly will die in its cocoon.

Heroic women were found in all social positions. At the professional school of Mme Poulin, women of all social levels organized the Society for the Victims of the War. They would have preferred to die rather than surrender, and dispensed their efforts the best way they could, while demanding ceaselessly that Paris continue to resist the Prussian siege.

Although I knew some of them well, I don't know who is still living, but during the Siege no one failed. They didn't become like those harpies the following May who dug out the eyes of our fallen comrades with the tips of their parasols.

Later, when I was a prisoner, the first visitor I had was Mme Meurice from the Society for the Victims of the War. At my last trial, behind the hand-picked spectators, among those who had to wedge themselves in, were two other former members of the Society, the large woman, Jeanne B—— and the petite Mme F——.

I salute all those brave women of the vanguard who were drawn from group to group: the Committee of Vigilance, the Society for the Victims of the War, and later the League of Women. The old world ought to fear the day when those women finally decide they have had enough. Those women will not slack off. Strength finds refuge in them. Beware of them! Beware of those who, like Paule Minck, go across Europe waving the flag of liberty, and beware of the most peaceful daughter of Gaul now asleep in the deep resignation of the fields. Beware of the women when they are sickened by all that is around them and rise up against the old world. On that day the new world will begin.

The Prussian siege continued; the days became dark and the trees lost their leaves. Hunger and cold reached more deeply into the houses of Paris.

On October 31, at the Hôtel de Ville the people proclaimed the Commune. The Committees of Vigilance from all over Paris organized the demonstration, and the people no longer cried out "Long live the Republic"; they cried out "Long live the Commune!" The Government of National Defense promised to hold meetings and elections and promised to take no reprisals against these demonstrators. It broke both promises. The word *Commune* was hushed up as effectively as some conjurer's trick, but experiences like that are necessary, for they let you see who the real enemy is. If we are implacable in the coming fight, who is to blame?

Another month went by and conditions became increasingly bad. The National Guard [best described as a half-trained Parisian popular militia] could have saved the city, but the Government of National Defense feared supporting the armed force of the people.

Early in December I was arrested a second time. That second arrest came when several women who had more courage than clairvoyance wanted to propose some unknown means of defense to the government. Their zeal was so great that they came to the Women's Vigilance Committee in Montmartre, using the name of a woman and of a group whom they had neglected to receive permission from, but if they had come to us with no recommendation at all to introduce them, it would not have mattered. We agreed to join them the next day in a demonstration in front of the Hôtel de Ville, but we made one reservation. We told them we would go as women to share their danger; we would not go as citizens because we no longer recognized the Government of National Defense. It had proved itself incapable even of letting Paris defend itself.

The next day we went to the rendezvous at the Hôtel de Ville, and we expected what happened: I was arrested for having organized the demonstration. I answered their charges by saying that I couldn't have organized any demonstration to speak to the government, because I no longer recognized that government. I added that when I came on my own behalf to the Hôtel de Ville, it would be with an armed uprising behind me. That explanation appeared unsatisfactory to them, and they locked me up.

The next day four citizens—Théophile Ferré, Avronsart, Christ, and Burlot—came to claim me "in the name of the Eighteenth Arrondissement." At this declaration, the reactionaries became frightened. "Montmartre is going to descend on us," they whispered to each other, and they released me.

Mme Meurice also came to claim me in the name of the Society for the Victims of the War, but she arrived after I had already left the prefecture.

It wasn't until January 19, when the struggle was almost over, that the Government of National Defense finally agreed to let the National Guard effect a sortie to try to retake Montretout and Buzenval. At first the National Guard swept the Prussians before them, but the mud defeated the brave sons of the people. They sank into the wet earth up to their ankles, and unable to get their artillery up on the hills, they had to retreat.

Hundreds stayed behind, lying quietly in death; these men of the National Guard—men of the people, artists, young persons—died with no regrets for their lost lives. The earth drank the blood of this first Parisian carnage; soon it would drink more.

Paris still did not wish to surrender to the Prussians. On January 22, the people gathered in front of the Hôtel de Ville, where General Chaudey, who commanded the soldiers, now had his headquarters. The people sensed that the members of the government were lying when they declared they were not thinking of surrendering.

We prepared a peaceful demonstration, with Razoua commanding our battalions from Montmartre. Because our friends who were armed were determined for the demonstration to be peaceful, they withdrew with their weapons, even though peaceful demonstrations are always crushed.

When only a disarmed multitude remained, soldiers in the buildings around the square opened fire on us. No shot was fired by the people before the Breton Mobiles fired their volleys. We could see the pale faces of the Bretons behind the windows, as a noise like hail sounded in our ears. Yes, you fired on us, you untamed Celts, but at least it was your faith that made you fanatics for the Counterrevolution. You weren't bought by the reactionaries. You killed us, but you believed you were doing your duty, and some day we will convert you to our ideals of liberty. You will bring to liberty the same fierce convictions you now are bringing to the reaction, and with us you will assault the old world.

The Breton Mobiles fired first; the people around the square of the Tour Saint Jacques became indignant as the bullets began to rain down on them, and they began to throw up barricades. Malézieux, his cloak riddled with bullet holes, took over as our leader. He was an old man now, a hero of June 1848. He remembered bygone days and bravely took command of the situation as if he had been draped in his June flag.

I stood in the middle of the square lost in thought. I looked at the accursed windows from which the Bretons continued to fire on us and thought, "One day you will be on our side, you brigands."

The bullets continued to make their hail-like noise. The square became deserted while the projectiles coming from the Hôtel de Ville dug into the ground haphazardly or killed people here and there.

Near me, a woman of my build, who was dressed in black and who resembled me, was struck down by a bullet. A young man who had come with her was also killed. We never found out who they were, but the young man had the intrepid profile of the Midi.

Gradually the square emptied. Many people did not want it to end like that, but we decided that this was not the time to attempt to overthrow the government.

On this January 22, Sapia was killed along with many others. P—— of the Blanqui Group had his arm broken. Passersby were killed like our own people, and over the fallen we swore an oath of vengeance and liberty. As a token of defiance, I took off my red scarf and threw it on a grave. A comrade picked it up and knotted it in the branches of a willow.

Six days after that January 22, the people having been raked by machine-gun fire and then raked with assurances that the government did not intend to surrender, the government surrendered to the Prussians. This time the shudder of anger that went through Paris did not abate; it prepared Paris for the coming months.

Chapter 9

The Commune of Paris

After Paris surrendered to the Prussians in January 1871, the other French forces agreed to an armistice, during which the Prussians allowed the French to elect a national government, there being some doubt whether the self-proclaimed Parisian government could speak for France as a whole. Expected to decide on the terms of the peace, that new government met first at Bordeaux and then moved to Versailles, just outside Paris. Monarchists dominated the new Versailles government, and until the divisions between those who supported rival pretenders to the throne became evident, it seemed likely that the Versailles government would reestablish a monarchy in which the dreams of republicans and revolutionaries would dissolve.

On January [*sic:* February] 22, the Committees of Vigilance were closed down, and newspaper publication was suspended. The Versailles reactionaries decided they had to disarm Paris. Napoleon III was still alive, and with Montmartre disarmed, the entrance of a sovereign, either Bonaparte or an Orleanist, would have favored the army, which was either an accomplice of the reactionaries or was allowing itself to be deceived. With Montmartre disarmed, the Prussian army, which was sitting in the surrendered forts around Paris while the armistice continued, would have been protected.

The cannon paid for by the National Guard had been left on some vacant land in the middle of the zone abandoned by the Prussians. Paris objected to that, and the cannon were taken to the Parc Wagram. The idea was in the air that each battalion should recapture its own cannon. A battalion of the National Guard from the Sixth Arrondissement gave us our impetus. With the flag in front, men and women and children hauled the cannon by hand down the boulevards, and although the cannon were loaded, no accidents occurred. Montmartre, like Belleville and Batignolles, had its own cannon. Those that had been placed in the Place des Vosges were moved to the faubourg Saint Antoine. Some sailors proposed our recapturing the Prussian-occupied forts around the city by boarding them like ships, and this idea intoxicated us.

Then before dawn on March 18 the Versailles reactionaries sent in troops to seize the cannon now held by the National Guard. One of the points they moved toward was the Butte of Montmartre, where our cannon had been taken. The soldiers of the reactionaries captured our artillery by surprise, but they were unable to haul them away as they had intended, because they had neglected to bring horses with them.

Learning that the Versailles soldiers were trying to seize the cannon, men and women of Montmartre swarmed up the Butte in a surprise maneuver. Those people who were climbing believed they would die, but they were prepared to pay the price.

The Butte of Montmartre was bathed in the first light of day, through which things were glimpsed as if they were hidden behind a thin veil of water. Gradually the crowd increased. The other districts of Paris, hearing of the events taking place on the Butte of Montmartre, came to our assistance.

The women of Paris covered the cannon with their bodies. When their officers ordered the soldiers to fire, the men refused. The same army that would be used to crush Paris two months later decided now that it did not want to be an accomplice of the reaction. They gave up their attempt to seize the cannon from the National Guard. They understood that the people were defending the Republic by defending the arms that the royalists and imperialists would have turned on Paris in agreement with the Prussians. When we had won our victory, I looked around and noticed my poor mother, who had followed me to the Butte of Montmartre, believing that I was going to die.

On this day, the eighteenth of March, the people wakened. If they had not, it would have been the triumph of some king; instead it was a triumph of the people. The eighteenth of March could have belonged to the allies of kings, or to foreigners, or to the people. It was the people's.

The people arrested General Lecomte, who commanded the soldiers that had moved against Montmartre, as well as General Clément Thomas, whose curiosity had led him to watch what he thought would be the degradation of Paris. Their very acts had convicted both of them a long time before. Clément Thomas's crimes extended as far back as the June Days of 1848, and he had reminded the people of his earlier actions when he insulted the National Guard. Lecomte, like Clément Thomas, owed an old debt he had to pay. His soldiers remembered, and vengeance came out of the past. The hour struck for them.

It will strike for many others, without the Revolution pausing in its course. The old world takes note of the reactionaries who die because of popular reprisals. It does not count our side's losses; it is not able to, because the sons of the people who fall are only stubble under sickles, only grass mowed in the summer sun.

Several of our side perished. Turpin, who was wounded near me on the eighteenth in the predawn attack on 6, rue des Rosiers, died at Lariboisière several days later. He told me to commend his wife to

Georges Clemenceau, the mayor of the Eighteenth Arrondissement, and I carried out his dying wish.

I have never heard Clemenceau's testimony at the inquiry into the events of March 18; we weren't able to read newspapers when he gave his evidence. Clemenceau's indecisiveness, for which people reproach him, comes from the illusion he holds that he should wait for parliamentarianism to bring progress. But parliamentarianism is dead, and Clemenceau's illusion is some kind of infection he caught from the Bordeaux Assembly. When that assembly became the Versailles government, he fled from it. Properly, his place is in the streets, and when his anger is finally roused, he will go there. That is what remains of his revolutionary temperament. His indignation at some infamy will bring him out of his illusions, as he came out of the Bordeaux Assembly.

Wouldn't it be better for the last parliamentarians who remain honest to follow the example of the great Jacobin, Delescluze? The attempt to work through parliaments has been going on for a long while, but parliaments, standing as they do in the midst of rottenness, can no longer produce anything worthwhile.

In the provinces people believed the stories Versailles spread about the Commune. After all, statecraft requires a government to create discord among the common people. The bosses give the common people enough to allow them to work, but too little to revolt. And between each periodic pruning they grow back as numerous and as strong as Gallic oaks. At any rate, some of our most committed supporters went from Paris to the provinces to explain the situation. Among those who went were women like Paule Minck. They worked as hard as they could. If the provinces had only understood the true situation, they would have sided with us, but they listened to the lies of the Versailles government. We in Paris even tried launching balloons filled with letters to the provinces. Some of them came down in the right places, but they were not enough.

Nevertheless, not everyone was fooled by the lies of Versailles. Lyon, Marseille, Narbonne, all had their own Communes, and like ours, theirs too were drowned in the blood of revolutionaries. That is why our flags are red. Why are our red banners so terribly frightening to those persons who have caused them to be stained that color?

Some people say I'm brave. Not really. There is no heroism; people are simply entranced by events. What happens is that in the face of danger my perceptions are submerged in my artistic sense, which is seized and charmed. Tableaux of the dangers overwhelm my thoughts, and the horrors of the struggle become poetry.

It wasn't bravery when, charmed by the sight, I looked at the dismantled fort of Issy, all white against the shadows, and watched my comrades filing out in night sallies, moving away over the little slopes of Clamart or toward the Hautes Bruyères, with the red teeth of chattering machine guns showing on the horizon against the night sky. It was beautiful, that's all. Barbarian that I am, I love cannon, the smell of powder, machine-gun bullets in the air.

I am not the only person caught up by situations from which the poetry of the unknown emerges. I remember a student who didn't agree with our ideas (although he agreed even less with the other side's), who came to shoot with us at Clamart and at the Moulin de Pierre. He had a volume of Baudelaire in his pocket, and we read a few pages with great pleasure—when we had time to read. What fate held for him I don't know, but we tested our luck together. It was interesting. We drank some coffee in the teeth of death, choosing the same spot where three of our people, one after another, had been killed. Our comrades, anxious about seeing us there at what seemed to be a deadly place, made us withdraw. Just after we left a shell fell, breaking the empty cups. Above all else, our action was simply one of a poet's nature, not bravery on either his part or mine.

During the entire time of the Commune, I only spent one night at my poor mother's. I never really went to bed during that time; I just napped a little whenever there was nothing better to do, and many other people lived the same way. Everybody who wanted deliverance gave himself totally to the cause.

During the Commune I went unhurt except for a bullet that grazed my wrist, although my hat was literally riddled with bullet holes. I did twist my ankle, which had been sprained for a long time, and because I couldn't walk for three or four days, I had to requisition a carriage.

It was a little two-wheeled buggy that looked fairly attractive. We harnessed it to a horse which, unfortunately, was used to the whip. The rotten beast refused to move when we treated him nicely. Everything was all right when we were only following a funeral cortège to a Montmartre cemetery at a walking pace, but after the funeral it was a different story. That damned animal wouldn't keep up even the slow jog which allowed him practically to go to sleep standing up. He simply stopped, which gave time for a group of imbeciles to gather around us and begin whispering to each other, "Ah. Here are some people who have a buggy. They're filthy rich. The upkeep of that buggy must cost a lot."

"Wait," said a friend who was riding with me. "Don't get down. I'll make the horse move." He gave a piece of bread and other encouragements to that monster, who began to munch on the bread while he rolled back his lips as if he were laughing in our faces. And he didn't budge an inch. At that point, with all due respect to those who, like me, are slaves to beasts, I applied the law of necessity and hit him with the whip, and he took off, shaking his ears, for the Perronnet barricade at Neuilly.

While I was going to Montmartre for the funeral, I hadn't dared to stop off at my mother's, because she would have seen that I had a sprain. Several days before the funeral, though, I had come face to face with her in the trenches near the railroad station of Clamart. She had come to see if all the lies I had written her to soothe her were true. Fortunately, she always ended up believing me.

If the reaction had had as many enemies among women as it did among men, the Versailles government would have had a more difficult task subduing us. Our male friends are more susceptible to fainthearted-ness than we women are. A supposedly weak woman knows better than any man how to say: "It must be done." She may feel ripped open to her very womb, but she remains unmoved. Without hate, without anger, without pity for herself or others, whether her heart bleeds or not, she can say, "It must be done." Such were the women of the Commune. During Bloody Week, women erected and defended the barricade at the Place Blanche—and held it till they died.

In my mind I feel the soft darkness of a spring night. It is May 1871, and I see the red reflection of flames. It is Paris afire. That fire is a dawn, and I see it still as I sit here writing. Memory crowds in on me, and I keep forgetting that I am writing my memoirs.

In the night of May 22 or 23, I believe, we were at the Montmartre cemetery, which we were trying to defend with too few fighters. We had crenelated the walls as best we could, and, except for the battery on the Butte of Montmartre—now in the hands of the reactionaries, and whose fire raked us—and the shells that were coming at regular intervals from the side, where tall houses commanded our defenses, the position wasn't bad. Shells tore the air, marking time like a clock. It was magnificent in the clear night, where the marble statues on the tombs seemed to be alive.

When I went on reconnaissance it pleased me to walk in the solitude that shells were scouring. In spite of my comrades' advice, I chose to walk there several times; always the shells arrived too early or too late for me. One shell falling across the trees covered me with flowered branches, which I divided up between two tombs, that of Mlle Poulin and that of Murget, whose spirit seemed to throw us flowers. My comrades caught me, and one ordered me not to move about. They made me sit down on a bench near the tomb of Cavaignac. But nothing is as stubborn as a woman.

In the midst of all this Jaroslav Dombrowski passed in front of us sadly on his way to be killed. "It's over," he told me.

"No, no," I said to him, and he held out both his hands to me.

But he was right.

Three hundred thousand voices had elected the Commune. Fifteen thousand stood up to the clash with the army during Bloody Week.

We've counted about thirty-five thousand people who were executed, but how many were there that we know nothing of? From time to time the earth disgorges its corpses. If we are implacable in the coming fight, who is to blame?

The Commune, surrounded from every direction, had only death on its horizon. It could only be brave, and it was. And in dying it opened wide the door to the future. That was its destiny.

Chapter 10

After the Commune

Somehow I managed to escape from the soldiers trying to arrest me. Finally the victorious reactionaries took my mother and threatened to shoot her if I wasn't found. To set her free I went to take her place, although she didn't want me to do it, the poor, dear woman. I had to tell her a lot of lies to convince her, and as always she ended up believing me. Thus I saw to it that she returned home.

They took me to the detention camp in the 37th [*sic:* 43rd] Bastion, near the Montmartre railroad. Even that far out, fragments of paper ash coming from the burning of Paris blew like black butterflies. Above us the lights of the fire floated like red crepe. And always we could hear the cannon. We heard them until May 28, and right up to that day we said to each other:

"The Revolution will take its revenge."

At the 37th Bastion, in front of the dust-filled square where we were penned up, there are casemates under a mound of green lawn. There, as soon as General de Gallifet arrived, the soldiers shot two unfortunate people in front of us. They resembled each other and must have been brothers. They both struggled until the shots rang out, for they did not want to die. They hadn't even been on our side. They had come out into the street, perhaps to insult us, and had been arrested. Before they were shot, they had said they weren't worried, because they were sure they'd be freed. Then General de Gallifet gave an order to shoot into the crowd if anyone moved. The two brothers were terrified and tried to flee. We cried out:

"We don't know them. They're not ours."

But it did no good. They were shot anyway. They weren't even able to stand up for the volley. They were so frightened that all they could say was that they were Montmartre merchants; they couldn't even remember their addresses so that they could commend their children to those of us who remained. We didn't think we could figure out who they were either. People thought that one of them was saying "Alas." I have always guessed that he said "Anne," and that she was his daughter. How many people were seized like this, how many who really were enemies of the Commune, like those two unfortunate men of Bastion 37?

After this execution we were lined up and marched off toward Versailles. As we arrived there, a bunch of bullies threw rocks at us as if we were rabbits, and a member of the National Guard had his jaw broken. One thing I owe to the cavalry who were guarding us: They pushed back the ruffians and their girl friends who had come to the prisoner-baiting. We didn't stop at Versailles, however; we were led beyond, south to Satory.

The prisoners filing past from Montmartre to Satory are present now in my mind. We were marching between the lines of a cavalry escort. It was night. Nothing could have been more horribly beautiful than the place where they made us climb down into the ravines near the Château de la Muette. The gloom, barely lit by the wan moon, transformed the ravines into walls. The shadows of the horsemen on either side of our long file formed a black fringe that made the path seem lighter. The sky, hovering with the promise of heavy rains on the morrow, seemed to press down on us. Everything became blurred and appeared dream-like—except for the horsemen who led the column and the first groups of prisoners. A sudden flash of light filtered from below between the hooves of the horses and lit them up; scattered red reflections seemed to bleed on us and on the uniforms. The rest of the file stretched out in a long trail of ink, ending in the murky depths of the night.

People said they were going to shoot us in those ravines, but the soldiers had us climb out, although I didn't know why. I felt no fear, for I was wrapped up in the picture I saw and no longer thought of where we were. Thrilled by my perceptions, I earned no merit at all for despising a danger I wasn't thinking about. Gripped by the tableau I only looked, and now I remember.

Satory! As we got there during a downpour which made the slope slippery, we were told: "Move! Climb as if you were charging up the Butte of Montmartre." And everybody climbed at full charge, and then we had to walk in front of some machine guns that they rolled after us. We told an old woman who was on the verge of hysterics, and who was in our group only because her husband had been shot, that the machine guns were only a formality they went through each time new prisoners arrived. We weren't so sure of this, but at least the woman fell silent. We believed the soldiers were going to kill us, and there would only be time enough for us to yell, "Long live the Commune" before we died. But then they pulled back the machine guns.

Satory! In the middle of the night the soldiers would call out groups of prisoners. They'd get up from the mud where they had lain down in the rain, and follow the soldier's lantern that led their way. They'd be given a pick and shovel to dig their own graves, and then they'd be shot. The echoes of volleys shattered the silence of the night.

Satory! The prisoners drank from their hands at the little pond when they were too thirsty and when the heavy rain which was falling on them had swept away the pink foam. There the victors washed their hands, which were often redder than those of butchers.

Who will record the crimes that power commits, and the monstrous manner in which power transforms men? Those crimes can be ended forever by spreading power out to the entire human race. To spread the feeling of the homeland to the entire world, to extend well-being to all people, to give science to all humanity—that will save humanity.

When I arrived at Satory the soldiers said they were going to shoot me the next day, in the evening; then the next day they said they would shoot me the day after. I don't know why they didn't, for I was insolent to them, as insolent as one is in defeat to ferocious victors.

Shortly thereafter, a group of us was sent to the prison of Chantiers at Versailles. As we were marching, a strange thing happened. A furious woman dashed in front of us, crying out that we had killed her sister, that she knew it, that there were witnesses. A cry rose up from our midst. It was her sister, who had been arrested by the Versailles government.

When we arrived at the prison of Chantiers, we were kept in a huge square room on the second floor, sitting on the floor by day and stretching out any way we could at night. At the end of two weeks they gave us bundles of straw, each of which had to do for two people. At night two lamps lit our morgue, where we hung up our rags and tatters on strings above our sleeping bodies. Above the room was a hole through which we climbed to the interrogation room; another hole led to the ground floor, where they kept the children who were prisoners, the children whose fathers they couldn't find. Some of those children, like Ranvier, were courageous and we were proud of them.

For a long time I was forbidden to see my mother, who came often from Montmartre without being able to speak to me. One day she was pushed back while she was offering me a bottle of coffee, and I threw the bottle at the gendarme who had pushed her. A nearby officer rebuked me, and I told him my only regret was that I had thrown the bottle at a tool of the government rather than at the head of it. They finally did allow my mother to see me, but it was a long time later.

At the prison of Chantiers I saw grotesque things. . . .

A deaf and dumb woman spent several weeks there, charged with having cried out, "Long live the Commune!" An old woman, both of whose legs were paralyzed, was charged with having built barricades. For three days, another woman just walked around the room, her basket under one arm and her umbrella under the other. In her basket were some poems that her employer had written in praise of the victors. Ironically, the soldiers believed those poems were in praise of the Commune, even one with a line that ran:

Good gentlemen of Versailles
Enter into Paris.

Inside the Prison des Chantiers, Versailles, 15 August 1871. Louise Michel is the third prisoner from the right, second row. (Photo. Bibl. nat. Paris)

But laughter quickly dies. The cries of the insane, uncertainty about relatives and friends whose fate was unknown, mothers left alone—all that I feel even now.

We were proud in defeat, and the ruffians and their girl friends who came out to see the vanquished as if they were going to look at animals in the Jardin des Plantes didn't see our tears. Instead, we sneered at their idiotic faces.

On the floor of our prison room there were so many lice they made little silver nets as they meandered about, going to their nests that resembled anthills. They were enormous lice, with bristling backs that were a little bit round-shouldered, so many lice that you believed you could hear the noise of their swarming.

Constantly guarded by soldiers, we women couldn't change our underwear easily (those of us who had any to change into). I was finally able to get some from my mother, who pushed it through the openwork gate in the courtyard.

I spent my nights looking at the tableau of this morgue. I have always been taken by views like that, so much so that I often forget people in the face of the horrible eloquence of things. Sometimes this morgue looked like dusk or dawn playing on a field where the crop had been harvested. I could see the empty stalks, thin bundles of straw, gilded like wheat. At other times, light mirrored off them. When daybreak paled the lamps, it looked like a harvest of stars.

On 15 June 1871, the worst forty of us were sent from the prison to the reformatory at Versailles. Mme Cadolle and Mme Hardouin have related what happened at Chantiers after we left.

Of course I was one of the worst forty sent to Versailles. We had to wait in the courtyard under a beating rain, and an officer said he was sorry. I couldn't keep myself from saying that making us stand in the drenching rain fitted in with all their other acts, and anyway I liked it better that way.

At the reformatory of Versailles, conditions for us forty were strangely eased. To get ready for the trial of the members of the Commune, the government tried a number of unfortunate women and sentenced them to death, although they had only been ambulance nurses. Because of her name, Eulalie Papavoine was sentenced to forced labor and was sent to Cayenne, even though she was not related to the legendary Papavoine. The Versailles government carefully kept from sentencing the boldest women to death; they didn't execute either Elisabeth Retif or Marchais, although they proved the two had conspired with each other, in spite of the fact that they had never met.

On the third of September, the eve of the first anniversary of the proclamation of the Republic, the sentencing of the chief members of the Commune was drawing to a close. By decree the governor general of

Paris had established the Third Military Court-Martial. Colonel Merlin was president and the members were Major Gaulet, Captain de Guibert, M. Mariguet, Lieutenant Caissaigne, Second Lieutenant Léger, Warrant Officer Labbat, Major Gaveau, and Captain Senart. The Third Military Court-Martial tried eighteen persons, among them Théophile Ferré.

Théophile Ferré, who once had been Clemenceau's deputy mayor, was the brother of my great friend Marie. In the *Dossier [sic: Cahiers] de la magistrature* by Odysse Barot I found an account of Théophile Ferré's arrest, and I quote those pages which were written under the vivid emotion of the horrible scene. People will understand why, when I am discussing these terrible sorrows, I quote friends who have related the events of those sad days instead of telling about them myself. Courage has limits, and one doesn't pass them unless duty demands it.

> There is a detail about which people do not know and which has not been written about until now: the manner in which Ferré's arrest took place and the way the authorities discovered his hiding place.
>
> All enquiries had been fruitless. The authorities had arrested five or six pseudo-Ferrés, just as they had shot five or six pseudo-Billiorays and five or six pseudo-Vallès.
>
> What did they do then? They went to the little house on the rue Fazilleau in the suburb of Levallois-Perret, where the former member of the Commune used to live with his parents.
>
> Théophile Ferré was not at the house, but the authorities had known when they went to Levallois-Perret that there was no chance of finding Ferré at his parents' home. Why did they go there? How naive you are! He lived there with his family, and what good is a family if it does not inform on and surrender its own?
>
> Needless to say, the authorities pushed their way brutally into the little cottage surrounded by its garden. Ah! Wait, I do not know if my pen will have the courage to finish. The other day business took me to Levallois, and when I passed down that street and came to that house, whose number suddenly came back to mind, I was forced to stop for a few minutes. Blood rushed to my head and sweat ran down my forehead; a simple memory caused waves of anger and rage to overwhelm me. Please excuse me for this involuntary emotion, but you will share that indignation, that anger, and that rage.
>
> The authorities entered the house. The father had left for his daily job, and only two women were there, the old mother and the young sister of the man they were looking for. The sister, Mlle Marie Ferré, was in bed, dangerously sick with a high fever.
>
> The authorities fell on Mme Ferré and questioned her harshly. They ordered her to reveal the hiding place of her son. She swore she didn't know it and that, if she did, it was terrible to tell a mother to betray her own son.
>
> They increased their pressure and used both gentleness and threats.

"Arrest me if you want to," Mme Ferré said, "but I can't tell you what I don't know and you will not be so cruel as to tear me away from my daughter's sickbed."

The poor woman trembled all over just thinking about that. One of the men smiled fleetingly, for her words had given him a diabolical idea.

"Since you won't tell us where your son is, we are going to take your daughter away."

Mme Ferré cried out in despair and anguish, but her prayers and tears were unavailing. The men set about getting her sick daughter up and dressing her, at the risk of killing her.

"Courage, mother," said Mlle Ferré. "Don't worry, I'll be strong. It will be nothing. They will have to let me go."

They were going to take her away.

Mme Ferré was faced with the horrible alternative of sending her son to his death or killing her daughter by allowing her to be taken off. In spite of desperate signs which the heroic Marie made to her, the hapless mother in a frenzy of grief lost her head in her anguish, hesitated . . .

"Be silent, mother! Be silent!" murmured the sick girl.

The authorities were taking Marie off. . . .

It was too much for her mother to bear. She broke down. Her reason became dark, and incoherent phrases escaped from her lips. The executioners listened for a clue.

In her hysteria the tormented mother let the address "rue Saint-Sauveur" slip several times.

Alas! No more was needed. While two of the men kept the Ferré home under observation, the others ran to finish the job. The rue Saint-Sauveur was sealed off and searched, and Théophile Ferré was arrested.

A week after the horrible scene at the rue Fazilleau, the courageous Marie was freed. But they didn't free her mother, who had become insane, and soon died in the asylum of Sainte-Anne.

At the court-martial, Théophile Ferré refused to have a defense lawyer, but the president of the court, according to law, appointed Maître Marchand to defend him. Ferré explained the role of the Commune, after having discussed the coup d'état prepared by the enemies of the Republic, who had gone so far as to deny Paris the right to elect its municipal council.

"Honest and sincere newspapers were suppressed," Ferré said to the court-martial. "The most patriotic among us were condemned to death while Royalists were preparing to divide France. Finally, during the night of March 18, they believed they were ready, and they tried to disarm the National Guard and arrest all republicans. Their attempt failed because it was faced with the complete opposition of Paris and even the mutiny of their own soldiers. The royalists fled and took refuge at Versailles.

"Paris was now free, and some vigorous and courageous citizens tried to reestablish order and safety at the risk of their lives. A few days later the population voted and created the Commune of Paris.

"It was the duty of the Versailles government to recognize the validity of the vote of Paris and to confer with the Commune about restoring tranquility. On the contrary, as if foreign war had not already given France enough misery and ruin, the government added a civil war. Breathing hate and vengeance against the people, the Versailles government attacked Paris and subjected it to a new siege.

"Paris resisted for two months, and then it was conquered. For ten days, without making any pretense at legality, the Versailles government authorized the massacre of citizens. Those terrible days remind us of St. Bartholomew's Massacre and surpassed the atrocities of June and December. When will the machine-gunning of people stop?

"Because I am a member of the Paris Commune, I am in the hands of the victors. They want my head. Let them take it. Free I have lived, and free I expect to die.

"I add only one word: Fortune is capricious. I entrust to the future my memory and my revenge."

Ferré was condemned to death. Of the eighteen defendants at that court-martial only he and Lullier were sentenced to death. Urbain and Trinquet were sentenced to life at hard labor. Sentenced to deportation to a fortification were Assi, Bilhoray, Champy, Regère, Ferrat, Verdure, and Grousset. Jourde and Rastoul were sentenced to simple deportation. Courbet was sentenced to six months and fined 500 francs, and Deschamp, Parent, and Clément were acquitted.

Another murder took place, too. Flourens was killed in an outpost as punishment for letting some men escape on October 31. They slipped away through windows, doors, and water closets, and he didn't join the hunt for the vanquished.

The Board of Pardons reviewed the verdicts of the court-martial, and that board is guilty of the volleys at the execution stakes. The fifteen members of the Board of Pardons were only fifteen executioners. If the soldiers were drunk with blood up to their ankles, the Board of Pardons had blood up to its belly.

Théophile Ferré and I were able to exchange a few letters from our prisons while we were both at Versailles. I still have some of them, and some of the poetry I wrote for him. The year of seventy-one! I have a notebook of black-bordered mourning paper in which Marie copied down some of my poems, a number of which she copied in red ink, red like blood. Marie had given this notebook to her brother Hippolyte, who lent it to me, but he won't get it back until I'm dead and the pages that are now blank are written upon.

I think I still have Ferré's last letter to me from his cell at Versailles. None of the house searches took those papers away from me, and my friends didn't want to disturb them because the people mentioned were either dead or prisoners. It is too painful to quote his letter; I will say only that Ferré, instead of being moved by his own fate, looked at liberty rising on the faraway horizon across the blood of 1871.

I do have a copy of the last letter Ferré sent to my dear Marie. This fragment came to me on May 24 of this year; I did not need to see the accompanying letter to guess that it came from you, my dear Avronsart.

Prison of Versailles, no. 6
Tuesday, 28 November 1871, 5:30 A.M.

My beloved sister,

In a few moments I am going to die. At the last instant, thoughts of you will be in my mind. I beg you to ask for my body so that it may be reunited with that of our unfortunate mother. If you can, have the hour of my burial put in the newspapers, so that friends can accompany me. Of course, no religious ceremony: I die a materialist, as I have lived.

Place a wreath on the tomb of our mother.

Try to cure my brother and to console our father. Tell them both how much I loved them.

I give you a thousand kisses and thank you for the attention you have never ceased to lavish on me. You must overcome your sorrow and, as you have often promised me, be equal to events. As for me, I am happy. I am going away to be done with my sufferings, and there is no reason to feel pity for me.

All yours,
Your devoted brother,
Th. Ferré

All my papers, my clothing, and other objects are to be returned, except for the money in the clerk's office which I leave to more unfortunate prisoners.

Th. Ferré

At seven o'clock on the morning of 28 November 1871, Ferré was assassinated on the plain of Satory along with Rossel and Bourgeois, who had been condemned to death in another trial. Here are the terms in which a reactionary newspaper related the heroic death of Ferré:

The condemned are very firm. Ferré, backed up to his post, throws his hat on the ground. A sergeant comes forward to place a blindfold over his eyes; Ferré takes the blindfold and throws it on his hat. . . . The three condemned remain alone. The three firing squads, which have just advanced, fire.

Rossel and Bourgeois fall immediately; as for Ferré, he stays standing for a moment and then falls on his right side. The surgeon-major of the camp, M. Déjardin, hurries over to the cadavers. He signals that Rossel is quite dead and calls the soldiers who are to give the coup de grâce to Ferré and to Bourgeois.

Finally the march past begins.

Marie recovered somewhat, and being the only member of the family who was free, she proved her courage by going from prison to prison as long as her brothers and her father were locked up, and she came to claim Théophile's body for burial.

Because of the letters Théophile and I had exchanged, the Prefect of Police sent me to Arras. By a maneuver of the prefect, a name was crossed off the list of those who were being sent to wait in faraway prisons, and mine was put in its place. I must say that the Military Tribunal didn't know about this, let alone approve it. I protested not against the prison, where we found much better treatment than at Satory or in the temporary prison camps, but against the squalid maneuvering of this transfer. I was under the jurisdiction of the Military Tribunal and not that of the Prefect of Police, who wanted to delay my trial indefinitely, while insulting me by trying the other women, Retif and Marchais, first.

On the day of Ferré's execution I was recalled from Arras. At the railroad station of Versailles I saw Marie, who had come to claim her brother's body. I was able to speak to her for only a moment. She was dressed entirely in black, and her thick brown curls stood out as if her skin was marble, for she was very pale. She showed neither tears nor weakness, but she looked like a corpse, and she was so cold to the touch! She was as cold as she was years later when I arranged her in her coffin.

The execution of Ferré prompted me to write to General Appert, under whose authority the trials were taking place.

Prison of Versailles
2 December 1871

Sir:

I finally believe that the triple assassination of Tuesday morning really happened.

If you don't want to go through the legal formalities, you already know enough about me to shoot me. I'm ready, and the plain of Satory is nearby.

You and all your accomplices know very well that if I get out of here alive I will avenge the martyrs.

Long live the Commune.

Louise Michel

But they didn't want to put me in front of a firing squad at Satory, and I am still here, seeing death mow people down all around me. No one who hasn't experienced this kind of emptiness can know what courage it took to live.

But no weakness! None! Long live the dead Commune! Long live the living Revolution!

In May 1871 the streets of Paris were dappled white as if by apple blossoms in the spring. But no trees had cast down that mantle of white; it was chlorine that covered the corpses. Now, the ground was all white again, this time with snow. On 28 November 1871, six months after the hot-blooded butchery had ended, the cold-blooded assassinations began.

The soldiers had become tired and perhaps their machine guns were breaking down. Now there would be an end to scenes of limbs half-covered with earth, an end to cries of agony coming from heaps of persons who had been summarily executed, an end to swallows dying poisoned by the flies that had been feeding in that enormous charnel house. Henceforth, murder would be done cold-bloodedly, in an orderly fashion.

We do not know the names of all those who died in the hunt and after. The enormous number of missing persons proves how minimal the official figures of the slaughter are. Sometimes now, in the corners of cellars, skeletons are found, and no one knows where they came from. People claim it is mysterious, but every out-of-the-way spot became a charnel house to the victory of the Versailles royalists.

And the plain of Satory. If it were excavated, corpses would be found there too. The royalists covered them with quicklime in vain, because plows will uncover them, and every stone upturned will reveal them.

As I write these pages, those places are only boneyards. Fifteen years ago they were slaughterhouses. And down in the catacombs under Paris, where the government chased the Communards with torches and dogs as if they were animals, there must be many modern skeletons among the ancient bones. Betrayals so numerous they were nauseating, stupid fear, disgust, the horror—all this was the aftermath of the Commune.

The trial of the members of the Commune was riddled with errors, but the main purpose of the appeal our lawyers filed with the Court of Cassation had been to test Versailles's justice to its end. None of the condemned counted on it, although the legal flaws were numerous. The prosecutor, Major Gaveau, insulted Ferré in the course of the trial by saying "the memory of a murderer." That same Gaveau twice vacated his seat as public prosecutor, did not appear even for a moment at the session of September 2, and did not attend the reading of the sentence, a sentence in which false documents appeared.

The members of the Commune did not conceal their acts. It was not easy to be found innocent, even when one had committed no crime, when people felt responsible for their own actions. Ferré carried his acts proudly and bore responsibility for them to the execution post at Satory. The others carried theirs to prison or to exile. Yet in order to convict the defendants, the authorities thought they needed to add forgeries that were established as false, forgeries that were so patently false that some were not even written in French.

By June 1872 the Versailles "justice" had delivered 32,905 verdicts. They had already condemned 72 persons to death, and sentenced another 33 to death in absentia. That made a total of 105 sentenced to capital punishment, and the Versailles "justice" kept on operating.

Forty-six children under the age of sixteen were put in reformatories. No doubt it was to punish them for what their fathers had been shot for. Small children, in the orgy of the fighting, had had their heads smashed against walls.

In the summer of 1873 they were still shooting prisoners at Satory. After a mockery of a trial in which I made no attempt to defend myself, I was sentenced to deportation to a fortification for life.

Chapter 11

The Trial of 1871

This chapter consists of an account of the trial as reported in the Gazette des Tribunaux *that Louise Michel included as an appendix to her memoirs.*

SIXTH COURT-MARTIAL BOARD (VERSAILLES)
PRESIDENT OF THE COURT: DELAPORTE, COLONEL, TWELFTH CAVALRY
SESSION OF 16 DECEMBER 1871

The Background of the Case against Louise Michel

The Commune had an insufficient number of men for protection against the loyal members of the National Guard, so it established companies of children known as Wards of the Commune. It also tried to organize a battalion of amazons. This group was never formed, but women wearing fanciful uniforms and carrying carbines at their shoulders could be seen preceding the battalions that went to the ramparts. Among those women who seem to have exercised considerable influence in certain quarters was Louise Michel, ex-schoolmistress at Batignolles, who never stopped displaying boundless devotion to the insurrectionary government.

Louise Michel is thirty-six years old, petite, brunette, with a very developed forehead which recedes abruptly. Her nose, mouth, and chin are very prominent, and her features reveal an extreme severity. She dresses entirely in black. Her temperament is as excitable as it was during the first days of her captivity. When she was first brought in front of the court-martial, she suddenly raised her veil and stared at her judges fixedly.

Captain Dailly was the public prosecutor for the Sixth Court-Martial. According to regulations, Maître Haussman was appointed to assist the accused in her defense, but she declared she would refuse the help of any lawyer.

The clerk of the court-martial, M. Duplan, read the following report:

Statement by the Clerk of the Court-Martial

In 1870, at the occasion of Victor Noir's death, Louise Michel began to display her revolutionary ideas. Because Michel was an obscure school-mistress with almost no pupils, it was not possible for our investigators to find out what her previous revolutionary activity had been or what her part was in the events leading up to the monstrous offense which terrified our unfortunate country.

To retrace the incidents of 18 March 1871 in their entirety would be useless, and this court, as its point of departure in the prosecution of Mlle Michel, will limit itself to determining precisely the part she took in the bloody drama whose theater was the Butte of Montmartre and the rue des Rosiers.

Louise Michel was an accomplice in the arrest of the two unfortunate generals, Lecomte and Clément Thomas. She was fearful that the two victims might escape. "Don't let them go," she cried out with all her might to the scoundrels who surrounded the generals. Later, when the murder had been committed, she showed her joy at the spilled blood, and dared to exclaim in the presence of the mutilated bodies, "It serves them right." Then, radiant and satisfied with her good day, she went to Belleville and La Villette to assure herself "that these neighborhoods were still armed."

On the nineteenth she returned home, after having taken the precau-tion of removing the National Guard uniform that could incriminate her. She felt the need to talk a bit about the events with her concierge. "Ah," she cried. "If Clemenceau had gotten to the rue des Rosiers a few instants sooner, they wouldn't have shot the generals. He would have been against it because he was on the side of the Versailles government."

Paris, in the hands of foreigners and rascals who had come from every corner of the world, proclaimed the Commune. Louise Michel, as secretary of the society called Improvement of Working Women through Their Work, organized the famous Central Committee of the Union of Women, as well as the Committees of Vigilance charged with recruiting stretcher-bearers—and, at the height of the struggle, women—to serve on the barricades and perhaps even some to be arsonists.

A copy of a manifesto found in the Town Hall of the Tenth Arron-dissement indicates the role she played in the aforementioned commit-tees during the last days of the struggle. The text of that manifesto reads:

> In the name of the Social Revolution that we acclaim, in the name of the demand for the right to work and the rights of equality and justice, the Union of Women for the Defense of Paris and the Care of the Wounded challenges with all its strength the shameful proclamation addressed to women which a group of reactionaries posted the day before yesterday.

That proclamation stated that the women of Paris are appealing to the generosity of Versailles and are requesting peace at any price.

No. The women workers of Paris have come to demand not peace but war to the death.

Today, reconciliation would be treason. It would be to deny all the aspirations of women workers who acclaim complete social change, the annihilation of all existing social and legal relations, the suppression of all special privileges, the end of all exploitation, the substitution of the reign of work for the reign of capital. In a word, they demand the emancipation of the worker through his own efforts.

Six months of suffering and treason during the Siege, six weeks of titanic fights against the united exploiters, waves of blood spilled for the cause of liberty—these are our warrant for glory and vengeance.

The present struggle can have only one result—the triumph of the popular cause. Paris will not pull back, for it carries the flag of the future. The final hour has struck! Give way to the workers! Enough of their executioners! Acts! Energy!

The tree of liberty grows tall, watered with the blood of its enemies! . . .

United and resolute, the women of Paris are matured and enlightened by the suffering that social crises bring. The women of Paris are deeply convinced that the Commune, representing the international and revolutionary principles of peoples, carries in itself the germ of Social Revolution. When the moment of greatest danger comes, the women of Paris will prove to France and to the world that they know how, at the barricades and on the ramparts of Paris, if the reactionaries force the gates, to give their blood like their brothers, to give their lives for the defense and triumph of the Commune—for the people.

Then, victorious, able to unite and agree on their common interests, working men and working women, interdependent and made one for a final effort . . . [The last phrase is incomplete.]

Long live the Republic of all persons! Long live the Commune!

Holding the positions cited above, Louise Michel directed a school at 24, rue Oudot. There, from her lectern in her rare spare moments, she professed the doctrines of free thought and made her young pupils sing poems she had written, among which was the song entitled "The Avengers."

As President of the Club of the Revolution which met in the church of Saint-Bernard, Louise Michel is responsible for the vote at the session on May 18 (21 Floréal, year 79). That vote was for:

The suppression of magistrates and the annihilation of the legal Codes, with their replacement by a commission of justice;

The suppression of religions, the immediate arrest of priests, and the sale of their goods and the goods of those fugitives and traitors who supported the scoundrels of Versailles;

The execution of an important hostage every twenty-four hours until Citizen Blanqui, an appointed member of the Commune, is freed and arrives in Paris.

It was not enough for this "passionate spirit," as the author of an imaginative account included in her dossier calls her, to stir up the people, to applaud assassination, to corrupt children, to preach fratricide, and to encourage crime; she still had to set an example and commit crimes herself.

Thus we find her at Issy, Clamart, and Montmartre fighting in the front line, shooting at government forces or rallying retreating rebels. The April 14 issue of the *Cri du peuple* proves this charge. "Citizen Louise Michel, who fought so valiantly at Moulineaux, was wounded at the fort of Issy." Fortunately for her, we add, the heroine of Jules Vallès came out of that notorious action with a simple sprain.

What was the motive that pushed Louise Michel down this irrevocable path of politics and revolution?

Clearly, it was arrogance.

Louise Michel was an illegitimate child reared by charity. Instead of thanking Providence for giving her the means to live happily with her mother, she surrendered to her heated imagination and excitable character. Breaking with her benefactors, she ran to Paris for adventure.

The wind of revolution began to blow. Victor Noir died. It was the moment for Louise Michel to enter on stage, but an anonymous role was repugnant to her. Her name had to draw public attention and be in the headlines of false proclamations and posters.

In conclusion, we must give a legal classification to the acts this devil-ridden fanatic committed during the period from the beginning of the frightful crisis that France has just undergone to the end of the blasphemous struggle in which the accused took part amid the tombs of the Montmartre cemetery.

She assisted, knowingly, the persons who apprehended the generals Lecomte and Clément Thomas. She assisted, knowingly, in the deeds that followed their apprehension: the torture and death of those two unlucky individuals.

Intimately linked with the members of the Commune, she knew all their plans in advance. She helped them with all her might and will. Moreover, she assisted them and even surpassed them when she volunteered to go to Versailles and assassinate the President of the Republic with the intention of terrifying the Assembly and, according to her, ending the fighting.

She is as guilty as "Ferré, the proud republican," whom she defended in such a strange fashion and whose head, to use her own words, "is a challenge thrown at your consciences—the answer to which is revolution."

She excited the passions of the crowd and preached war without mercy or truce. A she-wolf eager for blood, she brought about the death of hostages through her hellish plots.

Therefore, it is our opinion that there is sufficient cause to bring Louise Michel to trial for:

1. A crime, having the overthrow of the government as its goal.

2. A crime, having for its purpose the instigation of civil war through encouraging citizens to arm themselves against each other.

3. For having, during an insurrection, carried visible weapons and worn a military uniform and for having made use of those weapons.

4. Forgery of documents.

5. Use of a false document.

6. Complicity through provocation and planning in the assassination of persons held as hostages by the Commune.

7. Complicity in illegal arrests, followed by torture and death, and knowingly assisting the perpetrators of those deeds in the acts they committed.

These crimes are provided for in articles 87, 91, 150, 151, 59, 60, 302, 341, and 344 of the Penal Code, and article 5 of the Law of 24 May 1834.

The Testimony of Louise Michel

PRESIDENT OF THE COURT: You have heard the acts you are accused of. What do you have to say in your defense?

THE ACCUSED: I don't want to defend myself, nor do I want to be defended. I belong completely to the Social Revolution, and I declare that I accept responsibility for all my actions. I accept it entirely and without reservations.

You accuse me of having participated in the assassination of Generals Clément Thomas and Lecomte. To that charge, I would answer yes—if I had been at Montmartre when those generals wanted to fire on the people. I would have had no hesitation about shooting people who gave orders like those. But once they were prisoners, I do not understand why they were shot, and I look at that act as a villainous one.

As for the burning of Paris, yes, I participated in it. I wanted to block the Versailles invaders with a barrier of flames. I had no accomplices in that. I acted on my own.

I am also charged with being an accomplice of the Commune. That is quite true, since above everything else the Commune wanted to bring about the Social Revolution, and Social Revolution is my dearest wish. Moreover, I am honored to be singled out as one of the promoters of the Commune. It had absolutely nothing to do with assassinations or burning. I attended all the sessions at the Hôtel de Ville, and I affirm that there never was any talk of assassinations or burnings.

Do you want to know who the real guilty parties are? The police. Later, perhaps, the light of truth will fall on all those events. Now people naturally place responsibility on the partisans of Social Revolution.

One day I did propose to Théophile Ferré that I go to Versailles. I wanted two victims: M. Thiers and myself, for I had already sacrificed my life, and I had decided to kill him.

Question: Did you say in a proclamation that a hostage should be shot every twenty-four hours?

Answer: No, I only wanted to threaten. But why should I defend myself? I have already told you I refuse to do it. You are the men who are going to judge me. You are in front of me publicly. You are men, and I, I am only a woman. Nevertheless, I am looking you straight in the face. I know quite well that anything I tell you will not change my sentence in the slightest. Thus I have only one last word before I sit down.

We never wanted anything but the triumph of the great principles of Revolution. I swear it by our martyrs who fell on the field of Satory, by our martyrs I still acclaim here, by our martyrs who some day will find their avenger.

I am in your power. Do whatever you please with me. Take my life if you want it. I am not a woman who would dispute your wishes for a moment.

Question: You claim you didn't approve of the generals' assassinations. On the contrary, people say that when you were told about it, you cried out: "They shot them. It serves them right."

Answer: Yes, I said that. I admit it. In fact, I remember that I said it in the presence of Citizens Le Moussu and Ferré.

Question: Then you do approve of the assassinations?

Answer: Let me point out that my statement is not proof. I said those words with the intention of spurring on revolutionary zeal.

Question: You also wrote for newspapers, the *Cri du peuple,* for example.

Answer: Yes, I've made no effort to conceal that.

Question: In each issue, those newspapers demanded the confiscation of the clergy's property and suggested other similar revolutionary measures. Were those opinions yours?

Answer: Indeed yes, but note that we never wanted to take those goods for ourselves. We thought only of giving them to the people for their well-being.

Question: You asked for the suppression of the court system?

Answer: Because I had in front of me examples of its errors. I remembered the Lesurques affair and so many more.

Question: Do you confess to having resolved to assassinate M. Thiers?

Answer: Of course. I have already said that, and I claim it now.

Question: It seems that you wore various uniforms during the Commune.

Answer: I was dressed as usual. I only added a red sash over my clothes.

Question: Didn't you wear a man's uniform several times?

Answer: Once. On March 18. I dressed as a National Guardsman so I wouldn't attract attention.

Few witnesses had been subpoenaed, because Louise Michel had not disputed the acts she was charged with. . . .

Summation

CAPTAIN DAILLY, the prosecutor, spoke. He asked the court-martial to excise the accused from society, because the accused was a continuing danger to it. He withdrew all charges except that of carrying visible or hidden arms in an insurrectionary movement.

MAÎTRE HAUSSMAN, appointed to defend the accused, spoke. He declared that because of the formal wish of the accused not to be defended, he would simply put his faith in the wisdom of the court-martial.

PRESIDENT OF THE COURT: Accused, do you have anything to say in your defense?

LOUISE MICHEL: What I demand from you, you who claim you are a court-martial, you who pass yourselves off as my judges, you who don't hide the way the Board of Pardons behaves, you who are from the military and who judge me publicly—what I call for is the field of Satory, where our revolutionary brothers have already fallen.

I must be cut off from society. You have been told that, and the prosecutor is right. Since it seems that any heart which beats for liberty has the right only to a small lump of lead, I demand my share. If you let me live, I will not stop crying for vengeance, and I will denounce the assassins on the Board of Pardons to the vegeance of my brothers.

PRESIDENT OF THE COURT: I cannot allow you to continue speaking if you continue in this tone.

LOUISE MICHEL: I have finished. . . . If you are not cowards, kill me. . . .

The Sentence

After these words, which caused a great stir in the courtroom, the court-martial withdrew to deliberate. After a time, it returned and announced its sentence: that Louise Michel be sentenced to deportation to a fortified place.

Louise Michel was brought back into the courtroom and informed of the verdict. When the clerk told her she had twenty-four hours to petition for reviews, she cried out: "No, there is nothing to appeal. But I would have preferred death."

[This speech ends the excerpt from the *Gazette des tribunaux* reprinted in the Memoirs. Louise Michel later appended a short note.]

Observations

I shall limit myself to pointing out a few errors.

1. I was not reared by charity but by my grandparents, who thought it proper to do so.

I left Vroncourt only after their deaths, and I left to prepare for my schoolmistress's diploma. I believed that in this fashion I could be useful to my mother.

2. The number of my pupils in Montmartre was 150. That was stated by the authorities during the Siege.

3. Perhaps there is some use in noting that contrary to the description of my person given at the beginning of the account in the *Gazette des tribunaux*, I am tall, not short. In the times in which we live, it is proper to pass only for oneself.

Chapter 12

Voyage to Exile

While I waited for deportation, I was kept in the Auberive prison. Once again I can see that prison, with its enormous cell blocks and its narrow white paths running under the pines. There a gale is blowing, and I can see the lines of silent women prisoners with their scarves folded at their necks and wearing white headdresses like peasants. In front of the pines burdened with snow during the long winter of 1872–73, the tired women prisoners passed slowly by, their wooden shoes ringing a sad cadence on the frozen earth.

My mother was still strong then, and I waited for my deportation to New Caledonia without seeing what I have seen since: the terrible and silent anguish under her calm appearance. She was staying at her sister's in Clefmont, which was very near the Auberive prison, and I knew she was well. She brought me packages of cakes and cookies the way she used to do when I was a student at Chaumont.

How many little gifts her old hands sent me, even in the last year she was alive. We revolutionaries bring so little happiness to our families, yet the more they suffer, the more we love them. The rare moments we have at home make us intensely happy, for we know that those moments are transient and our loved ones will miss them in the future.

According to the few pages remaining from my journal of the trip to New Caledonia, we left Auberive on Tuesday, [5] August 1873, between six and seven in the morning. The night before we left my mother came to say goodbye, and I noticed for the first time that her hair was turning white.

When I left for exile I wasn't bitter about deportation because it was better to be somewhere else and so not see the collapse of our dreams. After what the Versailles government had done, I expected to find the savages in the South Pacific good, and perhaps I would find the New Caledonian sun better than the French one.

We were put on a train and while we were crossing through Langres on the way to Paris, five or six metalworkers with bare arms black up to their elbows came out of their workshop. One white-haired worker flourished his hammer and let out a yell that the noise of the railroad carriage's rolling wheels almost drowned out. "Long live the Commune!" he cried. Something like a promise to stay worthy of his salute filled my heart.

That evening we arrived in Paris in a prison carriage. As we were being transported from the Gare de l'Est to the Gare d'Orléans, I peered out and could see the little shop on the rue Saint-Honoré where my mother planned to live with a relative after my departure. We left almost immediately from the Gare d'Orléans, and the next day around four in the afternoon we arrived near the Atlantic coast at the prison of la Rochelle.

On August 8 we were put aboard a vessel, the *Comète,* to go the last thirty kilometers to Rochefort. Aboard the *Comète* we were treated like a vanquished enemy, not like evildoers, and some friendly people in small boats followed the *Comète* the entire way. We answered their salute from afar. As my last farewell I wanted to wave a red scarf I had saved since the Commune, but it was buried deep in my baggage, hidden from any search, and on deck I had only my black veil.

In the harbor at Rochefort we were put aboard the old warship *Virginie.* On Sunday, August 10, the crew let out the sails and weighed anchor while they sang the old war songs of Brittany. The rhythm of their songs multiplied their strength, and the cable rose while the men sweated. Their harmony became a force without which it would have been impossible to raise the anchor.

Until Monday we skirted the coasts of France. Then came the open sea. At first two or three ships were in sight on the horizon; then only one; then none at all. Two seabirds accompanied us for some time, but toward the fourteenth the last large ones disappeared. On the sixteenth the waves were strong. The wind blew a tempest, and the sun made a thousand flashes on the water. Two rivers of diamonds seemed to slide down the flanks of the ship.

It was really my ship then, alone under the heavens! Except for the trip between Chaumont and Paris, I had never traveled. Now I was taking a long voyage on a warship; I would never have dared to dream of such a stroke of good luck, especially with the state paying the cost. It was true that ultimately the cost was high: our people by the thousands fallen in the slaughter and mothers who believed they would never see us again. Still, to me, the sea was the most beautiful of spectacles, even though from infancy pictures and tales and especially my imagination had filled my mind with the ocean. I had dreamed of the ocean the way it truly was, and now that the reality had appeared, I was charmed and magnetized by its immensity. In my imagination I had loved the sea all my life; now I loved it as I really saw it.

For my first toys my grandfather had made me boats, beautiful little ones whose sails could be clewed up with cables of thick thread. In a poem about my childhood, I wrote about those toy boats my grandfather made.

As my first toys, he made me some boats.
Ships of great beauty with real sails and masts,
And we floated them through the cool of the pond.
We sailed them through hazards of monstrous brown toads,
Which sometimes turned and leaped on their decks
Down near the old elm where honeybees swarmed
In the hot summer sun, midst the roses of Provins.

....

How many white sails I saw as a child.
They swooped o'er the waves in my dreams of the night,
There was one in the starlight that floated alone,
A soaring white bird against blackest horizon.
How great was its beauty! I painted it brightly,
And stood struck with awe at its forest of rigging.
My grandfather said: "I will build you a ship,
A ship of great beauty with its heart made of oak,
For it is a frigate." . . .

But though he made me many lesser craft he never made that dream frigate with its oaken heart, and we never set it afloat in the pond near the red rosebushes with bees flying over its masts. He never built it, and yet on the real waves, after the defeat of the Commune, I recognized my dream frigate; it was the *Virginie*.

Anyone can try to explain this childhood dream. When I saw the ship from my imagination appear in the real world, I had already seen too many strange things to be moved by that new coincidence. I have seen things that made me think of Edgar Allan Poe or Baudelaire or the narrators of strange events; here I simply note that the *Virginie* breasting the waves under full sail was the very ship I had seen in my dreams.

On August 19 a black ship like the legendary *Naglfar,* the spectral ship of the North, came into view, sometimes crowding on sail and coming nearer, sometimes slipping back. It began to look as if it were lying in wait, and we wondered if its crew were liberators. It followed us in an intermittent fashion for two days. On the evening of the second day our vessel did some practice maneuvers and fired two blank cannon shots, and the strange ship faded into the night. For a little while longer it watched from a greater distance, its white sails shining like stars just over the horizon against the depths of shadow. Then it returned no more.

On August 22 sea swallows perched on our yardarms. We were in sight of Palma [*sic:* Las Palmas], Grand Canary Island, whose white houses seemed to grow out of the water. From the ships we could see mountains and more mountains, piled up and mixed with the clouds. From the anchorage at Las Palmas we could see some savage rocks, two forts, Luz and Santa Catarina [*sic:* Catalina], and some ruins which we were told were those of a customshouse. To the north, on a hill overlooking the bay, was the citadel.

The inhabitants came out to the ship in barges laden with enormous grapes, and they acquainted us with the monetary system of the Canaries. An ounce of gold or *quadruple* is eighty-four francs eighty centimes, a quantity of money none of us needed to worry about. Then there are quarters, eighths, and sixteenths of *piastres* and *piécettes* and *demi-piécettes*. There is also the *real*, nine of which are equal to a five-franc piece, and still others.

More interesting was the type of inhabitant. Two among them were magnificent. May science forgive me, but after looking in a number of scientific books, I don't think I'm mistaken; the natives were the Guanches, and their ancestors had lived in Atlantis. Perhaps the Canaries are the remains of Atlantis. Why not? The tormented ground there still shakes.

On the twenty-fourth we raised anchor at 9 A.M. We followed the reef and kept seeing mountain peaks without number and without end. In the deep gorges between them were forests or plantations of a somber green with delicate green spots. The bays lay open to the northwest wind. To the west we could see Tenerife in the distance and farther still we could see what appeared to be a blue summit lost in the sky, but we decided it must be masses of clouds.

I can smell the bitter odor of the waves. I can hear the organlike sound of the wind in the sails and the clatter of clearing for action and maneuvers. I can hear the whistles trilling as the sailors heaved up the anchor, snubbed it, and made it fast. I can hear the rough chafing of the cable and metal being bumped and the chants of the sailors who pushed at the capstan.

I see the ship tacking, and I see our ports of call, the Canaries and then Santa Catarina in Brazil before we turned southeastward. The sailors spread the topsails and hauled in the sheets to hoist them. Up on the yards the sailors let out the reefs, the canvas caught the wind and pulled away from the mast, and the land disappeared behind us.

We exchanged many letters and poems across the grates of the cages in which we were confined. Such actions were forbidden, but the guards did not enforce that rule. Because they treated us with consideration, we did not break their other regulations.

Until after my return from exile I saved much of that shipboard correspondence, but it has since been destroyed. The only fragments I still have are a few scraps of poetry I wrote and a wonderful poem that Henri Rochefort wrote to me, "To My Neighbor, Starboard Aft." I miss those scraps of paper on which the deportees wrote their simple letters and verses. There was one very pretty dedication that a comrade, a zealous Protestant, wrote on the flyleaf of some pious book that was scented with myrrh and cinnamon. I tore out the dedication and kept it, but I threw the book overboard. Some letters—a great many of them—were full of memories of those we left behind us. Those persons would be less free under the surge of the triumphant reaction in France than we would be in the Caledonian deserts.

The *Virginie* sailed on, ever southeastward. The sea was calm as an oilcloth, peacefully reflecting the shadow of the high yards. Then came the stormy seas of the Cape of Good Hope. On the mountains of waves all white with foam, all black in their depths, the eastern sun rose. At night millions of phosphorescent stars made constellations in the waves. How magnificent it all was!

There were albatrosses, the poor albatrosses that beat their wings against the ship or that the sailors caught with a hook. After snaring them, the sailors hung them up by their beaks until they died; any other method of killing them might let drops of blood spot the whiteness of their valuable feathers. Sadly, the albatrosses would keep their heads up as long as possible, rounding their swans' necks, prolonging their pitiful agony for a moment or two. Then with one last grimace of horror they opened wide their great, black-lidded eyes and died.

I wrote a poem to them:

Soar high in brilliant whiteness, birds,
Fly high above the roaring waves,
And beat your shining wings around
The tiny ship that glides away.

Float in a dream on the foaming sea,
Float like a scattered, roving fleet,
Gleam in the light of the shining sun,
For soon our men will capture you.

Men to glut their petty vices,
Defiling beauty, want your feathers.
They mean to torture you to death.
Poor flying birds, be fearful!

That sort of death is not given only to an albatross. Some men kill other men the same way, being very careful not to let the drops of blood soil either them or their victims.

The *Virginie* sailed through polar seas far south of the Cape of Good Hope, and the air itself was frozen under a black sky in which morning mingled with evening. With every swell the vessel creaked. The sailors sang old airs from Brittany as a magical chant to keep the cold from overtaking them, so that in the midst of polar cold, I smelled the breath of Brittany filled with the scent of genista in bloom.

Finally as we sailed across the Indian Ocean, the terrible cold slackened, and for week after week we sailed across the empty seas bound for New Caledonia.

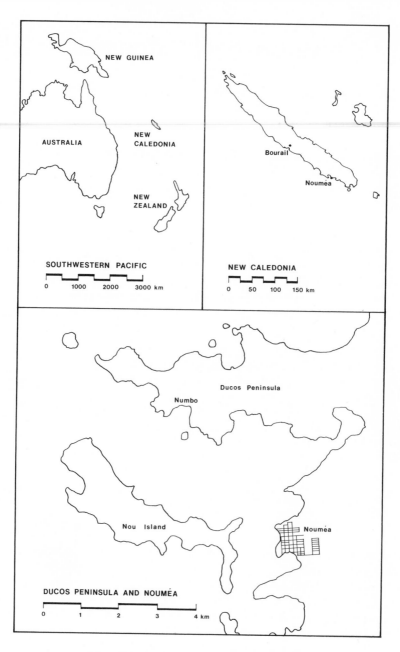

New Caledonia and the Ducos Peninsula

Chapter 13

Numbo, New Caledonia

Louise Michel was fortunate. Those persons sent to New Caledonia and sentenced to the most rigorous deportation lived under conditions that were tolerable, if not easy. Basically, the authorities restricted Louise Michel and her comrades to a small territory near Nouméa at the tip of the Ducos Peninsula. The issue of rations was insufficient, but the deportees were allowed to supplement their diets through their own efforts.

After Henri Rochefort's successful escape in 1874, the tyrannical Governor Aleyron replaced Governor de la Richerie, and the major problem of the deportees was an arbitrary administration which harassed them and cut off information about the world outside as much as possible. Medical care was minimal. Conditions, in fact, were more unpleasant than Michel suggests, but less severe than the government had intended.

Four months after the *Virginie* left France, we sailed into Nouméa through one of the gaps in the double rampart of coral which surrounds the island. Here, as at Rome, there are seven hills, which appeared blue under an intensely blue sky. To the south was Mt. Dore, with red crevasses of gold-bearing earth, and other mountain peaks were visible in all directions. One mountain had split in two, forming a V, and where the two arms of the V met, uprooted rocks had fallen backwards into some internal cavity. Those arid summits, those gorges torn from a cataclysm and still gaping wide, those volcanic cones from which flames spurted long ago and may erupt again—all that wilderness pleased me.

As usual, the authorities tried to separate the men from the women. At first they tried to send us women up the coast to Bourail while the men stayed on the Ducos Peninsula just outside Nouméa. The excuse they used was that conditions at Bourail were better, and for that very reason we protested bitterly. If our male comrades were going to suffer more on the Ducos Peninsula, we wanted to be there with them. The captain of the *Virginie* understood that we were right, and he made the authorities understand, too. Finally, on the captain's orders, the *Virginie*'s launch ferried us ashore.

I can still see all the details of the site. On the Ducos Peninsula we lived on the edge of the sea near the Western Forest. Nouméa was on the other side of the hills from Numbo, which was composed of earthen huts over which creepers formed arabesques. From a distance their random groupings among the trees were lovely. We heard the waves beating eternally on the reefs, and above us we saw the cracked mountain peaks from which torrents of water poured noisily down to the sea during the frequent great rains. At sunset we watched the sun disappear into the sea, and in the valley the twisted white trunks of the niaoulis glowed with a silver phosphorescence.

The men who had sailed with us had disembarked several days before we women did. When we were rowed ashore, they were waiting for us on the beach with other comrades who had come on earlier ships, and for more than a week we were honored guests, fêted from hut to hut.

Our first meal was with Père Malézieux, that old man of the June Days whose coat had been riddled by bullets on January 22. He had escaped from the slaughter without having any idea how he had survived, nor did we. I believe that the less you value your life, the more chance there is that you will keep it.

Lacour cooked a roast in a hole, the way the Kanakas do. Lacour was the comrade who had heard the Protestant organ playing one night at Neuilly near the Perronnet barricade. The organ had been answering the Versailles artillery, sometimes like a challenge, sometimes by imitating the diabolical thunder of the cannons. Lacour, along with five or six National Guardsmen, had pushed his way into the church oratory to threaten the person whose playing was attracting shells to the barricade. It was I, of course. Ordered to rest, I had gone into the oratory, which was close to the barricade; the organ was a good one—at that time only a few notes were broken—and I had never felt in greater form. Everyone rests in his own way. In my memory I could hear a few measures of that dance of the bombs, so Lacour was an old friend.

At another feast in our honor, one given by Henri Rochefort, I met a Kanaka for the first time. It was Daoumi, from Sifou. On Balzenq's advice, Daoumi had come dressed like a European in a high hat, which marred the effect of his wild man's head, and he was wearing kid gloves. With his hands thus imprisoned, Daoumi could not help Olivier Pain with the roast, nor could he help with the other preparations. That is how I was able to get him alone and have him sing a war chant to me while I fed leaves to a she-goat tethered to a castor oil plant.

Daoumi sang that war chant in the soft voice of the Kanakas. A threat howled through its tune in quarter tones, and the farewell at the end came out as a true cry; the Kanakas get those quarter tones from the cyclones, just as the Arabs draw theirs from the hot and violent wind of the desert.

Within the prison area on the Ducos Peninsula, the town of Numbo grew up little by little, each new arrival adding his own earthen hut covered with grass. Numbo, in the valley, was crescent-shaped, the eastern end being the top of the crescent and containing the prison, the post office, and the canteen. The other end, the western one, lay in a forest on low hills covered with salt-resistant plants. The middle of the crescent, running along the whole length of the bays from east to west, was where we built our huts.

Each person built his nest or dug his lair according to his own impulses. From a distance Bauër's hut was a beautiful villa. He had hung a basket in front of it filled with euphorbia that was sometimes cared for. Père Croiset had built a chimney for his hut, and with luck you could almost make coffee there to celebrate the anniversary of March 18 without making the roof go up in flames. G—— had ploughed up half the mountainside to plant crops; an onlooker would have thought he was watching the Swiss Family Robinson. In G——'s storehouse under a rock he kept a whole menagerie, in the midst of which his cat reigned supreme. At the very top of the mountain Burlot dwelt like a lookout. You could hear the sonorous cackle of his hen, which sang out like a donkey warning him of anyone entering his place.

Champy's hut on the western coast was so small that when several people sat down there it was like being in a basket. When the wind blew, as it did strongly enough to tear the horns off cattle in the forest and on Nou Island southwest of us in the bay, it made Champy's little basket dance.

Provins had a stupendous voice and would yell across from one bay to another, trying to chat with us across four hundred meters of water. We could hear him, but our responses couldn't reach him. He was the only one among us with such a powerful voice.

Père Malézieux had built his hut with his smithy at the edge of a large forest, which we called Père Malézieux's Forest. Near him lived Balzenq, a former staff member of Blanqui's newspaper, and in his hole full of crucibles, Balzenq distilled an essence of niaouli from the trees. At his hut you could almost believe you were visiting some alchemist. Bunant lived nearby and went into the woods with his hatchet in his belt; he and his wife both dressed like bandits.

All our operations were as primitive as the Stone Age. We had to make our own tools, improvising as best we could for the things we lacked or that weren't allowed in the camp.

When I was living at Numbo in a hut below the infirmary, I partially demolished an uninhabited hut to make it into a greenhouse. The guards were appalled at my audacity in daring to touch a building owned by the state. Even the deportees found my action a little brash, and speculated on what the governor—at that time de la Richerie— would do when he inspected the area and found out about it.

As it turned out, I was able to get his sympathy for my experiment when he came. I took him inside the greenhouse and showed him some trees standing in the best-lit corner. They were papayas which I had vaccinated with the sap of other papayas afflicted with plant jaundice, and I wanted to keep them hidden until my experiment was completed. Governor de la Richerie understood my experiment and gave orders that I be allowed to continue using the greenhouse.

I wanted to succeed with twenty trees before I talked about my experiment. That was important to me because even among the deportees, where all of us were suffering for having loved liberty, prejudice still remained. What would my comrades have said if I had talked openly about using vaccines on vegetables? Even when only very few persons knew what I was doing I kept hearing things like, "If it were true that vaccines could be used against all illnesses, professors of medicine would already have done it. Are you some sort of scientist that you are so busy on projects like this?"

Since that time scientists have tried vaccines for rabies and cholera, just as I tried it for plant jaundice in New Caledonia. Sap is like blood, and the same principles that govern diseases of the blood apply to the illnesses of plants. If boldness is useful to experimenters, it is most useful when it is employed to reason about the analogies that exist among all living things.

My four vaccinated papayas contracted jaundice, but they recovered. Perhaps they were the only ones which did not die of plant jaundice that year, especially on the peninsula. Before my experiment was complete, however, a new governor, the brutal and grotesque Aleyron, sent us women to the Bay of the West, and I don't know what became of my trees.

Governor Aleyron took over in 1874, following Henri Rochefort's escape, and the situation of the deportees worsened greatly. Governor Aleyron's time in office was a time of desperate madness. On one side of the area to which we were confined was the prison itself, and under Governor Aleyron the prison was always full. Many of our friends were locked up there for long periods. Odious things happened. The guards shot at any deportee who returned to his cabin after curfew, even if he was only a few minutes late. One unfortunate man who didn't have all his wits about him was shot at, the way somebody would have taken aim at a rabbit, because he came back a little late to his plot. At roll calls there were similar insults, and as punishment the deportees were deprived of bread.

The comical thing—there is always something comical—was that Aleyron set sentries around Numbo at night, and their calls in the midst of silence created an operatic effect. The sentries cast black shadows as they stood under the full moonlight which came over the peaks. Down from the top of the mountains we heard the clear night echo to, "Sentinels, take care." It was almost as if I were at a performance of the *Tour de Nesles* on an immensely enlarged stage, and I admit I enjoyed the spectacle greatly. Some of the sentries had beautiful, deep voices, and chance picked them to begin. But then their voices grew hoarse and the effect palled.

Even under Aleyron and Admiral Ribourt, who was on the island investigating Rochefort's escape, I was able to smuggle a few letters out. They described the illegal actions of Governor Aleyron, and they tell the story of our transfer from Numbo to the Bay of the West.

Numbo, New Caledonia
18 April 1875

Dear friends:

From the publicity given the revelations made by those who have escaped recently, you ought to know, more or less, the situation of the deportees. You ought to know about the abuses of authority which Messieurs Ribourt, Aleyron, and their consorts are guilty of.

Under Admiral Ribourt our letters were opened and read, as if the few persons who had survived the slaughter of 1871 still struck fear into the assassins across the ocean.

Under Colonel Aleyron, the hero of the Lobau barracks, a guard fired at a deportee sitting in his own hut. That deportee had unknowingly crossed the boundary to look for firewood. Earlier another guard had shot at Croiset's dog, which was lying between the legs of his master, and I don't know whether the guard was aiming at the man or the dog.

So many things have happened since then. It seems to me that I'm going to forget something, because there is so much to tell, but I'll remember sooner or later.

You have already learned that the guards cut off the bread ration of the deportees who showed up for roll call but did not line up in two rows in a military fashion. The deportation laws do not require them to line up that way, and their protest was vigorous but peaceful. It showed that the deportees had not forgotten solidarity, in spite of the divisions brought about among us by people foreign to our cause, whom the administrators have deliberately mixed with us. Since then, the guards have cut off supplies to forty-five deportees, allowing them to receive only bread, salt, and dried vegetables. Their only crime was showing their hostility to a job that existed solely in the officials' imagination.

Four women have also been deprived of supplies on the charge that their conduct and morality left something to be desired. That charge is false. The husband of one of those women, the deportee Langlois, responded vehemently because his wife had given him no grounds for discontent. For defending his wife against those slanders, he was sentenced to eighteen months in prison and fined 3000 francs.

Verlet says that the deportee Henry Place also spoke up for the woman who is his companion, the conduct of whom merits the respect of all the deportees. Place nevertheless was sentenced to six months in prison and fined 500 francs. Even worse, nothing can bring his child back to life. The child was born while Place was imprisoned awaiting trial, and it died as a consequence of the torments suffered by its mother, who was nursing it. Place was never allowed to see his child alive.

The courageous and dignified Cipriani was sentenced to eighteen months in prison and fined 3000 francs. Nourny was treated the same way for writing insolent letters to the authorities, letters that they clearly deserved.

Recently, Citizen Malézieux, the dean of the deportees, was seated one evening in front of his hut chatting with several deportees who work with him. A drunken guard accused him of disturbing the peace at night and struck him, whereupon Malézieux was put in prison.

Our beloved conquerors mix the droll with the harsh. They have drawn up lists to give deportees rewards for hard work or to cut off provisions from persons being disciplined. It turns out that the people who have worked the hardest since their arrival have been put on the list to be cut off from provisions. One deportee is on both lists at the same time: the list of those being punished for refusing to work and the list of those to receive rewards for special diligence, both lists being printed in the official *Journal de Nouméa*.

At the evening roll call a few days before Captain de Pritzbuer took over from Aleyron as governor, a guard with a bad reputation threatened the deportees with his revolver in his hand. That challenge and many others since merit the deepest scorn.

It is very probable that in the future there will be new lists of persons cut off from provisions. Work doesn't really exist because communications have been cut off for too long for anyone to try anything. Moreover, for some of the deportees to continue their old professions would require some basic expenditures which it is impossible for them to make.

Telling all these things will serve to tear the veil completely away from the events in New Caledonia. It will show just where the hatred of the victors can descend, and that is useful to know. But not to imitate them, for we are neither butchers nor jailers. We need to know and publicize the exploits of the party of order so that its defeat will be complete.

Farewell. I'll see you soon, perhaps, if the situation requires those of us who don't value our lives highly to risk them to escape, so that we can tell people about the crimes our lords and masters are committing here in New Caledonia.

Louise Michel, number 1

At the end of this letter of 18 April 1875 I went on to talk about an escape plan Mme Rastoul and I had worked out. Mme Rastoul lived in Australia, and we developed our plan through letters we smuggled from the Ducos Peninsula to Sydney and back hidden in the bottom of a box of sewing materials.

The plan was that one night after roll call I was to climb over the mountain and get to the Northern Forest. There I would get on the road that ran through the Northern Forest, and if I observed three or four risky precautions as I followed it, I would finally enter Nouméa through the cemetery. Meanwhile, Mme Rastoul would arrange for someone to smuggle me aboard the mail packet to Sydney. When I arrived in Sydney I would tell about the actions of Aleyron and Ribourt, inspiring the English, I hoped, to send a brig crewed by bold sailors. I would return on the brig to rescue the other deportees, or if I failed to move the English, I would return alone.

It was the sewing box containing the plan which failed to return. When I finally came through Sydney after I was legally repatriated, I learned from Mme Rastoul (now Mme Henry) that at the moment when I was supposed to receive the message to carry out our escape plan, someone handed our sewing box over to the authorities.

I have no idea why the New Caledonian administration never spoke to me about those plans for escape they had intercepted, but it may have been one motive behind sending us women from Numbo to the Bay of the West.

A month after I wrote the letter to my friends about the evil acts of Governor Aleyron and his guards, we women were ordered to move from Numbo to the Bay of the West, which is also on the Ducos Peninsula, and I wrote another letter describing those events.

Ducos Peninsula
9 June 1875

Dear friends,

Here are the official transfer papers I have spoken to you about. We consented to the transfer only after our protests had been satisfied. We protested two points: first, the way the transfer was ordered; and second, the manner in which we were to live in the new huts.

Whether we occupied this corner or that corner of the peninsula made no difference to us, but we couldn't endure the insolence of the first order the administration posted, and we had the right to set our conditions and not consent to change residence until those conditions were met.

That is what we did.

Here is a copy of the first order, dated 19 May 1875 and posted at Numbo. That was the way we got the government's orders—by proclamation.

19 MAY 1875

BY ORDER OF THE GOVERNMENT THE DEPORTED
WOMEN WHOSE NAMES FOLLOW WILL LEAVE THE
CAMP OF NUMBO ON THE TWENTIETH OF THE CURRENT MONTH
TO GO TO LIVE ON THE BAY OF THE WEST IN THE
LODGINGS ASSIGNED TO THEM

LOUISE MICHEL, NUMBER 1
MARIE SCHMIT, NUMBER 3
MARIE CAILLEUX, NUMBER 4
ADÈLE DESFOSSÉS, NUMBER 5
NATHALIE LEMEL, NUMBER 2
MME DUPRÉ, NUMBER 6

We protested. Here are our two letters of protest, the first from Mme Lemel.

Numbo, 20 May 1875

The deportee Nathalie Duval (Mme Lemel) does not refuse to live in the hut to which the administration assigns her, but she wishes to call attention to the following points.

First, she cannot move herself;

Second, she cannot procure the wood necessary for cooking her food and saw it up herself;

Third, she has already built two hen houses and cultivated a garden;

Fourth, through the authority of the law on deportation which reads, "The deportees will be able to live in groups or in families," the deportees have the right to choose the persons with whom they wish to establish relationships. The said deportee Nathalie Duval (Mme Lemel) refuses communal life except under those conditions.

(signed) Nathalie Duval (Mme Lemel), number 2

I sent the authorities my protest, too.

Numbo, 20 May 1875

The deportee Louise Michel, number 1, protests the measure which assigns a domicile far from the camp to the women deportees, as if their presence in the camp was a scandal. The same law governs both male and female deportees; no unmerited insult should be added.

I cannot go to this new domicile unless the administration publicly posts its motives for sending us there.

The deportee Louise Michel declares that if those motives are insulting, she will be obliged to protest to the end, no matter what happens to her.

Louise Michel, number 1

The day after our protests, we were warned to be ready to move during the day, an order we hastened not to obey. We were firmly resolved not to leave Numbo until the authorities acceded to our just protests. We declared we were ready to go to the prison if they wished, but we would certainly not bother to move as they had ordered. We affirmed, however, that once the insolent proclamation was corrected and our lodgings arranged in such a way that we wouldn't disturb each other, we had no reason to prefer one place to another.

The head guard was very annoyed with us. Toward evening he came on horseback so he would appear more imposing, but his horse kept breaking wind, which spoiled the effect. And then, bored with the long pause his master made in front of our huts, the horse ran back to the military camp more swiftly than his rider wished.

Three or four days later, the governor and the territorial commanding officer came to our huts. They promised to accede to our demands by putting up a second proclamation, and they agreed to separate us in little huts where we would be able to live in twos and threes as we wished. Thus at the Bay of the West we would be allowed to group ourselves according to our trades.

They fulfilled a part of their commitments immediately, but so long as they weren't met totally, it was impossible for them to make us leave Numbo. Their problem was that there were no places for us in the prison, so they decided to meet our demands completely. Now we are at the Bay of the West. It is sad for Mme Lemel, who is so sick she can scarcely walk. That's why I'm not rejoicing in the nearness of the forest I love so much.

Without passion or anger, that is the story of our transfer.

Louise Michel, number 1
Bay of the West, 9 June 1875

The administration gave in to our rebellion because it would have had greater problems if it had not; there was no special prison in which to keep a half-dozen women. But in June 1875 I made a new beginning at the Bay of the West.

Chapter 14

The Bay of the West

When I was forced to go to the Bay of the West, I had a greater opportunity to observe the countryside that I loved. Between the Western Forest and the sea, there is a band of volcanic rocks, some standing like the menhirs at Karnak, others affecting monstrous poses, one even looking like an enormous rose with a few broken petals. At high tide the sea prevents people who are fearful of the water from prowling around. Dominating the Western Forest is the signal post. Covered with swallows resting on its supports, the signal post appears from afar to be a gigantic tree with spreading branches, and from their resting places the talkative swallows gossip with each other.

The forest was beautiful. Lianas cover it with creepers twice a year, their branches floating in the air or thrown in mad arabesques. Almost all of them have white or yellow flowers, but different varieties of liana have differently shaped leaves. Some are like arrowheads in the tarot, others like lanceheads, and still others like grape leaves. Others have leaves that look like cut glass.

There is another creeper with grape leaves which are fragile and transparent and covered with a sort of down, like a French plum. It has flat, checkered seeds covered with a vermillion fruit, like the jellyfish that cyclones scrape up from the bottom of the sea and throw on the beach.

The woods are red with indigenous tomatoes about the size of French cherries. They climb high up through the shade, and, like strawberries, they put out fruit where the sun reaches through. There are figs which smell like ashes, fat mulberries covered with an odorless white coating like sugar, and yellow plums with an enormous round pit. Most people said the fruits weren't fit to eat, but I liked them; indeed, I preferred them to European fruit. I particularly liked gathering them from bushes between the rocks in the profound silence of the forest. Then all I needed was a light breeze from the sea and some good letter from my mother or Marie in my pocket.

There are berries which look like black currants. They have a fragrant aroma, although each cluster of fruit yields scarcely half a drop of juice. It has the bouquet of a very strong madeira, and I believe it could be fermented to make a liquor that would comfort the sick.

When I walked in the Western Forest, I saw few niaoulis, which are uncommon there but plentiful on the high slopes that crown the Ducos Peninsula. On dark nights the niaoulis give off a phosphorescence, and in the light of the full moon their branches rise up weeping like the arms of giants crying over the enslavement of the earth.

In the midst of the Western Forest, deep in a gorge between little knolls still impregnated with the bitter odor of the sea, there is an immense tree very like a European olive tree, and its branches stretch out horizontally, like a larch. No insect ever lands on its bitter-tasting black leaves, and no matter what the time of day or season, there is a grottolike coolness in its shadow, refreshing to thought as well as body. Above it, enveloping a whole rock with its archings, was a banyan tree, which was cut down in the last year of our exile. Never have I seen stranger insects than those that lived in the clefts of worn-away rock under the shadow of that banyan tree. If we hadn't been forbidden to have alcohol, I would have been able to preserve some of them.

Once and sometimes twice a year a gray snow enveloped the peninsula, sometimes ankle deep and whirling around. It was locusts. Noise scared them away temporarily, but they always returned, and eventually they devoured the forests and the cultivated lands alike. Leaves, vegetables, tender grass, old bushes—everything except the trunks of the trees was eaten.

If they appeared a second time, it was because the eggs of the first wave had hatched in the bushes. They remained there wingless for a time before flying out to devour the second crop and then to go off elsewhere to destroy the vegetation of some other area, lay eggs, and die. Perhaps men could sweep the locusts into deep trenches, and cover them with enough earth to blanket the smell; then the locusts would become a rich fertilizer.

Nothing was as beautiful as the gray and turbulent snow of the locusts. Their uniform color filled the whole sky, and the insects filtered the sun's rays, making it look as if the sunlight were coming through a sieve. From the sky, gray flakes fell in a strangely blurred chiaroscuro.

Only as a last resort did the locusts attack the castor oil plants that grew everywhere; and often they left those plants completely untouched. So castor oil silkworms could be raised in New Caledonia, and they are esteemed in the Indies almost as highly as the mulberry silkworms. For ten years I wrote asking scholars to send me castor oil silkworm eggs. In telling this story I beg the pardon of those savants who sent them to me, but they always sent the eggs first to Paris. From there they came through the mail to me half across the world, and they always died in transit. Yet ships came to Nouméa which had just stopped at the very places from which those eggs had been sent to France. During the last year of my exile, after thoroughly cursing the manners and customs of scholars who do nothing the simple way, I found some castor oil plants covered with worms that looked like silkworm moths. Perhaps silkworms exist in the wild in New Caledonia, and I will know someday.

New Caledonia is the paradise of spiders, too, among them a silk-spinning spider. It spins a tent of gauze and might be useful for mankind. The natives respect spiders because they think spiders destroy cockroaches. They even allow an enormous, black, hairy-legged variety to run free in their houses for that purpose. The Kanakas also esteem a fat white spider, which looks like a giant hazelnut, for its fine taste; they esteem it as highly as the locusts, which they eat like shrimp.

Another spider is a real monster. It exploits the work of little spiders who live in its web and repair it. Does the big spider eat them eventually? Probably, unless their work is more profitable than the nourishment they provide.

At the top of the high knolls in the Western Forest, enormous rocks have collapsed like the ruins of fortresses and have been covered over with pink heather, fragile creepers, and fragrant flowers. Among those ruined rocks lives a brown spider, as hairy as a bear. The female attaches the male to her web, and when he no longer pleases her, she devours him. That is the opposite of the human species.

No New Caledonian insect has a venom that affects humans yet; they have known man for too short a time. Even the animals that use poisons against each other cannot harm man.

Even the water serpents pose no threat to man. Their fangs are too short, and their species is disappearing everywhere. Those serpents are large and very beautiful. Some have white and black rings; others have patches of white and black. Some of us tamed them, and for a long time I kept one in a water hole I dug, but I had to let it go free because my old cat was terrified by it and constantly provoked it by spitting in its face. The serpent might have ended up by smothering her in its coils; certainly it followed her movements with its little reptile eyes filled with an expression that held very little sympathy.

On the mountain slope near the prison was the post office, its veranda covered with creepers. To send a letter to France and have it answered took six to eight months. At the end of my stay in New Caledonia, it regularly took only six months. On mail days, we climbed that hill anxiously at the exact hour set. Oh dear, beloved letters! With what ecstasy I received them. My mother wrote me the longest letters, and I awaited news from her with great joy.

Another frequent correspondent was M. de Fleurville, the inspector of the Montmartre schools, who had taken charge of my affairs in Paris—mostly a certain number of debts. At his own expense he got my *Contes d'enfants* published; I had written it while I was in the Auberive prison. M. de Fleurville wrote to me in New Caledonia about new discoveries because he knew we were not allowed newspapers.

I am reliving those days. I am walking down the hill with my letters in my hands: Marie's, full of flowers; M. de Fleurville's, a good half of which he devoted to scolding me the way he had in Montmartre; my mother's, in which she assured me she was still strong. At the beginning of last December she was still telling me she was well, just as she had during those years in New Caledonia, and forbidding anyone to tell me about her illness.

Coming back from the post office to the Bay of the West, I am following the edge of the sea. The pungent and powerful odor of the sea fills the air and smells good. Walking on the path, I hear guitar music coming from L——'s hut played on the guitar Père Croiset has made here in Numbo. It is so nice on shore, but I cannot keep from thinking about the prisoners on Nou Island only two kilometers away across the water. They are forced to live under the most severe conditions and are far more afflicted than we are. It is there that the best of us are locked up. We are hungry for news of them, but news is difficult to get through a thousand obstacles.

I see those silent beaches at the edge of the sea, where suddenly a fight between crabs splashes the water under the mangroves. Nothing but wild nature and deserted waves exists any more.

And the cyclones. Once you've seen them you are sated with the terrible splendors brought by the fury of the elements. It is the wind, the waves, the sea, which the old songs sang about. A cyclone seems to carry you away amidst the howling of a terrible choir; wings carry you, and they beat between the dark of the sky and the black of the waves. Sometimes an immense red fork of lightning tears the shadows and leaves a glimmer of purple against which the blackness of the waves floats like a mourning band. Thunder, the harsh sounds of the waves, the alarm gun firing in warning, the noise of water pouring in torrents, the enormous blast of the wind—all that is only one sound, immense and superb, the orchestra of frenzied nature.

Our first cyclone took place at night. Those are the most beautiful ones. On the Ducos Peninsula the barometer had fallen to its lowest point. No single refreshing breeze stirred, and the air had announced the coming cyclone since morning. The animals became uneasy, and everybody took his beasts into his own house. Having taken in my goat and my cats, I got an idea which I wanted to tell to Perusset, a former ship captain. There was no time to lose.

With some difficulty I followed the path to Numbo. Evening was falling, and the storm was beginning. I got to his house, one of the first houses on the side of the Western Forest where I used to live, and knocked.

"Who's there in this weather? Idiot," came from within. "Who's there?" Still grumbling, Perusset opened his door.

"I came to look for you," I said.

"Why?"

"The boat that guards the harbor isn't rowing around any more. It won't be in the harbor the rest of the night. On a raft we could float off with the cyclone and be carried to the next landfall. Sydney, probably. To an old sea dog like you they would give a brig to sail back and get the others."

But I flattered Perusset in vain. I called him an old salt, an old pirate, and so forth, but my vocabulary was soon exhausted. Perusset simply looked at me silently. He was a scholar, and knowledge makes you think; it is a bar to action, for it prevents you from surrendering yourself gladly to the unknown.

Finally, very gravely, he said, "In the first place we have nothing to make a raft with."

"There are some old barrels," I said. "We could fasten them together."

"Where do we get them?" he asked.

"Wherever we find them," I said. "At the canteen. Wherever."

"Even if we had them, how do we know where we'll land?"

"Luck," I said. "We must take our chances."

"A thousand to none we'd die."

"Well," I said, "we'll take the one chance you call 'none.' "

Thus we argued while the storm unfolded and the rain began.

"Do you want me to escort you back?" Perusset asked. He was uneasy about the path.

"No," I yelled. "I don't need you." I slammed his door shut in his face. I heard his lamp fall, poor old man. He opened the door, but I had already moved away, and I cried from afar, "I'm with many others." I told him five or six names. "Go back. Eight of us are leaving."

"Are you sure?"

"Of course, I wouldn't lie."

But it wasn't true. I was all alone, and when you're angry it's better to be alone. Keeping to the rocks, I returned to the Bay of the West. How beautiful it was. I no longer thought about Perusset or anything else. I looked not only with my eyes, but with all my heart.

Like night grabbing day the sea rose up on the rocks where I stood. Enormous claws of foam, completely white, stretched out toward me. From the waves came a sound like a death rattle deep in someone's chest. I finally returned to my hut and changed clothes because mine were soaked.

The young people who were my students gradually gathered at my hut as the storm increased its intensity. They were afraid something would happen to me, so they came.

"We almost got bowled over by the wind," they said.

"I know," I answered.

And, I reflected, if only I had thought of those young people to crew my raft. If only Perusset's title of sea captain hadn't dazzled me. For there certainly was no question of navigating during a cyclone; you only surrender to it. Those young people would have found what we needed to make a raft, and then we would have tempted fate. Now there was no longer time to do it.

I began to look around to see as much as I had eyes for, to absorb this night in which everything collapsed, moaned, howled. Whatever you see at any given moment has its usefulness and beauty. Across the torrents of rain, as if across a crystal veil, the lightning bolts showed splendid with horror.

How silent it was the next day! Thrown together in the river mouth were flotsam torn from the bowels of the sea and pieces of wreckage from the peninsula and Nou Island. And the chance for escape during the cyclone had passed, for the guard boat had resumed its monotonous patrol.

On a branch torn from the forest a female bird sat on a nest above her little ones. The cyclone had carried them away without destroying their nest, and the little birds had not fallen out during their terrible voyage; the mother bird must have held them pressed down under her body. Among humans during fires or other disasters, some terrified parents forget their children while fleeing. I picked up the branch and fastened it to a gum tree as well as I could. The birds would be better off there than on the ground.

Month by month, deportees kept arriving at the Ducos Peninsula. When I first got there, few of the condemned of the Commune had yet been sent out. They continued to arrive until just before the amnesty which the people forced the government to grant.

From the time we first arrived, each mail brought illusions to the homesick and those hopes pushed them into their graves. Those exiles could have mastered their yearning to return if only they hadn't nurtured premature hopes which disillusionment later crushed. In vain we cautioned them that the average deportation lasts ten years. We told them too much blood had flowed for the government to allow us to return. But they preferred to dream those fallacious dreams that killed them rather than to listen to the voice of reason. Too many times I walked in funeral cortèges dressed in a clean white frock, the flower of a wild cotton plant in my buttonhole, mourning some father of a family of little children, for during the first days of exile it was the fathers of small children who were most likely to leave for the deliverance of death.

When I had disembarked on the Ducos Peninsula the first person I had asked about was Verdure. I had seen him only once since 4 September 1870, when we had gathered saplings for liberty trees from the garden of the Tuileries. My mother kept one of them alive for several years, but it perished in the glacial winter just before my return. During the days of the fighting, we hadn't had enough time to see our friends, and I had hoped to find Verdure in New Caledonia and help him to teach the young people. But just before my arrival Verdure had died of grief at receiving no news from home. Only a few days after his death a bundle of letters arrived for him. Poor Verdure! Now he sleeps over there, and I took over his pupils alone.

Many of the best of us have stayed on in New Caledonia because they fell into the great sleep. Some of those ghosts are good, others terrifying. Muriot, the suicide, sleeps under a niaouli which twists its white, desolate branches like the limbs of some specter. Blanche Arnold, who lived like the sweet flowers on the liana, died on the voyage home. She does not lie in the ground; instead she sleeps under the waves. In the earth of New Caledonia little Théophile Place lies in his coffin, his tiny hands folded around the stanzas written in honor of his birth. Over his tomb, a eucalyptus grows. There lies Eugénie Tiffault, a beautiful girl with dark blue eyes who died at the age of sixteen. For her tomb Henri Lucien made a terra cotta statue which survived the cyclones until after our departure. The comrades on New Caledonia cultivated flowers on all the graves.

Down the hill from the cemetery, mangroves intertwine, sometimes beating back the ocean, sometimes being recaptured by the waves. Above the cemetery is a rock of rose marble on which I would have liked someone to have inscribed the names of those buried there.

Wreaths from France still cover the grave of Passedouet, the journalist. Passedouet died a little before I returned; he had been sick a long time, and his memory had failed. In spite of all his wife's care, it seemed that his last moments were approaching and that he would never leave his bed again, so I was astonished when I encountered him at the Bay of the West, when only the evening before I had seen him look very ill. Now his mind was clear. He stopped to rest at the women's huts in the forest, and he chatted almost the way he used to do, but he was very pale, and his legs were trembling.

I didn't dare to tax him with explaining how he had undertaken this trip alone, but I suspected his wife must be very uneasy over his absence. So I proposed that I return with him to Numbo, where he lived, and he accepted.

Leaning rather heavily on my arm, he walked very well. When we reached the heights between the Ndié Bay and the Bay of the West, from where we could see the buildings of the convict prison on Nou Island, reddish on the horizon, Passedouet drew himself up to his full height. He stretched out his long, gaunt arm toward the prison, and said to me, biting off each syllable:

"Proudhon was right. Every reform we've ever tried to make keeps the same causes for disasters, the same inequalities, the same antagonisms. Proudhon said it: 'The men who produce everything get only poverty and death in return.' The best commercial treaties of a nation only protect exploiters. People will end all that. But how much pain, how much evil. . . . "

Now reciting Proudhon word for word, now developing ideas in short phrases separated by rather long intervals, Passedouet remained standing there with his arm stretched out toward Nou Island. It was the Passedouet of the old days. But he was a phantom getting ready to rejoin the slaughtered of '71. Several times he repeated: "Proudhon. Proudhon."

Then he became silent, and said almost no word after that. We walked on to Numbo where, as I had expected, they were looking for him. He lived only a few more days, and we never knew why he had come to the Bay of the West.

But that is the way I remember him now: standing on the heights, his arm outstretched toward Nou Island and giving the last light of his reason, the last breath of his body, to the day of deliverance.

And it will come.

That same hope for liberty and bread was in the hearts of the Kanakas. They rebelled in 1878, seeking liberty and dignity. Not all of my comrades approved of their rebellion as strongly as I did. One day Bauër and I were talking about the revolt of the Kanakas, a burning question on the Ducos Peninsula. We started speaking so loudly that a guard ran over from the post office thinking that a riot had broken out. He withdrew, very disconcerted, when he saw there were only two of us.

As a general statement, Michel's explanation for the Kanaka rebellion is sufficient, but more specifically, the French settlers were displacing the natives from the land; the introduction of a large number of cattle caused serious problems. The natives felt that French labor practices were, at best, deceptive, and the French males were casual in carrying off native women. Precipitating the insurrection was a serious drought in some areas in 1877, which caused French cattle to destroy native crops.

That argument was about not only the Kanakas, but also about a Kanaka play. Bauër accused me of wanting to put on a Kanaka play, and I didn't deny it. We deportees had a real theater on the hill above Numbo. It had its directors, its actors, its stagehands, its sets, and its board of directors. This theater was a masterpiece, given the conditions under which we were living. Every Sunday we used to go to the theater. We put on everything there: dramas, vaudeville, operettas. We even sang fragments of an opera, *Robert the Devil*, although we didn't have all the score.

True, the leading women usually had deep, booming voices, and their hands kept searching in their skirt pockets as if they were looking for a cigar. Even my court-martial dress, which was very long, left their feet uncovered to the ankles, for some of our leading ladies were tall. They lengthened their skirts finally, and then nothing was lacking in their costumes.

Wolowski trained the chorus. They were talking about an orchestra when I left the peninsula for Nouméa. I had my own ideas for an orchestra: I wanted to shake palm branches, strike bamboo, create a horn from shells, and use the tones produced by a leaf pressed against the lips. In short, I wanted a Kanaka orchestra, complete with quarter tones. Thanks to knowledge I had gotten from Daoumi and the Kanakas who brought supplies, I believed I knew enough to try. But my plan was blocked by the Committee of Light Classical Theater. Indeed, they accused me of being a savage.

To some comrades I seemed to be more Kanaka than the Kanakas. They argued a bit, so to make the situation a little more interesting, I spoke of putting on a Kanaka play whose text was wearing out my pocket. I even talked about performing the play dressed in black tights, and I added a few more details designed to exasperate those people. The incident took its normal course, rousing my adversaries and amusing me deep within.

The revolt of the tribes was deadly serious, but it is better if I say little about it. The Kanakas were seeking the same liberty we had sought in the Commune. Let me say only that my red scarf, the red scarf of the Commune that I had hidden from every search, was divided in two pieces one night. Two Kanakas, before going to join the insurgents against the whites, had come to say goodbye to me.

They slipped into the ocean. The sea was bad, and they may never have arrived across the bay, or perhaps they were killed in the fighting. I never saw either of them again, and I don't know which of the two deaths took them, but they were brave with the bravery that black and white both have.

There is the legend—perhaps it is a story—of Andia, the bard with long hair, Andia the Takala, who sang his songs and was killed in combat by the side of Ataï [a historical figure, the leader of the insurrection of 1878]. Andia had an olive complexion, and the build of a dwarf with an enormous head and crooked legs; his body was as crooked as a niaouli, but his heart was brave. In his blue eyes the light sparkled, and he died for liberty at the hands of a traitor, when Ataï, too, was struck down. May traitors everywhere be cursed!

From the traditions of the Kanakas or from the resources of his musical ear, Andia discovered, or rediscovered, the lute. The Kanakas have their bamboo and shell instruments, and they also have a bagpipe; the legends say it was first made by Naïna from the skin of a traitor. In this tradition, Andia made a lute, with strings of catgut taken from one of the degenerate, wild descendants of the cats Captain Cook abandoned in the forests here.

It took a traitor and a white military expedition to kill Ataï and Andia. Under Kanaka practice a chief can be struck only by a chief or by someone appointed by another chief. One chief had sold out to the whites and appointed Segou to kill Ataï, even giving him the weapon with which to kill him. Segou went out with the white militia columns and spotted Ataï between the huts and Amboa; Ataï was returning to his own encampment with some of his people. Segou ran out from amidst the white soldiers and pointed out the great chief Ataï, who was recognizable because of his snow-white hair. Ataï had his sling wrapped around his forehead and carried a gendarmarie saber in his right hand and a small axe in his left. Around him were his three sons and the bard Andia, who was armed with a short spear.

Ataï turned to face the column of whites and noticed Segou.

"There you are," he cried out.

The traitor Segou faltered for a moment under the look of the old chief, but then, wanting it all to be over, he threw his short spear at Ataï and it pierced the old chief's right arm. Ataï raised his axe in his left hand as his sons were shot down around him, one killed and the others wounded.

Andia lunged forward crying out, "A curse on you. A curse on you," but he was shot dead instantly.

Then Segou moved in against the wounded Ataï, and with his own axe struck blow after blow, the way he would have chopped at a tree.

Ataï fell, and Segou grabbed at his partially severed head. He struck him several more blows, and Ataï was finally dead. Seeing Ataï fall at Segou's hands, the Kanakas unleashed their death cry in an echo to the mountains. The Kanakas love the brave.

Ataï's head was sent to Paris, but I don't know what happened to the bard Andia's.

To keep memory alive, I have translated one of Andia's war chants.

The *Takata*
    Gathered *adouéke* in the forest,
    Adouéke, the shield herb,
    In the moonlight, *adouéke*,
    The war herb,
    The spirit plant.
The warriors
    Divided *adouéke*.
    It makes them fierce
    And charms their wounds.
The spirits
    Of their fathers
    Make a storm.
    They are waiting
    For the brave.

> The brave
>   Are welcome.
>   Friends or enemies,
>   They are welcome
>   Beyond this life.
>   Those who wish to live
>   Go back.
> War is come.
>   Blood will flow
>   Over the earth
>   Like water.
>   The *adouéke*
>   Must be blood.

The Kanakan Insurrection of 1878 failed. The strength and longing of human hearts was shown once again, but the whites shot down the rebels as we were mowed down in front of Bastion 37 and on the plains of Satory. When they sent the head of Ataï to Paris, I wondered who the real headhunters were; as Henri Rochefort had once written to me, "the Versailles government could give the natives lessons in cannibalism."

After I had stayed on the Ducos Peninsula for five years, first at Numbo and then at the Bay of the West, I was allowed to go to Nouméa as a schoolmistress. There it was easier for me to study the country, and I was able to see Kanakas of various tribes. I even had some in my Sunday classes, a whole horde of them at my house in Nouméa.

Shortly after I left the peninsula, some of my friends who had been at Nou Island arrived there, and I went back to welcome them. It was a joyful occasion for the deportees. We loved them more than the others because they had suffered more. That made them as proud as they had been during the May Days. We sat at the edge of the sea on rocks, and events came back to us, rising like the waves.

After the human beehive of Paris, any crowd looked small to us. After we had crossed the entire world to New Caledonia, any voyage seemed short to us. Days became crowded together without our really thinking about them, as if we turned the hourglass each year. Days fell upon days in the silence, and all the past swirled around us like the gray snow of locusts.

Chapter 15

Nouméa and the Return

During my exile I used to let my mind return to France. From time to time down there in New Caledonia, with my gaze fixed on the sea and my thoughts free in space, I used to see the years gone by. I inhaled again the odor of roses in the yard, the hay just mown and lying in the summer sun, and the bitter reek of hemp. I saw it all again: thousands of details which had made no impression on me when they had occurred floated up from the depths of my memory. I discovered the sacrifices my mother had uncomplainingly made for me. She would have given me her very blood as piece by piece she had let me take everything we possessed so that I could promote ideas she didn't share. All she ever wanted was to live near me in some quiet corner, in some village school lost in the woods.

Now that I have returned to France I let my thoughts roam free in space to New Caledonia. After the cyclones I witnessed there, I no longer gaze at the European storms I used to love so much. I had seen my first cyclone at night while I was on the Ducos Peninsula. I saw my second cyclone by day at Nouméa. It was beautiful, but less grand than the cyclone at night had been, even though sheet-metal roofs went flying about like immense butterflies. The sea clamored with rage. The rain soaked us; it didn't fall so much as pour down like an ocean. The needle of the compass went wild and searched for north with anguish. Great gusts of wind struck in the midst of the roar of sea and rain, and yet the dramatic effect was less awesome; perhaps I was becoming as sated with storms as I was with other things.

I had pardoned Perusset a long time before for failing to help me escape during the first cyclone, and while I was living in Nouméa he died. Although he had done many other bold things, he had refused to help me escape, perhaps because he felt he had trusted his luck too often, and to have put blindly to sea would have been to provoke fate. Men, like beasts, have an instinct that warns them of danger, and when we think too much, we lose that ability. A horse has no hesitation in surrendering to instinct and can find the road hidden beneath the snow when its lost rider loosens the reins in desperation. Perhaps if Perusset had listened to me, we would have arrived in Sydney the way other waifs have dropped anchor there.

The authorities allowed me to leave the Ducos Peninsula and move to Nouméa early in 1879. Those who had a profession and could be self-supporting were given a measure of freedom; so I went to Nouméa to teach. There I taught not only the children of the white colonists, but also the Kanakas, and among those I taught was Daoumi's brother.

It was fitting that I should teach him, because Daoumi was the first Kanaka I had met in New Caledonia, when he had come to Rochefort's banquet. After that first meeting with Daoumi, I saw him again many times. To practice European life he got a job at the canteen on the Ducos Peninsula, and when I talked to him I got him to tell me the legends of the Kanakas, and he gave me vocabulary lists. For my part, I tried to tell him the things I believed it was most important for him to know.

Daoumi himself, though he was the son of a chief of Lifon, was almost European through living with whites. He knew how to read perfectly, his writing wasn't any worse than many others, and even under the miserable stovepipe hat which he had had the naiveté to burden himself with, he had the air of Othello.

He introduced his brother to me, a magnificent wild man with glittering teeth and wide phosphorescent pupils. He was dressed in the Kanakan manner, which is in nothing at all, and he spoke French, which is harsher than Kanakan dialects, with difficulty.

There is a story that a certain white woman loved Daoumi and nearly died of grief when her parents refused her permission to marry him. When I went to Nouméa, I found that the white girl who had loved Daoumi was still living, but that Daoumi had died, and Daoumi's brother had taken over the project of learning about European life. It is he who will return to his tribe with knowledge, and he who will derive the benefits from it.

That handsome wild man had begun to dress in a strange costume he believed was European. He had already learned how to read, and he came to my house to learn to write. There we used to speak about Daoumi and of the long-shadowed past of his tribe.

I do not know if the traditions which say that another race lived where their own was established are founded in fact or not, but the legends that are connected with them are too numerous for there to be no truth in them, all things considered. I don't know the evidence for the argument that people make about some mainland Asian tribes being the same type as some Oceanic ones. But I believe that the so-called albinos seen by Cook and others in this part of the world were not albinos, but the last representatives of an Aryan branch, having long hair and, most of all, blue eyes, which are not albino characteristics. These Aryans, lost in some migration or in some geological revolution, lived on, marrying among themselves and among the Oceanic tribes. That inbreeding and intermarriage together are what explains their extinction and the rickety forms of their last representatives.

There were many legends that I learned from Daoumi and his brother. Daoumi's brother and I also spoke of the short future that loomed before his race, when untutored and unarmed men faced our greed and our innumerable means of destruction. Seeing the lofty, resolute mind and the courageous and kind heart of Daoumi's brother, I wondered which of us was the superior being: the one who assimilates foreign knowledge through a thousand difficulties for the sake of his race, or the well-armed white who annihilates those who are less well armed. Other races giving way before our arms is no proof of our superiority. If tigers and elephants and lions suddenly covered Europe and attacked us, they would triumph in a storm of destruction and would seem superior to us.

At my school in Nouméa on Sundays, I got to know the Kanakas firsthand. They are neither stupid nor cowardly, two characteristics common in the present century. Curiosity about the unknown is as strong for them as it is for us, perhaps even more so, and their perseverance is great. It isn't rare for a Kanaka to puzzle for days—I've even seen them spend years—over something that interests him, trying to understand something, and finally come and tell you, "Me understand what you say other day." Time for them is always measured the same: 'other day.'

In their minds, like blank pages, many new things could be inscribed, perhaps better than in ours. Ours are confused by doctrines and blurred by erasures.

Lively methods must be used to teach the Kanakas; they're necessary for any young mind. Even educated persons learn more quickly if their teachers use dramatic colors rather than arid lists. In any case, the Kanakas don't have the time or the facilities to wear out their pants on schoolbenches. For one thing, they have no pants.

Reading, mathematics, and the elements of music can be taught with a pointer against wall charts. With the pointer the teacher can single out letters or numbers, or using a pencil tip, can draw notes on a staff. This technique produces a spirited atmosphere, which facilitates understanding.

The Kanakas learn writing almost intuitively. If the teacher makes the words with movable letters, the blacks will write the words in an acceptable way very quickly. I say 'acceptable' with assurance, because the Kanakas have a marvelous dexterity for writing as well as for drawing.

Their sense of numbers is unlike ours. Ours has been shaped by our voyages and our crowds which have accustomed us to large numbers. Their sense of numbers is of small ones only. It is impossible for them to put a specific number on a large quantity—even one that is still small to us. Their word is 'numerous'—that which can no longer be numbered precisely.

At Nouméa I had a piano. Some of the keys were silent, and unless someone sang constantly to cover up the gaps in the melody, you couldn't use it. Boeuf finally rebuilt the piano for me as a true instrument, and at the very end of my stay I was able to use it properly. But before it was repaired the piano served me as a teaching method that produced good results. With this piano whose broken hammers or strings made some notes in a run silent, the pupils realized there were gaps, and filled them in with their own notes. Sometimes they sang notes from the piece they were studying, and at other times they searched out their own musical phrases to fill the gap. Thus they created motifs which were often strange and sometimes beautiful. Since I'm on the subject, let me add that I tried out this method on my regular schoolchildren as well as in my Sunday class for the Kanakas.

From time to time on Sundays, when I was teaching my Kanaka classes, I noticed the head of M. Simon outside my window. Then I could be sure that shortly I would receive the white paper, boards for wood carving, notebooks, and everything else we lacked. In addition M. Simon would see to it that I got tobacco, firecrackers, and other treats for the Tayos.

At my Sunday classes there were tall Tayos, whose protruding ears had been lulled by the wind from the sea blowing through the palm trees and filled with the noise of storms. After they have reflected for five or six years over the little we have taught them, perhaps they will find from that little bit the wherewithal to astonish us. Leave them alone and let them dream about what they've learned. If, instead of civilizing childlike peoples with muskets, we sent schoolmasters to the tribes—as M. Simon, the mayor of Nouméa, wanted to do—the tribes would have buried the warstone a long time ago.

Throughout the world there are too many minds left uncultivated, just as good land lies fallow while much of the old cultivated land is exhausted. It is the same for human races. Between those who know nothing and those who have a great deal of false knowledge—those warped for thousands of generations by infallible knowledge that is incorrect—the difference is less great than it appears at first glance. The same breath of science will pass over both.

When I returned to Europe from New Caledonia, the pen-wielding crows attacked me with various calumnies. Some hate-maddened idiot arranged for a newspaper (I forget which one) to print infamous things about my work in Nouméa. Those enemies had already tried to put their lies across in a gathering where, purely by chance, some former deportees from the Commune who knew better were present, so the attack was without success, or without the sort of success they had anticipated.

Now they hoped for better luck through the publication of their lies. They did not dream that thousands of persons had watched my life day by day in New Caledonia. It was another Caledonian, M. Locamus, a lawyer and former town councilor and officer at Nouméa, who answered those charges against me. Because my anonymous slanderers have been so persistent, I am obliged to reprint M. Locamus's letter, even though it is flattering. Is it worth the trouble? Yes, because all the witnesses will soon be dead, and we ought to keep our reputations pure for the sake of the Revolution, which will live eternally. Shaking off specks of mud is not useless, so here is a clipping that prints M. Locamus's letter:

Citizen Locamus, formerly a town councilor at Nouméa, sends us the following letter. We believe we must publish it, even though our friend Louise Michel needs no testimonial to protect herself against the foul vilifications against which her whole life stands in evidence.

Paris, February 27

Dear Editors:

I have just read in the *Intransigeant* a few lines from Louise Michel's response to her slanderers. I have not read the calumny, but I am convinced, as you are, that it should only be scorned. Nevertheless, because Louise Michel has deigned to answer it, I feel it is my duty to discuss the subject; also, Nouméa is far away, and the response to those slanderers would come too late from there.

Happily, there are some former Nouméans in Paris. I am one, and as town councilor of Nouméa, with responsibility over public education in 1879 and 1880, I must now give a certificate of esteem and satisfaction to our former town schoolmistress.

The Board of Municipal Public Education was composed of three persons: M. Puech, an important merchant; M. Armand, a pardoned deportee, and me. The lay schools we inaugurated in the colony produced excellent results. By virtue of a governmental decree issued by the interim mayor, M. Simon, Louise Michel was invited to assist us, and she discharged her duties with unfailing devotion. Her assistance was most useful for us.

I shall add that Louise Michel's conduct and attitude at Nouméa inspired respect and admiration even from her political enemies.

Sincerely,
P. Locamus

In 1880, after I had spent a year and a half in Nouméa, the government granted a general amnesty to us Communards. At the same time that I heard the news of the amnesty, I received word that my mother had had her first attack. Weariness had overcome her, and she was fearful she wouldn't live to see me again. I, too, was afraid that I would arrive too late. My voyage home, therefore, was sad, and I came on deck only rarely. But the voyage was beautiful.

We were landed at Sydney and there, thanks to the lessons I had given and to help from a few friends, I was able to request passage on a mail packet rather than a slow sailing ship. That way I would get to my mother's side more quickly. The French consul at Sydney had not yet made up his mind to repatriate me with some others scheduled to go on the mail packet. I told him that, in that case, I would be obliged to give lectures on the Commune for several days, so that I could use the fees for my trip. He preferred to send me with twenty others on the *John Helder,* which was leaving for London.

I don't know the inward nature of the consul at Sydney, but in Holland I have seen a painting of a Flemish burgomaster, peaceably seated in front of a beer mug. It is exactly the consul's portrait: his coloring, his pose, his profound calm. Standing in front of that portrait I understood him better than I had in front of his person in Sydney. I understood how our ideas appeared subversive to him, and the goodness which was hidden deep in his face would have made him prefer to allow me to leave as quickly as possible, so that I could see my mother again.

With Mme Henry as my guide I was able to see a bit of the territory surrounding Sydney before I sailed. There are great expanses of solitude cut by wide roads. Only the forest can be seen, the forest full of gum trees and eucalyptus. They say the whip-snake and others are common there, but we saw none, perhaps because it was the end of the southern winter and those animals feared the cold. I saw no kangaroos either, and they would have interested me much more. Those wide, beautiful roads cutting through the forests must keep wild animals away.

Sydney is already an old city; when the *John Helder* put into Melbourne even that place seemed like a European town, one washed by waves. I still have a notebook on which Mme Henry and her children, Lucien Henry, and other friends wrote inscriptions to me. When I stopped in Melbourne, some strangers came to visit us, and they wrote their names there, too. My twenty traveling companions on the *John Helder* also inscribed their names in that notebook, and those are the only pages left in it. The other pages were plucked out on the *John Helder* for sketches of my fellow passengers.

A large proportion of those sketches were ones I made of the frail and darling English babies, of which the third-class passengers had a great collection. The poor always have swarms of children; nature makes up in advance for young shoots mowed down by death. The mothers, English-women as blonde as the children, asked me for the sketches, and it was only proper for me to give them away. A few sketches of sailors with enormously wide shoulders met the same fate. I have only one sketch left, one I made near the Isthmus of Suez, looking over a sandy desert where the rocks seem like a sleeping Isis. In my sketch is the eternal sand, and then rocks whose corrugated surface looked like the bark of a niaouli. They form walls against which there is a caravan at rest, and camels stretch their necks out on the sand.

On that trip there was one English lady who took special care of some unfortunate girls who had been turned into prostitutes. People heaped shame on them because they were prostitutes, as if the victims and not the assassins deserved that shame.

I brought five of my oldest cats with me from Nouméa, giving three others that were younger and more beautiful to friends. They had made the crossing from Nouméa to Sydney on the bare deck, sheltering from the cold in a crate. As we sailed into cold regions where the wind blew harsh and icy—it was winter in the antipodes—they rubbed up against each other, probably missing the warm sun of their homeland. They had some sort of comprehension that they had to abstain from loud demon-strations either there or aboard the *John Helder,* onto which I smuggled all five of them, crowded into a parrot cage. They spent the whole crossing attached like ornaments to the shelf that formed my bed. They never cried out, and were satisfied with fussing over me sadly.

Once in London, in front of a fire, with an enormous bowl of milk my friends brought them, they began to stretch out, yawning. Only then did the large red tom and the old black female express their unfavorable impression of the Dutch ship. As for the three little cats, they looked at the fire with adoration.

The *Figaro* and other ludicrous newspapers, instead of taking as much trouble as they did to add burlesque episodes to my return, would have done better if they'd opened their eyes wide enough to see that when we came down the gangplank in London, my friends and I each had something under our arms disguised to look like briefcases. Well hidden in our coats were five cats.

Three of them are still alive, the old black female and two of the little ones. Let anybody laugh who wants to; they are something alive left from home. For me they have become a cherished souvenir—as much as anything could be to the heart of someone who has before him only a solitary life and a destroyed home. But perhaps it's better that it is so, because when there is nothing, you don't look back anymore.

The exiles in London welcomed us warmly. We hadn't seen each other for ten years, and meeting that way, it seemed as if we were reliving the days of the Commune.

While en route I had gotten a letter from Marie that my mother had recovered somewhat when my return was announced. I was happy to be among my friends again, but I was in too much of a hurry to see my mother again to linger in London, and I left immediately for Paris.

With my tickets paid for and ten francs in my pocket, my London friends took me to the railroad station, from where we were to take the train that connected with the boat to Dieppe. The London railroad station had been set ringing by our singing of the Marseillaise. We continued to hear its echo as our train left, and English sensibilities weren't offended by it. So long as we could hear it we responded, and no one reproached us for our song. At Dieppe friends were waiting for us at the station, and at the first stop after Dieppe my dear Marie and Mme Camille B—— joined us.

I have a few documents concerning my return that Marie kept for me. Here is a letter I sent to Rochefort and Olivier Pain, which describes my arrival in Paris:

Dear Citizens Rochefort and Pain,

I have received a telegram from Pain asking for some details concerning my arrival [on November 9].

I don't remember much of my arrival at Paris. I do remember that I embraced all of you, but because I was disoriented at the prospect of seeing my mother again, I didn't wait to listen to any speeches, and I didn't really understand anything of what was going on before we came to the Saint-Lazare station. I saw only that great rumbling crowd that I used to love so much and which I love even more now that I have returned to civilization. I heard only the Marseillaise, and a new and strange idea came to me: that instead of sending this beloved crowd to another slaughter it would be better to risk only one person. The nihilists were right.

I also hasten to express my gratitude and to say that, with the ten other deportees who also returned yesterday, we had a similar welcome in London from the exiles there which nearly prepared us for yesterday. It proves what good friends we are and how well we remember each other across time, exile, and death.

I'm writing to Joffrin about the meeting in Montmartre at the same time that I'm writing you. I can attend no other meeting before that one. It was in Montmartre that I marched before; it is with Montmartre that I march today. But you know very well that if I agree to be the object of one of those receptions—which really isn't a high reward for a whole lifetime—I don't want it all addressed to me personally. I want it in honor of the Social Revolution and all the women of the Revolution.

I embrace you with all my heart.

Louise Michel

I had come home.

Chapter 16

Speeches and Journalism
November 1880 — January 1882

I stayed in Lagny with my mother for almost two weeks, and then I returned to Paris to my first formal meeting. When I had come back to France the Social Revolution had been strangled. It was a France whose rulers mendaciously called themselves republicans, and they betrayed our every dream through their "opportunism."

It had begun ten years before in the drawing rooms of the Elysée, when Foutriquet [President Adolphe Thiers] went in front with the Duke de Nemours. In the course of the evening the Count and Countess of Paris, the Duke of Alençon, and the Prince and Princess of Saxe-Coburg-Gotha all came. The presence of these princes of Orléans was the occasion for that reception, the third dinner party that M. Thiers, the Orleanist President of the Republic, had given. After him as president came MacMahon, Marshal of the Empire. The more things change, the more they remain the same.

That was the situation after my return, when I made my first speech. I gave it in the early afternoon of November 21 at the Elysée-Montmartre.

Today at one o'clock, the first meeting in honor of Louise Michel took place.

At one-thirty, Louise Michel went to the rostrum and cried out: "Long live the Social Revolution!" Then she added: "The Revolution was killed, but now it is reborn." The audience responded with "Long live Louise Michel!" and "Long live the Revolution!" and people brought several bouquets to the heroine.

Citizen Gambon declared that the Commune was more alive today than ever, and that France would always be at the head of revolutions. Joan of Arc, he said, was a victim of the ingratitude of a king, and Louise Michel had been the victim of the ingratitude of the Republic.

Louise Michel then spoke again. "Let us hope that we will never again see Paris transformed into a river of blood. When all those people who maligned the Commune are no longer here, we will have been avenged. When the Gallifets and all the others have fallen from power, we will have served the people well. No longer do we wish vengeance through blood. To shame those men will suffice.

"Religions vanish in the blowing wind, and when they do we become masters of our own destinies. We accept the ovations given us, but not for ourselves. We accept these ovations FOR THE COMMUNE AND THOSE WHO DEFENDED IT. . . .

"So that the Revolution will triumph, we will accept into our ranks all those people who want to march with us, even if they opposed us in the past.

"Long live the Social Revolution!

"Long live the nihilists!"

Those cries were repeated by the audience, and people added:

"Long live Trinquet!"

"Long live Pyat!"

"Long live the Commune!"

I remained, and will always remain, faithful to my principles. Here is the report of another speech ten days later.

1 December 1880. Yesterday a private lecture to benefit those persons who had received amnesty took place in the Graffard hall.

Citizen Gérard thanked Louise Michel for the assistance she had given in organizing this meeting. He saluted the "principle of hate" in her "which alone makes great revolutionaries and great events," and presented her with two bouquets.

Louise Michel responded that she accepted the bouquets in the name of the Social Revolution and for the women who had fought for their freedom. "It is the people that I salute here," continued Citizen Michel, "and in the people, the Social Revolution."

Applause and cries of "Long live the Commune!" interrupted her.

"The time when they machine-gunned people at Satory is now in front of our eyes. We still see the men who judged us, as well as the murderer of Transnonain, the Bazaines, and the Cisseys.

"At the end of the road those men whom we believed lost forever are now coming back, holding their heads higher than ever. The Reaction is no more than a corpse the government lifts up, and we will crush it like a snake when it tries to pass among us.

"Today it is destiny that is advancing. It is the people, still convicts dragging their chains, who will deliver us from the men who have been corrupting us, and the people themselves will win their liberty."

In 1881 a general election took place. Paule Mink and I were proposed as candidates, though as mere women we were forbidden to vote or hold office. Even if men had voted for us, we would have been ineligible to take office and our candidacy, therefore, was a dead candidacy. I wrote about that subject.

THE ILLEGAL CANDIDACY

Citizens, you ask Paule Mink and me what we think of dead candidacies. Here is my answer, and I think Citizen Mink will agree with me.

Dead candidacies are both a flag and a demand. They are pure idea, the idea of the Social Revolution soaring without individuality, an idea that can be neither struck at nor destroyed, an idea as invincible and implacable as death.

Illegal candidacies are just. Dead candidacies are great, like the Revolution itself. As for women being candidates, that is a claim, a demand that comes from the eternal slavery of the mother who must raise men and make them what they are. But what does that matter? We are all part of the same slavery, and we fight the same enemy.

For my part, I do not bother with particularist questions. I stand with all groups which attack the cursed edifice of the old society, whether with pick-axe, land mine, or fire.

I salute the awakening of the people, and I salute those who by dying have opened wide the gates of the future so that the Revolution can pass whole through those gates.

Louise Michel

Here is a second article on my being a candidate.

Seeing my name among those proposed as candidates, I feel obligated to respond. I cannot oppose the candidacy of women, because for women to be candidates affirms the equality of men and women. But, faced with the seriousness of the situation, I must repeat that women ought not to separate their cause from that of the rest of humanity; instead, they must take a militant part in the great revolutionary army.

We are combatants, not candidates. We are brave and implacable combatants—that's all there is to it.

To propose the candidacy of women is enough to do in support of the principle. But because those candidacies won't come to anything—and even if they should come to something, *they would change nothing in the situation*—I must ask our friends to withdraw my name.

What we want is not a few scattered outcries asking for a justice that will never be accorded without force. We want the entire people and all peoples to stand up for the freeing of all the slaves, whether they call those slaves women or workers.

There are three possible courses of action. Those who still hope for a favorable outcome through the ballot can vote for workers. Or they can abstain. But those whose heart is full of a seething disgust for this empire-in-miniature, this government that is called a republic, should acclaim the sacred principle of the Social Revolution. They should revive the names of their representatives who were assassinated in 1871.

It is still a question of waking from sleep. It is a sinister sleep, in which we will not allow the people to remain, because when the people sleep, empires are created and opportunism increases. Certain persons find it expedient that the daughter of the people should be in the street, exposed to rain and shame, so that the daughter of the rich is safeguarded; it pleases them to lead men in herds to the slaughterhouse and women in herds to the brothel. We want no more buying and selling of human flesh that is to be stuffed into the mouths of cannon or used to sate the appetites of parasites.

We proclaim very clearly: no more questions of personalities, not even questions of sex; no more egotism; no more fear.
The brave must go to the front of our march, and the faint-hearted, when they realize where we are going, can fall away.
                                                    Louise Michel

I had no interest in cooperating with the opportunist republicans, even when their motives were good. Shortly after my return from New Caledonia, the Chamber of Deputies requested me to give testimony on conditions there, and I refused.

                                                    Paris, 2 February 1881

Chairman, Board of Inquiry into the System of Convict Deportation in New Caledonia
Chamber of Deputies, Tenth Committee

Dear Sir:
Thank you for the honor you do me in calling me as a witness concerning prison conditions in New Caledonia.
While I approve of shedding light on those faraway torturers, I will not go to the Chamber of Deputies to testify against those bandits Aleyron and Ribourt as long as M. de Gallifet, whom I saw shoot prisoners, dines with the President of the Republic at the Palais-Bourbon.
In New Caledonia, if the jailers deprived the deportees of bread, if overseers with drawn revolvers insulted them at roll call, if guards shot at a deportee returning to his garden plot in the evening, still, those officials were not sent over there to put us on beds of roses.
But at this time when Barthélemy-Saint-Hilaire is a cabinet minister and Maxime du Camp is in the Academy; when Cipriani and young Morphy are expelled and so many other iniquities are being committed; when M. de Gallifet can draw his sword over Paris again; when the same voice that called for every severity of the law against the "bandits of la Villette" asks for the absolution and glorification of Aleyron and Ribourt—I'll wait for true justice to come first.
                                                    Sincerely,
                                                    Louise Michel

In January 1881 I wrote a letter to *Le Citoyen* which they published on January 28. The problem was that the amnestied, heroic defenders of the Commune could find no work, and no work meant that they were starving. I helped with efforts to relieve their terrible suffering. The first part of my letter, however, did not talk about soup kitchens for the exiles.
The first part of my letter talked of a paltry thing, but it might amuse the reader. Various newspapers were repeating a stupid phrase they attributed to me: "When the pigs are fattened, you kill them."

Amidst several other images, I had said that when a wild boar is degraded by being fattened, it becomes a domestic porker. That's all I said. But now every time that anyone made an allusion to pigs, the reactionaries claimed that a personage in the government was being insulted. It was forbidden to name anything fat. I couldn't even mention Vitellius, and sometimes I wasn't even thinking of the personage in question. If he were alive, I wouldn't say so little about him.

Anyway, here is my letter to *Le Citoyen:*

> It has now become an historic phrase: "The pigs shouldn't get fat." At least that was how the newspaper *Le Gaulois* quoted me. They did not get their money's worth, because when they reported what I said—although they got more than half, I admit—they made it almost polite, while my intention was to be worse than the original offense. That offense is committed by the friends of a certain high personage who say that their master is attacked each time the name of the animal in question is pronounced. They express themselves crudely, while we are giving them a good example by using the proper word for a domesticated wild boar.

That was the first part of my letter. The second part became more serious.

> Let us not forget those who are hungry and cold, the brave people who prevented the return of the Empire in 1871 and who are walking the ice-cold pavement without work and without shelter.
>
> Some devoted citizens are talking about establishing a soup kitchen to be kept in operation until next March. There every amnestied person could find one meal daily to keep from dying of hunger. The project would be financed by a speech at which an enormous audience would raise the money.
>
> In addition, if a hundred or two hundred families or men by themselves could each give an unemployed amnestied person a place to sleep until next March, then the people themselves would save the lives of their brothers returning from prison or exile.
>
> That would be a first step in the people's learning to act for themselves.
>
> Louise Michel

This second part of my letter, the part about founding a soup kitchen for the exiles, put on paper a dream we hoped to make real even though we had no money. All we had were speeches and the devotion of those who had work and would help those who were not working. And then from among those people who would find in our midst the few crumbs that occasionally save a life, some might have helped others in their turn.

I had no money myself. A few idiots invented lies about my having horses and carriages, or that I got income from lands and so forth. I had to put up with that sort of nonsense during the entire three years I was free after my return from New Caledonia. My mother and I would get insulting letters after people had asked me, futilely, for three or four hundred francs, or even for several thousand francs—when there weren't even a hundred sous in the house. My mother often cried about it. But my account book is open, and it has always been open.

To make money, I would have had to sell my writings, and I had no time to run from publisher to publisher. I was dividing my time between staying near my sick mother and going to meetings. That is why I used to collaborate with people who had the time to find a publisher.

I wrote a letter alluding to these matters to M. Fayet: "As for the fears you express about my future, don't worry. I won't need charity."

Then I continued my letter with a comment on how tyranny might come to an end at last. "You have enough of my verses from the old days to recognize that I have always thought that it was better for one person to perish instead of a whole people."

The last few lines of this excerpt are and always will be true. As for thinking that one person is nothing compared to all the people, I have always believed that way. Tyrannicide is *practical* only when tyranny has a single head, or at most a small number of heads. When it is a hydra, only the Revolution can kill it.

Perhaps 'practical' is the wrong word to use. We are nothing more than bullets more or less well adapted to the struggle and are not worth the trouble of being considered as anything more. There is no prohibition against wanting to live only as long as one is useful and to prefer dying upright rather than in bed.

Although we are still savages ourselves, we are nevertheless trying to make the world clean for those who are coming. The Revolution will be the flowering of humanity, as love is the flowering of the heart.

Those who will be alive then will march in the epic, and they alone will know how to tell it, because they will have done it; and they will have the artistic skill to tell it, because the sense of the arts which is now rudimentary will have developed in everybody.

In those years just after my return from New Caledonia I was concerned with more than indicting opportunist politicians and trying to ease the destitution of returned deportees; I also speculated about the power of strikes. I wrote a series of articles on strikes and what their effects would be. Among my favorites was a piece I wrote on conscripts going into the army. I have always dreamed of sheep refusing to become wolves, and in this article I wrote of conscripts who would refuse to become assassins.

The Strike of the Conscripts

As if there weren't a social question here! Little children are born in the same beds where their fathers are dying, and to relieve that horrible misery Public Assistance sends one franc per person. To print up and display one single speech costs the people thirty-four thousand francs. It is the people who pay, always the people.

The people should be satisfied, however, because they are told they are "sovereign," an opportunistic word in which to hide the other phrase that is really being spoken no less opportunistically, "the vile multitude."

Trick election laws are applied when it is a matter of getting the herd to elect Badinguet the Third or Opportunist the First, and not used when the question concerns some right by which the "sovereign" multitude could solve social questions.

If "majority rule" were applied properly there would be a way to resolve social questions other than by selling the daughters of the people to brothels or by slitting the throats of the sons of the people on some battlefield to satisfy some opportunistic pleasure. There would be a better way to resolve social questions than by starving old workers as if they were worn-out horses at Montfaucon.

As if there weren't a social question here! Now the people are enchained through having been made to believe that they are free. The social question could be summed up in one single act of will by the people. That act need be no more than a passive one, and would bring no repression, for although an army can be shot, or all the inhabitants of a city can have their throats cut, no one would dare to attack an entire nation.

If every one of a heroic people were to use his full authority to shut down the vice squad lists, the lists that make certain girls commit suicide—properly!—rather than have their names put down. . . .

If an entire people were to refuse to send its sons into hazardous undertakings that might end up as future Sedans; if the conscripts were to strike, it would silence the potentates who claim they are fertilizing the soil with blood. It makes the land fertile only for them. If the conscripts were to strike, they would force kings and dictators to take Boulogne's flag, Membrin's helmet, and Marlborough's saber and go off to war by themselves.

Rather than do that, those potentates would solve the problems they had hoped to exploit to maintain themselves in power. The authorities would solve them so they would not have to leave their peace and quiet and their lives at the trough.

Now that the wind is at war, if the authorities, using the new law on "freedom of the press," came to arrest me at the bedside of my sick mother—to arrest me when I have seen the Franco-Prussian War, in which generals were bought and sold and in which great battalions had their spirit broken by forced marches—I would still scream out the cry that fills my soul:

Conscripts, strike!

Louise Michel

Marie Ferré stayed with my mother when I went to meetings, and in the spring of 1881 I was able to travel through France to speak to the various revolutionary groups that had invited me. On April 21 I spoke to the Workers' Union of Amiens, and one newspaper reported it this way:

The Workers' Union of Amiens had delegated fifty of its members, led by Citizen Delambre, to welcome Citizen Louise Michel at the railroad station. More than five hundred persons joined the delegation. The Workers' Union had organized a meeting at the Longueville Circus for that afternoon, and fifteen hundred persons attended.

Louise Michel went to the speaker's platform after a few words from Citizen Hamet, who was presiding over the meeting. She described the sufferings of the working class, and condemned the conduct of those who govern us.

"The men in power today," she said, "are Jesuits masquerading as republicans. They send soldiers to Tunis to kill them, as was done at Sedan.

"I claim the rights of women and not of men's servants. If some day our enemies catch me, they must not let me slip away, for I don't fight like an amateur. I'm fighting as people do when they are absolutely determined that it is time for social crimes to end. That is why I will be pitiless during the struggle and why I wish no mercy for myself. I am fooled by neither the lies about universal suffrage, nor the lies about the concessions they appear to be giving to women.

"We women are half of all humanity. We fight on the side of all the oppressed, and we will keep our share of equality, which is only just.

"The earth belongs to the peasant who cultivates it; the mine to those who dig it; all belongs to all—bread, work, science. The freer the human race is, the more it will draw riches and power from nature.

"The 'vile multitude' has the numbers, and when it decides to do it, it will be the force which sets people free instead of overburdening them."

Following Louise Michel's speech Citizen Gauthier explained his ideas on the question of capital and labor.

During that same spring I went through the Midi. At Bordeaux, I was with Cournet, and I remember that at one small meeting where various groups were represented, someone raised the question of death.

"We shall die standing," Cournet cried out. He alluded to the commotion that would ensue when the Revolution attacked the old, empty shell from all sides. The day when that happens, everyone will give of himself—the young, those returning from the slaughter, probably the last Blanquistes. These persons bound together will all support the revolutionary forces like an army. At the head of their march, those of 1871 will take their place along with the anarchist groups. "We," said Cournet, "have the right to die standing, too."

Those who were mown down on the red anniversary at Père Lachaise should not complain. They were following the blood-speckled flags, and they died without ever stopping the struggle. They died standing.

I knew only vaguely what had happened at Père Lachaise on May 26, because I hadn't read the newspapers for two years. Nothing other than what happened was possible. The prohibition against displaying the forbidden flags foreshadowed what was to come.

O my friends, I hope that none of you is crazy enough to dream of having any power whatever after the people are victorious. Every time someone possesses power, every single time, it leads to events like those at Père Lachaise. When authority has been dressed in the cloak of Nessus, you smell the stench of Charenton.

This time the people must be the masters. The feeling for liberty will develop. Perhaps it would be better for the people if all of us who lead the fight now should fall in battle, so that after the victory, there will be no more general staffs. Then the people could understand that when everyone together shares power, then power is just and splendid; but unshared it drives some people mad.

A friend quoted a newspaper passage to me that he wanted me to know about. Savages, drunk with wine and blood, are applauded just as the assassins were applauded in 1871. People egg them on because not enough murders have been committed yet.

I hope that our side, the day after our victory, or even at the very moment when we attain it, will have other things to do than to duplicate those shameful acts.

The Revolution is terrifying, but its purpose is to win happiness for humanity. It has intrepid combatants, pitiless fighters, and it needs them. The Revolution is pulling humanity from an ocean of mud and blood, an ocean in which thousands of unknown persons serve as feasts for a few sharks, and if the Revolution has to cause pain to achieve its victory, it is necessary. To pull a drowning person from the water, you do not choose whether you are pulling him by the hair or in some way he finds more comfortable.

One item deserves prominent notice in my memoirs: the affair of the newspaper *La Révolution sociale*. Because of the revelations people have made, it is a matter of honor for me to bring up the matter.

What none of us knew at the time was that the Prefect of Police, Louis Andrieux, had financed a revolutionary newspaper by supplying funds to a Belgian named Serraux. Andrieux did this to give himself a way to watch over revolutionary groups more closely. His idea was stupid. His plan to destroy us by founding *La Révolution sociale* destroyed him as much as us. It was a strange thing for an intelligent man to do, to fight us this way. If we followed his example and established a reactionary newspaper the way he established a radical one, people would think we should be sent to the madhouse at Charenton.

I knew the ostensible program of *La Révolution sociale* from the editorial printed in its first issue, and it was most attractive. Anarchy is not a new idea; writers long before Saint-Just believed that a person who makes himself a leader commits a crime.

Here is a fragment from the editorial statement printed in the first issue of *La Révolution sociale*. Who would have believed that the Prefect of Police, M. Andrieux, was on the paper's editorial committee?

The Revolutionary party ought to organize itself solidly on its own ground, with its own arms, without borrowing anything from its enemies' institutions, sophistries, or procedures. It ought to prepare itself so that once the "heroic times" have returned, it can lay siege to the State, lay siege to the fortress which defends and protects the avenues of privilege, and not leave one stone upon another.

FROM EACH ACCORDING TO HIS STRENGTH, TO EACH ACCORDING TO HIS NEEDS. We believe that society is neither innate nor immanent, but is a human invention whose purpose is to struggle against the deaths that nature brings otherwise. Above all, society ought to benefit the weak and surround them with a special solicitude to compensate for their inferiority. Consequently, the goal we propose and hope for is the creation of a social order in which the individual, so long as he gives all he can give of devotion and work, will receive all he needs.

Let the table be set for everyone, and let each person have the right and the means to sit down to the social banquet. Let everyone eat at that banquet as his choice and appetite direct without anyone measuring out his serving according to the amount he can pay.

Before the Congress at London in July 1881, Emile Gautier and I got some anonymous warnings about agents of M. Andrieux, but who believes anonymous letters? To be sure, I had asked some of my London friends to go to see a woman who, they said, had advanced money to M. Serraux. Our friends found the lady in an apartment that gave them the impression of having just been furnished, but with only that impression and no other proof, they could not support the accusation. The lady gave them some reasonable explanation, and neither my London friends nor I were led to believe she represented M. Andrieux. But it doesn't matter; the trap he set for us did more harm to those who set it than it did to us.

Now, even though M. Andrieux has confessed his deception publicly, I still need to clear the air. When I found an anarchist paper after my return, I blindly accepted an invitation to participate in writing it. M. Serraux offered me the chance to write for *La Révolution sociale,* but if he had not, I might have tried to submit my material to the paper anyway.

I admit I had great confidence in M. Serraux, and it was only recently that I learned of the trap. I must say, however, that M. Andrieux could have lied and accused my friends and me, but he did not do it. He was far less opportunistic than many others in his party.

Let me quote from one article published in *La Révolution sociale.* My original title was "To M. Andrieux." I did not know that it was unnecessary to publish it for him to read it. Someone, perhaps Andrieux himself, retitled it "Silence the Villain."

SILENCE THE VILLAIN

The traiter Andrieux, when he named me at the inquest that took place at Arbresles, has inspired a rejoinder. The villain made some costly admissions. He admitted that he let my companions and me return to France so that he could have us under his butcher's paw. He wanted to dishonor us with degrading charges so he could murder us an inch at a time.

Nouméa is too far away for Andrieux to be able to satisfy his hatred against the wrecks of the Commune. On his own authority at Lyon he had people arrested or murdered by his soldiers. But he ran out of victims and he had to get some new flesh for his club-wielding helpers. That was the reason he voted for the amnesty. He said so. He prides himself on it.

We must have justice against the one who is kept as a public executioner, the one who serves as the butchers' valet for all sorts of repression. Does anyone believe that the French people will put up with what the Russian peasants refuse to accept? No. Like the Russian peasant we know how to die, but not how to live under the whip. It is a question of wounds that men who call themselves political realists do not feel; otherwise, that gallows salesman would have been hit as many times as there are fists on the city council. Because it is impossible for the men who work for the government to do anything about him, it is up to those of us who are independent to get justice done.

Louise Michel

I do not have the last issue of *La Révolution sociale*. I would like to have the last two or three articles I did, especially the last one. That one I did with the intention of having the authorities break up the newspaper. I told M. Serraux that was my idea, and now I understand why they did not want to. Who the devil could have guessed that the Prefect of Police was behind it all?

I have said enough to make it clear that I was above questions of personality. The affair of Foutriquet's statue left me completely indifferent, also. [Andrieux was aware of, or instigated, a plot to blow up a new statue of President Thiers; the plan came to nothing when the explosives failed to go off.] To keep the misfire from being blamed on a man, I wanted to attribute it to a child. At that age, if the hand is unsure, the child is corrected, and then it doesn't matter. If Andrieux deceived us, our frankness will break the trap, and it will not sully the Revolution.

The most perfidious part of Andrieux's plan failed. Like other comrades, I had inserted in the newspaper several letters in which I declared I would write insults only against the government and I would refuse to deal with any insults stupidly addressed to other groups scattered along the path of revolution.

I have always made war against bad principles. As for particular men, they do not count. Andrieux and his lackeys who tried to set traps for us are having the trap turned on them.

Only this morning did I become aware of a little maneuver they had. When there were articles that especially attacked personalities instead of ideas (which is completely opposed to the way I see things), they would put a few adroitly cut words of mine in an epigraph. Then people were led to attribute the rest of the article to me. Personal hatreds were generated by that technique.

The rest of 1881 I spent making speeches, attending an international meeting in London, and writing for various newspapers. In January 1882 the silent poor spoke out on the anniversary of the great Blanqui's death, and I was arrested. I have copied the story of the trial from *L'Intransigeant* of 7 January 1882, because the affair was not reported in the *Gazette des tribunaux*.

POLICE COURT

Louise Michel was the first accused called. The valiant citizen was entirely self-possessed, and in her own voice she answered the judge's questions in a very precise manner.

"You are charged with insulting policemen," said M. Puget, the judge.

"On the contrary, it is we who should bring charges concerning brutality and insults," Louise Michel said, "because we were very peaceful. What happened, and doubtless the reason I am here, is this: I went to the headquarters of the police commissioner and when I got there, I looked out a window and saw several policemen beating a man. I did not want to say anything to those policemen because they were very overexcited, so I went up to the next floor and found two other policemen who were calmer. I said to them, 'Go down quickly. Someone is being murdered.' "

The judge said, "That story does not agree with the depositions of witnesses we're about to hear."

Louise Michel answered, "What I've said is the truth. When accusations against me have been true, I've admitted things far more serious than this."

The first witness called was a police constable named Conar. He said that when he got to the police commissioner's he found two women, one of whom was Louise Michel. He testified that she said to him, "You are hoods and deadbeats."

"That's a lie," said Louise Michel. The police constable persisted in claiming his account was true. Louise Michel repeated that she was telling the truth and could say nothing more.

Regardless of the police constable's story being a lie, the court sentenced Louise Michel to two weeks in prison for violating Article 224 of the Penal Code.

My friends were right to believe that I could not have said the words attributed to me. I said, "Someone is being murdered," not some slang phrase, and the word "deadbeat" isn't in my vocabulary. Nevertheless, I spent two weeks in the middle of January 1882 in jail, while my mother waited for me.

Chapter 17

The Death of Marie Ferré

Marie Ferré had lived for a decade after the horrible events surrounding the arrest of Théophile. Persons whose brothers or fathers were sent to New Caledonia or to exile elsewhere know her devotion and indefatigable courage. At London the refugees had spoken to me about a few days she had spent there as if, by seeing her, they saw friends again who had disappeared during the slaughter. I believe they loved Marie more than I did, but none of us has her any longer.

After I was arrested for the incident on Blanqui's anniversary, Marie Ferré fell ill. Her heart had been weak for ten years, any emotion was dangerous for her, and after she suffered a short illness, death came for her on the night of 23–24 February 1882.

At 47, rue Condorcet in Paris, there is a red room shaped like a lantern. Marie, when Mme Bias rented the room, told me about it. "It's a real nest," Marie said. "You'll see how peaceful it is there." It was a nest—the nest of her death.

Her illness had not seemed serious at first. We did not suspect it was going to have such a terrible conclusion, but it was in that little red room shaped like a lantern that we lost her.

After I had served my two-week sentence, I was released. When I found that Marie was ill, I was a little upset that she didn't come to stay with me until she recovered, but she told me, "I shall be well in my little red room. After a few days it will all be over."

It was indeed all over. If God existed, he would be truly a monster to strike such a blow.

Her bed was opposite the door, with its head against the wall. During the two days while her body was laid out there, someone across the hall who didn't know what was happening never stopped playing the violin. That's the way it is in cities where each building is a city in itself. The sound of that violin sank into my heart.

In front of her bed we laid Marie in her coffin, well wrapped in my large red shawl, which she used to like. Someone had given it to me in case I needed to make a banner, and it made her shroud. It's the same thing now.

Here is the way the newspapers of 28 June [*sic:* February] 1882 described the funeral of Marie Ferré.

Yesterday morning at 9 o'clock, the funeral of the courageous Citizen Marie Ferré took place. She was the sister of Théophile Ferré, who was murdered by the reactionary bourgeoisie for his participation in the Commune.

The life of Marie Ferré was one of self-abnegation and devotion to the cause for which her brother died. Thus it was with respectful admiration that a great number of friends yesterday followed this martyr to the revolutionary faith to her last resting place. . . .

The cortège was made up of a thousand persons, among whom were Henri Rochefort, Clovis Hughes, Hubertine Auclert, Camille Bias, Cadolle, and Louise Michel. . . .

When the funeral procession reached the cemetery at Levallois-Perret, several persons made speeches: delegates from revolutionary groups, social studies circles, free thought associations, and the Committee of Vigilance of the Eighteenth Arrondissement. . . .

"History," Jules Allix said, "will associate the memory of Théophile Ferré with the great and sublime devotion of his sister Marie, and it is her simple and great life that we salute here.

"Frail and gentle like all women, she was as strong as the most courageous man.

"We salute you, Marie Ferré. Your memory will live in spite of the care you took to hide yourself. We the tortured, we the banished and exiled, form a procession here for you. It will last until the day when we will glorify our martyrs who died to make liberty grow for those who remain.

"The crowd that is pressing around your tomb, dear citizen with the wonderful spirit, is making a greater eulogy to your life than all the speeches today. May you be honored, Marie Ferré. We ask that we may imitate your example, so that instead of martyrdoms alone, we will win the final triumph. Long live the Republic! Long live the Revolution!"

The sad moment ended with a few words from Emile Gautier and me. I said to the crowd: "Citizens, we place this tombstone over the very heart of the Revolution. Let us remember. Let us always remember!"

Gautier concluded the ceremony: "You have said it very well, Louise. Let us remember. May memory come back to life and make us glimpse the dawn of the days when liberty, equality, and justice will reign."

When Marie Ferré died, the revolutionary women of Lyon who had been calling themselves the Louise Michel Association took the name Marie Ferré Association. Thank you, just and valiant women of Lyon.

Among the fragments of 28 February 1882 there are many touching pages written about the heroic and impressive friend whom we had lost. Henri Rochefort reminisced about her at length.

When I saw Marie again after my return from exile, I had been keeping in my mind an ineradicable memory of the young girl from my days in prison, and her unexpected death brought it back to my attention.

I see her again, gliding like a shadow in her black clothing along the corridor that led to the visiting room in the jail. Rossel, Théophile Ferré, and I were usually all together in a set of cubicles which were arranged like a sort of prison wagon. Because all three of us were marked for execution, we were locked up next to each other on the first floor of the prison with two guards who had uneasy eyes staring curiously at us through open spy-holes.

In the visiting room Mlle Rossel, Mlle Ferré, and my children waited, sharing their common anxiety. When they found out I had been sentenced only to deportation for life, I shall never forget the look of sympathetic longing the two young girls gave my children. It seemed to say, "Your father is only going to have to end his days six thousand leagues from here among man-eating savages. You're fortunate!"

Like Delescluze's sister, Ferré's sister struggled bravely against the bitterness of regrets, and then she fell, vanquished.

When the clerical calendar that the mailman brings us each year is replaced by the republican calendar, the name of this martyr will shine there among the most memorable. If ever civil baptism replaces religious baptism, decent women will honor her virtue and her memory by dedicating their children to her.

The last fragment I want to give is a poem I wrote to Marie's memory just after her death.

In Memory of Marie Ferré

We have to admit that she is dead.
From the gates of jail, we'll see her no more.
The door to cold nothing will never reopen.
These words shall go where tears can't reach.
To speak her name will take us back
    To all those we have lost.

Marie was modest, brave, and proud,
A contrast of charm we often admired.
It's over now; and in her tomb
She sleeps forever; our last smile
Held in her heart; and beneath the stone
    My heart is buried alive.

Betwixt bleak skies and stony earth
A few rare treasures are fleetingly ours
Before pale death swoops in to steal.
We stand beneath our crimson flags
And mourn the loss of those we love,
    Too soon taken to the tomb.

Revolution; beloved mother who devours us
Giving equality, take our broken destinies
And make of them a dawning. Make liberty
Fly above our cherished dead. When the bells
Of ominous May ring out again, wake us
    To your luminescent clarity.
                    Louise Michel
February 1882

After the terrible blow of Marie's death, I thought I would die. My mother still remained alive then, my mother and the Revolution. As I write these lines, I have only the Revolution.

Chapter 18

Women's Rights

All the women reading these memoirs must remember that we women are not judged the same way men are. When men accuse some other man of a crime, they do not accuse him of such a stupid one that an observer wonders if they are serious. But that is how they deal with a woman; she is accused of things so stupid they defy belief. If she is not duped by the claims of popular sovereignty put forth to delude people, or if she is not fooled by the hypocritical concessions which hoodwink most women, she will be indicted. Then, if a woman is courageous, or if she grasps some bit of knowledge easily, men claim she is only a "pathological" case.

At this moment man is master, and women are intermediate beings, standing between man and beast. It is painful for me to admit that we are a separate caste, made one across the ages.

For many years the human race has been lying in its cocoon with its wings folded; now it is time for humanity to unfold its wings. The human race that is emerging from its cocoon will not understand why we lay supine so long.

The first thing that must change is the relationship between the sexes. Humanity has two parts, men and women, and we ought to be walking hand in hand; instead there is antagonism, and it will last as long as the "stronger" half controls, or thinks it controls, the "weaker" half.

How marvelous it would be if only the equality of the sexes were recognized, but while we wait, women are still, as Molière said, "the soup of man." The strong sex condescends to soothe us by defining us as the beautiful sex. Nonsense! It's been a damned long time since we women have had any justice from the "strong" sex.

We women are not bad revolutionaries. Without begging anyone, we are taking our place in the struggle; otherwise, we could go ahead and pass motions until the world ends and gain nothing. For my part, comrades, I have refused to be any man's "soup," and I've gone through life with the masses without giving any slaves to the Caesars.

Let me tell men a few truths. They claim man's strength is derived from woman's cowardice, but his strength is less than it appears to be. Men rule with a lot of uproar, while it is women who govern without noise.

But governing from the shadows is valueless. If women's mysterious power were transformed into equality, all the pitiful vanities and contemptible deceptions would disappear. Never again would there be either a master's brutality or a slave's perfidy.

The worship of force which exists today reminds me of savages and dawn-age peoples. In New Caledonia I saw warriors loading their women as if they were mules. Whenever someone might see them, they posed haughtily, carrying only their warrior's spear. But if the gorges and mountains closed up and hid them from view, or if the path were deserted, then the warrior, moved by pity, would unload some of the burden from his human mule and carry it himself. Thus lightened, the woman breathed deeply; now she had no more than one child hanging on her back and one or two others hanging on her legs. But if a shadow appeared on the horizon—even if only a cow or a horse—quickly the load went back on the woman's back, and the warrior made a great pretense of adjusting it. Oh dear, if someone had seen him—a warrior who thinks women are worth something! But most women after a lifetime of being treated like this no longer wanted anything more.

Is it not the same everywhere? Human stupidity throws old prejudices over us like a winding-sheet over a corpse. Are there not stupid arguments about the inferiority of women? Maternity or other circumstances are supposed to keep women from being good fighters. That argument assumes people are always going to be stupid enough to butcher each other. Anyway, when a thing is worth the pain, women are not the last to join the struggle. The yeast of rebellion which lies at the bottom of every woman's heart rises quickly when combat stirs it up, particularly when combat promises to lessen squalor and stinks less than a charnel house.

Calm down, men. We are not stupid enough to want to run things. Our taking power would only make some kind of authority last longer; you men keep the power instead, so that authority may wither away more quickly. I must add that even "more quickly" will still be too long.

We women are disgusted, and further villainies only inspire us to act. We jeer a little also. We jeer at the incredible sight of big shots, cheap punks, hoods, old men, young men, scoundrels—all turned into idiots by accepting as truth a whole heap of nonsensical ideas which have dominated the thinking of the human race. We jeer at the sight of those male creatures judging women's intellects by weighing the brains of women in their dirty paws.

Do men sense the rising tide of us women, famished for learning? We ask only this of the old world: the little knowledge that it has. All those men who wish to do nothing are jealous of us. They are jealous of us because we want to take from the world what is sweetest: knowledge and learning.

I have never understood why there was a sex whose intelligence people tried to cripple as if there were already too much intelligence in the world. Little girls are brought up in foolishness and are expressly disarmed so that men can deceive them more easily. That is what men want. It is precisely as if someone threw you into the water after having forbidden you to learn to swim or even after having tied your arms and legs. It is all done under the pretext of preserving the innocence of little girls.

Men are happy to let a girl dream. And most of those dreams would not disturb her as they do now if she knew them as simple questions of science. She would be in fact more truly innocent then, for she could move calmly through visions which now trouble her. Nothing that comes from science or nature would bother her. Does a corpse disturb people who are used to the dissecting room? When nature, living or dead, appears to an educated woman, she does not blush. There is no mystery, for mystery is destroyed when the cadaver is dissected. Nature and science are clean; the veils that men throw over them are not.

Englishmen have created a race of animals for slaughter. "Civilized" men prepare young girls to be deceived, and then make it a crime for them to fall, but also make it almost an honor for the seducer. What an uproar when men find an unruly animal in the flock! I wonder what would happen if the lamb no longer wanted to be slaughtered. Most likely, men would slaughter them just the same, whether or not they stretched their necks out for the knife. What difference does it make? The difference is that it is better not to stretch your neck out to your murderer.

There is a roadside market where men sell the daughters of the people. The daughter of the rich is sold for her dowry and is given to whomever her family wishes. The daughter of the poor is taken by whoever wants her. Neither girl is ever asked her own wishes.

In our world, the proletarian is a slave; the wife of a proletarian is even more a slave. Women's wages are simply a snare because they are so meager that they are illusory. Why do so many women not work? There are two reasons. Some women cannot find work, and others would rather die of hunger, living in a cave, than do a job which gives them back less than enough to live on and which enriches the entrepreneur at the same time.

Prostitution is the same. We practice Caledonian morality, and men don't count women for much here either. There are some women who hold tight to life. But then, forced on by hunger, cold, and misery, they are lured into shame by the pimps and whores who live from that kind of work. In every rotten thing, there are maggots. Those unfortunate women let themselves be formed into battalions in the mournful army that marches from the hospital to the charnel house.

When I hear of one of these miserable creatures taking from a man's pocket more than he would have given her, I think, "So much the better." Why should we close our eyes? If there were not so many buyers, that sordid market would not exist. And when some honest woman, insulted and pursued, kills the scoundrel who is chasing her, I think, "Bravo, she has rid others of the danger and avenged her sisters." But too few women do it.

If women, these accursed—even the socialist Proudhon said they can only be housewives and courtesans, and indeed they cannot be anything else in the present world—if, as I say, these women are often dangerous, to whom does the blame belong? Who has, for his pleasure, developed their coquetry and all the other vices agreeable to men? Men have selected these vices through the ages.

We women have weapons now, the weapons of slaves, silent and terrible. No one has to put them into our hands. It is done.

I admit that a man, too, suffers in this accursed society, but no sadness can compare to a woman's. In the street, she is merchandise. In the convents, where she hides as if in a tomb, ignorance binds her, and rules take her up in their machinelike gears and pulverize her heart and brain. In the world, she bends under mortification. In her home, her burdens crush her. And men want to keep her that way. They do not want her to encroach upon either their functions or their titles.

Be reassured, "gentlemen." We do not need any of your titles to take over your functions when it pleases us to do so. Your titles. Bah! We do not want rubbish. Do what you want to with them. They are too flawed and limited for women. The time is not far off when you will come and offer them to us in order to try to dress them up a little by dividing them with us.

Keep those rags and tatters. We want none of them. What we do want is knowledge and education and liberty. We know what our rights are, and we demand them. Are we not standing next to you fighting the supreme fight? Are you not strong enough, men, to make part of that supreme fight a struggle for the rights of women? And then men and women together will gain the rights of all humanity.

Beyond our tormented epoch will come the time when men and women will move through life together as good companions, and they will no more argue about which sex is superior than races will argue about which race is foremost in the world. It is good to look to the future.

This chapter is by no means a digression. As a woman, I have the right to speak for women.

Chapter 19

Speeches Abroad,
1882 – 1883

During the year after Marie's death, I made speeches not only in France but also in Belgium, Holland, and England. More or less true accounts exist of the speeches I gave in Brussels in October 1882. They went very well except for the third or fourth speech. At that one some young fool who claimed his name was Fallou caused a disturbance. To explain why no one knew him in Brussels, he declared ingenuously that he had come from Paris the same time I did. To the crowd he stated that I had written an article in *La Révolution sociale* proposing the erection of a statue to M. Thiers!!! He claimed he had the issue that proved his allegations, and a large number of people believed his nonsense, even though the only article I had ever written about Thiers was one that began, "The little squirt has been castrated."

In spite of the objects that "friends of order" threw at the rostrum, I finished my speech. The incident showed by the very example people had before their eyes that those "friends of order" understood "order" to mean their right to knock down people like myself who claim that bees should not have to work forever for hornets.

Reactionaries have raised two questions about my foreign speeches which would be laughable if our principles were not involved. One question is, Where did I get the money for my trips? and the other was, What did I do with the money I made?

The money for the trips came from Henri Rochefort when whatever group that invited me did not furnish it. He lent me the money, which I have never paid back, and any money I received over my expenses I gave to the sponsoring group. Other friends bought my railroad tickets. Receipts? Both in New Caledonia and since my return, I have made it a practice to keep receipts or documents which would establish, if necessary, what I have done with the various sums I have been given to dispense, but the revolutionary groups know what was done with the money. They know I kept nothing for myself.

I'd like to quote a piece from *L'Intransigeant*.

We've seen a report in the magazine *Voltaire* which reads: "Revolutionary propaganda brings in a great deal of money. Mlle Louise Michel's three speeches at Brussels each got her 500 francs, or 1500 francs for all three. At prices like those, calls for revolt have become a pretty good deal."

Not only have we seen that report, but one of our kind readers, astonished at the princely gifts Citizen Louise Michel is giving to Chagot's victims through us, has asked us for information about her means of support. That gentleman feels Louise Michel has a knack for uttering "charming bits of nonsense" and making "pleasure trips at the expense of fools exploited by a committee of scoundrels." . . .

To this gentle reader we shall limit ourselves to submitting a few figures which the *Voltaire* is also at liberty to use for its own purposes.

Over and above the cost of the first speech and independently of what was earmarked for the work of revolutionary propaganda, *L'Intransigeant* received a hundred francs to give to the exiles of 1871.

Over and above the cost of the second speech, a hundred francs were given to the Barinage miners. Another hundred francs went to the socialist press in Antwerp, and the remainder, three hundred francs, the "princely gift," was featured yesterday at the head of the list of contributors for the accused of Chalon-sur-Saône and their families.

There certainly was no less democratic or worthwhile use made of the proceeds of the third speech.

Is our gentle reader satisfied?

I'm obliged to get quotations from friends because I can find the truth nowhere else. I delete things that are too flattering to me when I can; they are only exaggerations in response to the exaggerated hatred my enemies express, and I do not deserve that flattery—although I'm not a monster. I just follow my own inclinations, the way everybody and everything does.

We are the product of our own times, that's all, and each of us has his good side and his bad. It does not matter what we are so long as our work is great and covers us with its glory. In the midst of the things we begin, what our own lives are does not matter. What counts is what will be left for humanity when we have disappeared.

Two weeks after my speeches in Brussels, I spoke at Ghent. Our friend Deneuvillers has told the story of what happened that day in Ghent. I'm going to quote his account from revolutionary pride, not personal pride. It shows the conduct of the people compared to the conduct of those who are their exploiters, consciously or unconsciously.

Louise Michel at Ghent

Louise Michel gave a speech Wednesday at the Mont-Parnasse hall, the proceeds from which were earmarked for the socialist cause. Three thousand comrades were present and gave an enthusiastic welcome to the speaker, who talked on "Revolutionary Proselyting."

Then she left to go to deliver a speech at the Hippodrome in a bourgeois and reactionary setting. The brave and courteous people of Ghent wanted to form a procession around her to protect her from hecklers, but Louise Michel told them: "We must not allow the enemies of the people to believe that any one person from our ranks is an idol. We should form processions only for the Revolution. That's why I ask you to let me go on by myself."

The workers who heard her at Mont-Parnasse were composed and enthusiastic, but the reactionaries at the Hippodrome were wild and furious. For three days the delirious Catholic clerics had been preparing howling choristers to prevent people from hearing her. Only wide open mouths yelling out furious cries could be seen, along with enough raised clubs to make Pietri envious.

There was a comic side to the Hippodrome speech; as a souvenir of the clerical arguments the speaker was able to keep a two-kilogram piece of a bench which had been thrown at her head.

The Catholic packs gathered in the streets where they bayed after the trail of socialists. They tried to murder the person the Catholics thought was their leader, the courageous Anseele, and he escaped from their hands only because we intervened in the fight. . . .

Deneuvillers

In Ghent after I had witnessed the magnificent spectacle of the guilds marching, I saw during the night, which added to the setting, a medieval scene in a medieval city. It came after my speech that caused so much furor. One part of the hall in which I was speaking was occupied by policemen sent from Paris, and a person, like the conductor of an orchestra, signaled them when to make a racket. Students from Catholic universities occupied the upper parts of the hall, and with their ears conspicuous against the shadows, they howled out in unison every time the conductor raised his baton. If only there had been some real bellowing at that concert, but all the police and students did was yelp.

My friends forced me to leave that concert, and their decision was wrong. Those raucous little fellows would finally have lost their voices, and the reasonable parts of the room would have been able to judge their conduct at the end. To my regret, I obeyed the wishes of my friends and left, but it was painful.

They pushed me into a cab which immediately pulled away, but Jeanne, a friend who was accompanying me, had been separated from me in the turmoil. I kept trying to make the cab driver turn back for her, but for half an hour he whipped on his horses without answering me or admitting he heard me or even felt me pulling on his arm.

I finally prevailed upon the driver, and he turned back, driving through "Messieurs the scholars," who were throwing stones at the meeting hall. The windows of the cab were broken, the horse was hardly able to move, and now and again outlined against the black night, a young head, flushed with the drunkenness of the chase, pushed its way through the fragments of the carriage's windows and howled out some insult. The old phantom city behind them opened out dead black to my view.

Amidst my concern for my friend Jeanne, I thought about the old Ghent of the fourteenth century, the days of the van Arteveldes, when the guilds used the axe to kill those they believed were seeking power, and I looked out at the somber banks of the canal. It all made a magnificent spectacle, framed between the water and the night. In front of the meeting hall were the students and those who kept watch over them, all of them milling around. The Middle Ages were alive still.

Very worried about Jeanne, I got down from the cab to ask them if they had seen the tall brunette who had been with me and to ask what they had done with her, because I was the one they wanted to kill. A few of them became serious and began to make inquiries. Then a police superintendent helped me to search for Jeanne.

He was a police superintendent from Ghent, and not at all like the policemen who had migrated from Paris to bellow at my speech. He told me not to get involved in any way with what was going on other than to look for Jeanne, and in fact it was he who located her. I remember that when he found that the students were acting improperly he placed himself in front of me, to my great astonishment, and he helped me move through the packed mass. That surprised me, because I fully expected to be led off to prison for having been insulted. That's what the police would have done in Paris.

The newspapers recognized the evenhanded honesty of those Belgian police.

> The spectacle of fevered madness lasted until evening. The mob thought that by stifling a speech they had saved religion and society.
>
> Without the protection of the burgomaster and the police chief, who proved they had truly heroic devotion to principle by intervening in the fight at the Circus and even up to the railroad station, we do not know what might have happened to our friend, Louise Michel.

I traveled to Holland, also. Besides our friends, of whom I have such good memories, there were scholars who were curious to see close up what species of animal we revolutionaries are. They undertook their studies in good faith. I also met enemies who were sincere because they knew about us only through gossip in reactionary newspapers. They were astonished at having been deceived and ended up by understanding revolutionaries.

In Holland, the motherland of the brave, I also saw Freemasons, and it seemed to me that Freemasonry had undergone a rejuvenation. During the courageous proceedings of the Freemasons in 1871 I had gotten the impression of an assembly of specters drawing themselves up on the ramparts in front of the royalists who were butchering the Revolution. It was grand and coldly beautiful. Later in New Caledonia I saw the Freemasons again; there they had been revitalized by the influence of the tropics. They seemed to be moved by a great desire for progress and were going to a lot of pains to take part in it, there where the sun was warm.

But more and more, it is clear that societies based on rites, or hampered by any rites whatever, will not last until the emergence of the only viable fellowship—that of revolutionary humanity. Rite-bound societies will assist that birth only as ghosts.

An isolated life can be interesting only as it relates to the multitude of lives that surrounds it. Only crowds, with each person free in the immense harmony, are worthwhile now.

Two months after this northern trip, just after the beginning of 1883, I went to London to give a series of speeches. The travel expenses were paid by Citizens Otterbein of Brussels and Mas of Anvers, and I have not paid them back yet.

At London, I lived with our friends Varlet, Armand Morceau, and Viard the way I had done during the conference of 1881, and as always they spoiled me a bit. It is impossible for me to spend money when I go to London; they spend it. As for the proceeds from the speech, our friends know what was to be done with them. For a gathering of revolutionary groups, the hall we rented was very expensive, and what we came up with had to be supplemented. *L'Intransigeant* added more yet, because we had promised our friends of '71 who had become infirm that there would be a small remembrance for them.

The proceeds were small. Some time ago we made a plan to create a very modest refuge where old and starving former exiles could find a little bread and a few drops of broth. With no qualification other than destitution, those poor people who had become unable to work or to whom people had refused work could receive food and find shelter. Many of the Communards are proud, and some of them had already taken the path of Père Malézieux. With the proceeds from our meetings, we hoped to support a home for these exiles, owned by the exiles themselves, and if we had received sufficient funds, perhaps we could have saved a few desperate persons.

Even the most aristocratic and reactionary English newspapers reported my London speeches quite impartially. Perhaps that relative kindness was owed to the bad faith of the bourgeois gutter press of France. Nothing puts people in a better light than to say too many bad things about them. After a good round of violent criticism, exaggerations are immediately noticeable.

As for the accounts of my London speeches in the opportunistic press of Paris, they were all based on the same stereotype. They did not need to send reporters. It was enough for them to know the name of the meeting hall where I was speaking, the subject treated, and the group that had organized the meeting to permit them to fix up their accounts of the "revolutionary craze" in their good old-fashioned way.

Because my London lectures were given in rich neighborhoods where people knew about me only through the legend my enemies had invented, my British audience was quite astonished at finding me neither so ill-mannered nor so ridiculous as it had heard. Those who saw me in England did not recognize in the slightest the horrible portrait of me they had been given. Also, all the newspapers, even the aristocratic *Pall Mall Gazette,* were extremely courteous to me.

One thing that surprised them was that I did not share the current British ideas on workhouses, but they were incorrect when they thought they saw me contradict myself on on this point. They thought I was enthusiastic about the workhouses, and that's not what I think of them. I only stated the pleasure I felt over England's considering it a duty to be concerned about people who have neither food nor shelter. The thing that struck me—and I immediately said so—was the care with which in some workhouses, Lambeth for example, they soften the refuge where old Albion piles its poverty.

The English will wait on their own little island until the rest of Europe has had its revolution, and then, not imitating the stupid mistakes others have committed, England will do everything at once. Albion will rise suddenly and light the sacred fire. The winds from abroad will cause the sacred fire to burn more brightly and will make it a dawning.

So that their antiquated institutions will last longer, the English warm them up with the enthusiasm of women. Women direct the workhouses now, and in the future there will be women in Parliament. But the green branches on the old tree cannot rejuvenate the rotten trunk.

There is one workhouse where the old and the poor are happy; it is one in which the woman who directs it feels that liberty is necessary if the destitute are to stay alive like other people. "There are no rules" is written in big letters on the wall, and the place is more orderly than anywhere else. The clock directs people. At the time for meals or work or a walk, everybody goes freely where he must, the same way a person in his own house goes to his own meal or his own work.

I will not name the people in England who showed me their sympathy. They will remember that evening of the black London winter on which a cloud of fog floated. Raindrops condensed in an unceasing mist and now and again came in broad sheets. They will remember a frozen evening in the large, cold meeting hall in front of a cold and correct audience drawn from a grand neighborhood of immense palaces under which the wretches have holes like animals. But despite that, I felt an impression of human honesty persisting regardless of the accursed chains that people interminably fasten on each other.

The audience did not share my beliefs, but they were sincere. I do not know why, but they seemed like a family to me, even as serious and cold as they were. Then, as I had done long ago during my childhood at Vroncourt, as I had done when I was a young schoolmistress and sat on the hearth-stone at Mme Fayet's while I let everything in my heart break free, I began to talk unrestrainedly. In this large, cold meeting hall in London, I spoke freely about the scenes of my life which came to mind—from Vroncourt to New Caledonia, and at that moment those past things were truly present.

My English friends, Miss M——, Miss X——, Miss F——, do not believe for a minute that I have forgotten you. Do you really believe, Miss M——, that the book in which you wrote the words of the old Jacobins—"neither God nor master"—could ever have been destroyed? I certainly still have it. I also have "The Song of the Shirt" translated into French so well by you, Sir T. S——.

London! I love London, where my exiled friends have always been welcomed, London, where old England, standing in the shadow of the gallows, is still more liberal than the French bourgeois republicans are.

Maybe those French opportunists really think they are liberal. Do you suppose that everybody who commits crimes against the people is conscious of what he is doing? Among them are persons who are deluding themselves and who wish to reward themselves for virtue and intelligence. Intelligence, nonsense! Wisdom is found in the people.

It is quite true that today the people do not know any science, but considering the mess science is in now, that's all right. Science today is only opening its buds. Tomorrow it will be wonderful, and tomorrow science will belong to everybody. Today, if the people do not know this or that little bit of information, at least they are not stubborn about believing, for example, that glowworms are stars. That's something.

Chapter 20

Speeches in France, 1882 – 1883

In the summer of 1882 I made a lecture tour through northern France with Jules Guesde, in connection with a strike. The trip had some merry moments. In one café a dozen men came over and made a circle around us, looking at us the way curious animals do. I took out my sketch pad and began to draw their mugs. I wrote underneath the sketches "Skillful Stool-pigeon," "Fool," and "Spiteful Stool-pigeon." They weren't informers any more than we were, but they were so stupid, looking at us the way they did. One of them came and peeked over my shoulder; the others did too, and then we were rid of them.

During the journey, there was another moment of comedy when one fellow went on and on telling another man about the burials of famous men he had seen; nobody could have been as complete a fool as this fellow was. I wondered if he was in earnest. When I realized he was, I became fearful that Guesde would find a way to disturb the bird, but he didn't, and the fellow ended his recital of hopes for funeral processions with the wish that Victor Hugo, whose age he worked out, would soon give him another spectacle.

After having stirred that prospect around for a long time he began on another subject: Thiers. That mournful crow certainly had a gift for conversation. He was talking to a man who had a neck as red as a turkey's and who was watching him admiringly, and so was a young woman with big, round eyes. Then a traveling salesman who was neither affected nor boastful straightened him out by telling some truths to the fellow who was deploring the miseries of the "poor bosses."

At the meeting we had come to attend, the chief of police, all dressed up with his sash of office, placed himself near Guesde and me. Clearly believing the tales the reactionaries were telling about us, he seemed astonished at how calm our friends kept the meeting. It is true that the four sergeants-at-arms appointed to keep order in the hall were all the size of Hercules, and one of them picked up a lower-middle-class troublemaker and put him under his arm the way you carry a cat. That troublemaker was giving a signal for the start of a racket, but the Hercules carried him out before anyone did anything. The other reactionaries calmed down magically.

In September 1882 there was a meeting at Versailles. Quite a group of us anarchists went there together. We were prepared for the worst, but we thought it was our duty to go to Versailles and memorialize there the execution grounds at Satory and the wall at Père Lachaise. I still have a letter I wrote about this meeting which was published in *L'Intransigeant.*

[24] September 1882

Concerning the incidents which occured at the meeting organized last Sunday at Versailles by a revolutionary socialist group, Louise Michel sends us the following note:

Did our friends expect us to get a different reception? We don't need to talk about the Revolution to people who are revolutionaries; we need to tell people who aren't revolutionaries about it.

Since we began at Versailles, I don't see any obstacle to our ending up in some place like Brittany, which is even more reactionary. Soon we will go to all the royal provinces. Maybe some of the people there will greet us with pitchforks, but our publicity will win others over to the Social Revolution. All their Breton obstinacy will turn toward the truth, and all their fanaticism will be directed toward the future instead of the past.

I've thought about conquering Brittany for a long time, ever since 22 January 1871, when I stood in the courtyard of the Hôtel de Ville. That day, more than ten years ago, I looked up indignantly at the broad, pale faces of the Breton boys glued against the windows of the building which once had been and again would be the home of the democratic Commune. In accordance with Trochu's plan, they fired at us then from those windows with great conviction, but we will recruit those Bretons too, like all the others, for the Revolution. We will recruit the king's faithful, just like all other proletarians.

Louise Michel

That article in *L'Intransigeant* went on to print another of my letters:

Yesterday our friend, Citizen Louise Michel, addressed a letter to the editor-in-chief of *L'Intransigeant,* commenting on an article entitled "Memories of Satory."

To Citizen Rochefort.

My dear traveling companion,

I congratulate you for your article today. How could those people imagine that the pursuit and cries of an ignorant pack of dogs could alarm me when I have the image of Satory in my mind? It would be just like amusing myself by grumbling when I was on the Ducos Peninsula, as I looked at Nou Island visible at the horizon.

Once again we are able to declare that our adversaries have no serious arguments. They use shouts, which is an admission that they have lost.

Still, the crowd was picturesque. The most striking figure was a limping beggar who stretched himself out on his crutches like a spider and screeched against the enemies of property. You've seen Callot's painting "The Beggars," haven't you? You would have thought that the fellow had been pulled out of the frame. There were also a few big, funny-looking creatures that looked like the monsters that form the retinue of the goddess of the sea, and some street urchins, among whom there was more than one future insurgent. All in all, they made up the whole tableau of human stupidity.

No matter. This scene will have made its contribution by bringing us more than one listener. Things have an eloquence that words lack.

Louise Michel

At another meeting, this one at the de la Perle meeting hall, I believe, someone managed to break a window and throw a smoke-bomb behind the speaker's rostrum. If we had not dealt with it immediately and told the audience it was a trick of the police or of idiots, it would have caused the crowd to rush toward the one very small exit, and there would have been some accidents. It turned out to have been the work of idiots. Ashamed of what they'd done, they later sent me their apologies, which I read publicly, of course without mentioning their names.

There were many other meetings; accounts of them are in one of Marie's notebooks. Among them was one at the Graffard meeting hall. Speaking of that, there is a painting of me in the Grévin Museum entitled "Louise Michel at the Graffard Meeting Hall." Why the Graffard, I don't know; that title is given to other portraits and caricatures. I certainly have been at the Graffard hall, as I have been at almost every other meeting hall in Paris, but it seems to me that your face does not change from one speaker's platform to another.

"Louise Michel at the Graffard Meeting Hall" is again the inscription, I believe, under the portrait that a very young painter, the son of Mme Tynaire, stubbornly persisted in doing for the Salon. I let him do it in spite of the distress I felt at posing during that time, for it was immediately after Marie's death. I did not want to thwart a child who had talent, and I was sure the Salon would accept it for two reasons. The first and foremost was that he painted very well. The second, and the one on which I counted, was that his portrait of me resembled, feature for feature and especially expression for expression, not me, but an old prisoner named Mme Dumollard whom I had seen in '72 at the Auberive prison.

I'm aware of my own ugliness, but between my ugliness and the portrait I'm speaking of—a portrait which was magnificently painted and which doesn't resemble me at all—there is a difference that can be checked simply by comparing it to any of my photographs.

The reactionaries must have rubbed their paws together and said, "What a fright." It made me laugh until someone was stupid enough to tell my mother about several incidents, the knowledge of which pained her, but her distress was relieved when a simple-minded man, absolutely dressed to the teeth, a stupid man as stiff as a wooden doll, appeared at the door of 45, boulevard Ornano, where my mother and I were living.

"Mlle Michel?" he asked, forgetting to take off his stove-pipe hat and beating his right hand with a small stick.

"I am she," I said.

"No, you aren't her."

"I'm not me?"

"Well! I know Louise Michel. I saw her portrait in the Salon."

"So?"

"So! Try not to make fun of me. A woman who has horses and carriages doesn't open her own door. Go and get her for me. I repeat: It isn't her who is opening this door."

"It's she who is closing it," I said. Whereupon, as this stupid man wasn't all the way inside, I pushed him completely outside and slammed the door in his face. He blustered a little from the other side of the door, and then I heard him going down the steps, still shouting insults.

People did say that I had horses and carriages, and people appeared to believe that I made money from my speeches. Because the persons who organized the meetings know what was done with the profits, I confess that I spent hardly any time worrying about that spiteful, stupid talk.

In October 1882 I went to Lille to speak in connection with the strike of the women spinners there. They were all around us at the speaker's platform, all those female workers from the cellars of Lille, whose cheap shoes protect their feet so little from the water, and who are killed by work before their time. They were asking for only ten or fifteen centimes more a day to continue their horrible life. Those ten or fifteen centimes for bread would be sufficient for those who work so hard to support the rich.

Those poor workers are just like the silkworm, which is boiled when it has spun its cocoon. When their labor is finished, those workers, too, must die. Like the silkworms, their lives must stop with the thread. How will they exist in their old age? Won't their daughters be chained to the same torture before they are scarcely out of their cradles?

The rich must use and abuse their flocks. Both the silkworms and the daughters of the people are made for spinning; the worm will be boiled, and the girl will die or become twisted like green wood that has been bent. All they wanted was ten or fifteen centimes for a little bread, and they earned billions for others.

All the strikers had to do was hold out for one week more and the exploiters would have given in, but to last a week longer the strikers needed two thousand francs. That was why I went to Lille to make a speech. Thanks to the reactionaries who paid for their seats so that they could come to insult me, we made the two thousand francs in one lecture alone. I asked the organizers of the speech to put that money away safely, and then I was able to announce to the gentlemen who had bought tickets that we had what we needed. Thus, they were free either to listen to me or to spend their time howling, either of which was perfectly all right with me because we already had the two thousand francs that we needed.

That frank explanation calmed them down, and the speech took place without further incident. Around one in the morning I was able to take the train and return to my mother. For the tomb of Marie Ferré I brought back a sacred souvenir—a bouquet the workers of Lille had given me.

Unfortunately, at the end of the week a few evil persons made some gullible workers believe that others had gone back to their workshops, and they believed it was their duty to do the same. Once back in their capitalist prison, they saw they had been fooled, and then it was too late for them, but the lesson will not be lost.

Just after the turn of the year, in January 1883, was the trial of the sixty-eight anarchists in Lyon, fifty-four of whom were prisoners, the other fourteen being tried in absentia. Because the reactionaries could not figure out a crime to accuse them of, they were indicted for being affiliated with the International, which had been dissolved in 1876. The trial was a travesty.

It began on January 9 and Prince Kropotkin, Emile Gautier, Bordat, Bernard, and forty-three others of the accused issued a manifesto which Gautier had written.

Manifesto of the Anarchists

What is anarchy and what are anarchists?

Anarchists are citizens who, in a century where freedom of opinion is preached everywhere, have believed it to be their right and duty to appeal for unlimited liberty.

Throughout the world there are a few thousand of us, maybe a few million, for we have no merit other than saying out loud what the crowd is thinking. We are a few million workers who claim absolute liberty, nothing but liberty, every liberty.

We want liberty; we claim for every human being the right to do whatever he pleases and the means to do it with. A person has the right to satisfy all his needs completely, with no limit other than natural impossibilities and the needs of his neighbors, which must be respected equally with his.

We want freedom, and we believe its existence incompatible with the existence of any power whatsoever, no matter what its origin and form, no matter whether it be elected or imposed, monarchist or republican, inspired by divine right, popular right, holy oil, or universal suffrage.

History teaches us that every government is like every other government and that all are worth the same. The best are the worst. In some there is more cynicism, in others more hypocrisy, but at bottom there are always the same procedures, always the same intolerance. There is no government, including even the ones that appear the most liberal, which does not have in the dust of its legislative arsenals some good little law about the International to use against inconvenient opposition.

Evil, in the eyes of anarchists, does not dwell in one form of government more than any other. Evil lies in the idea of government itself. The principle of authority is evil.

Our ideal for human relations is to substitute a free contract, perpetually open to revision or cancellation, in place of administrative and legal guardianship and imposed discipline.

Anarchists propose teaching people to get along without government as they are already learning to get along without God.

Anarchists will also teach people to get along without private ownership. Indeed, the worst tyrant is not the one who locks you up; it is the one who starves you. The worst tyrant is not the one who takes you by the collar; it is the one who takes you by the belly.

No liberty without equality! There is no liberty in a society where capital is monopolized in the hands of an increasingly smaller minority, in a society where nothing is divided equally, not even public education, which is paid for by everyone's money.

We believe that capital is the common patrimony of mankind because it is the fruit of the collaboration between past and present generations, and that it ought to be put at the disposal of everyone in such a way that no one is excluded and in such a way that no one can hoard one part of it to the detriment of other people.

In one word, what we want is equality. We want factual equality as the corollary of liberty, indeed as its essential preliminary condition.

To each according to his rights; to each according to his needs.

That is what we want; that is what our energies are devoted to. It is what shall be, because no limitation can prevail against claims that are both legitimate and necessary. That is why the government wishes to discredit us.

Villains that we are, we claim bread for all, knowledge for all, work for all, independence and justice for all.

That was the manifesto of the anarchists. I was in London when the trial began, but I arrived in time to go to several of the last sessions and to see the prosecutor, M. Fabreguettes. When I looked at his angular profile, with his arm raised and the wide sleeve of his robe rolled up, and heard his biting words, I thought of an engraving I had dreamed in front of during my childhood, an engraving of the Grand Inquisitor, Tomás de Torquemada.

I have only one account of the speeches I gave at Lyon during the trial, and I no longer remember which newspaper it was taken from:

Telegraphed from Lyon, 19 January 1883

Yesterday evening in the Elysée meeting hall, Louise Michel gave a lecture for the benefit of the families of the detained anarchists.

The meeting proclaimed Kropotkin and Bernard as honorary chairmen.

When Louise Michel started her speech, she stated that only force can transform society, since force is being used to destroy it.

At Lyon, she said, anarchists are in the dock. In England they are members of the House of Commons.

Louise Michel said she had brought back a resolution signed by the French refugees in London protesting against the trial at Lyon and declaring their solidarity with the accused and their theories. But because she knew she was under police surveillance, she had destroyed the piece so as not to compromise anyone.

Louise Michel developed at length her ideas on the situation of women in present society.

The chairman put the order of the day—the taking up of arms to defend oneself against the bourgeoisie—to a vote. It was adopted.

At this point a person named Besson requested that the journalists present be expelled. Louise Michel protested, saying that liberty must be equal for everyone.

Another speaker requested the assembly to pass a motion in favor of acquitting the anarchists. The chairman answered that that matter was the business of the court and not of the assembly. Such a resolution could not be passed without the consent of the persons accused.

The meeting adjourned in the midst of cheering by those present.

Of course, the court found Kropotkin and all the others guilty. The idiocy of the charge was no defense, and Kropotkin and the main defendants were sentenced to five years' imprisonment.

With all this in my mind I returned to Paris at the end of January 1883.

Chapter 21

The Trial of 1883

Several weeks after the trial at Lyon, it seemed to me that I would have been an accessory to cowardice if I did not use the liberty I was allowed—I don't know why—to call up a new and immense International which would stretch from one end of the earth to the other.

On 9 March 1883 there was a mass demonstration at the Esplanade of les Invalides, after which Louise Michel led a number of demonstrators across Paris. For that, she was accused of rioting and looting. A massive police hunt for her in Paris and throughout Europe ensued while she remained comfortably hidden at the home of the editor of L'Intransigeant, M. Vaughan. On March 30 she surrendered herself in a farce designed to make the police look as foolish as possible.

I stayed in hiding for three weeks. While certain reporters claimed they were chatting with me in a house where I wasn't present, others saw me at a pleasure party in the Bois de Boulogne, where I wasn't either. I was living with the families of my friends Vaughan and Meusy, from where I made my way to my mother's, dressed as a man. In those clothes I would have been able either to stay hidden in Paris or take my mother abroad. I would even have been able to continue to publicize the Revolution. Wearing men's clothing, I had often gone to meetings from which women were excluded. Dressed in a National Guard's or soldier's uniform during the Commune, I went many times to places where people hardly expected to have to deal with a woman.

You, my friends, who gave me hospitality after the demonstration at les Invalides as if I were a family member, when you read this, remember that I was sorry to cause you so much trouble. Your true spirit was revealed when you sheltered me from the searchers, but I had to face trial. We must be implacable, especially concerning ourselves. Lies are too shameful.

Louise and Augustine, remember that you agreed, and you told me that I was right. I haven't forgotten, and I know you will feel that same way always. If your brothers will need courage for the things they'll see, you will need a hundred times more. Women must have dry eyes today where men might cry.

And you, you other little boys and girls, do you really believe I have forgotten you? If Paul and Marius one day become what I believe they will, they, too, will need courage. May the one who is a poet and the one who is a musician go their way in sunlight.

And you, Marie and Marguerite, you, too, my little ones, you are coming to that great moment when humanity is on the march, and you must not weaken. It will be so much the worse for you, but the better for humanity.

Let me get back to my trial. Several of our friends offered to defend me, but each one of us must explain his own thought himself. Then, too, it was impossible for me to choose between those who had already defended our friends the way free men should be defended, and Locamus, who had defended the deportees called before the colonial courts at Nouméa.

So many times we saw Locamus pass by us, going away to prison in handcuffs, with his clients having been acquitted at the cost of his being sentenced for insulting the judiciary. He prized those theatrics and made the courts do it to him so that the whole process would look ridiculous. As he was being taken away, Locamus used to laugh in a way that made you laugh, too. He swaggered, just like Lisbonne in his convict's uniform. The only difference was that Locamus, standing straight, used to shake his great curly head, and Lisbonne, striking out with his crutch, raised his head under his mane. Both of them looked like lions.

As the trial progressed, I was conscious of how bothersome it was to speak to a court when you are only one of several persons accused. You have to be very careful, because the prosecutors wait in ambush over your sentences to get them to serve, when possible, as ammunition for prosecuting the others. I hope I avoided that trap.

There were a number of young people disguised as lawyers—perhaps they were newly created lawyers—who gathered together like a classical chorus to stare at me and laugh or do other things like that. I hope that the three or four who stopped shouting insults themselves have not allowed themselves to be reenlisted in the band that insults the dead. I hope that they won't look at things through the wrong end of their opera-glasses again, and that the names of Vallès, Rigault, Vermorel, de Millière, Delescluze, and so many others who have been students just like them will sometimes come to their minds.

At my trial I used to think of Erasmus's *Praise of Folly*. The scepters of fools were missing, but the sound of the little bells that dangle from them tinkled in your ears. The obtuse jurors were bewildered by the indictment, in which they had been told that if they did not convict me their shops would not be safe. I was accused of the burlesque charge that

I had laughed on their doorsteps. Youngsters came to insult me, but some of them were pacified and left—perhaps captured by the Revolution, which blows through the courts.

It is not me, messieurs, whom you condemned. You know very well that I was not acting from motives of personal gain. It is my old mother whom you condemned to death—and she is dead now.

Let me give myself justice here. The accusation that I laughed was only a decoy. They did not want to accuse me of anything else because a woman is killed more quickly by ridicule. Let's get the facts straight. What people prosecute me for is my ideas. That is why I quoted the complete Manifesto of Lyon in the last chapter. I share *all* of the ideas written there.

This is justice. Now that I have quoted that manifesto and confessed that the ideas in it are the same as my beliefs, justice is done. I therefore have no need to worry any more about commenting on the details of my trial, although I will quote the transcript.

At my trial it was agreed that I laughed on a doorstep one day when people were asking those inside for work. I did this, although my mother had begged me to wait until she was dead before I took part in any more demonstrations.

Here is the record of the trial taken from the *Gazette des tribunaux.*

SUPERIOR COURT OF THE SEINE DISTRICT
M. RAMÉ, PRESIDING JUDGE
SESSION OF 21 JUNE 1883

Louise Michel, Jean-Joseph-Emile Pouget, and Eugène Mareuil are charged:

1. With having been the leaders and instigators of looting committed by a band in Paris in March 1883, the said looting having been committed by force and the loot consisting of loaves of bread belonging to the married couple Augereau, who are bakers;

2. With having been, at the said time and place, the leaders and instigators of forceful looting committed by a band, the loot consisting of loaves of bread belonging to the married couple Bouché, who are bakers;

3. With the similar looting, the loot consisting of loaves of bread belonging to the married couple Moricet, who are bakers.

THE QUESTIONING OF LOUISE MICHEL

Question: Have you ever been prosecuted?
LOUISE MICHEL: Yes, in 1871.
Question: That can't be mentioned any more. Those deeds were covered by the amnesty. Have you been convicted since then?

MICHEL: I was sentenced to two weeks in prison for the Blanqui demonstration.

Question: Do you take part in every demonstration that occurs?

MICHEL: Unfortunately, yes. I am always on the side of the wretched.

Question: Because of that habit you went to the demonstration at the Esplanade of les Invalides. What result did you hope for?

MICHEL: A peaceful demonstration never produces results, but I thought the government would follow its usual policy and sweep the crowd with cannon fire, so it would have been cowardly of me not to go.

Question: You recruited your followers for that demonstration. Did you know Pouget?

MICHEL: I had met Pouget at some meetings.

Question: Pouget was your secretary. He was supposed to distribute brochures propagating your ideas in the provinces. He acquired a name as one of your followers.

MICHEL: They are not, properly speaking, followers. Some people are curious about our ideas.

Question: You were the leader of a small demonstration that followed the general demonstration, but let's take care of your participation in the general demonstration first. You went to les Invalides and you met Pouget there?

MICHEL: Yes, monsieur.

Question: Had you planned with Pouget and Mareuil to go to the Esplanade?

MICHEL: No, monsieur. We met by chance.

Question: Wasn't the demonstration only for unemployed workers?

MICHEL: Yes, monsieur.

Question: Did you think that this demonstration could provide work?

MICHEL: I've already told you, no. I went there out of duty.

Question: The demonstration was dispersed. Isn't it true that at that moment you decided to make your own little demonstration?

MICHEL: It wasn't a demonstration. I wanted to make people hear the cry of the workers.

Question: You asked for a black flag?

MICHEL: Yes, and someone brought me a black rag.

Question: Who gave it to you?

MICHEL: A person I didn't know.

Question: You don't find a flag so easily and accidentally on the Esplanade of les Invalides.

MICHEL: All you need to do is find a broomstick and a black rag.

Question: It was easy to find because the demonstration had been prepared in advance. Who had prepared that flag?

MICHEL: No one. Even if somebody had, you know quite well that I wouldn't point him out.

Question: Didn't you leave the Esplanade with the intention of making a disturbance?

MICHEL: I simply put myself at the head of a group.

Question: Were Pouget and Mareuil part of it?

MICHEL: Yes, they were determined to protect me.

Question: What was your purpose in crossing Paris with a black flag? Did you believe you could get bread for the workers that way?

MICHEL: No, but I wanted to make people see that the workers didn't have any and that they were hungry. The black flag is the flag of strikes and the flag of famines.

The judge ordered the bailiff to go to the table of exhibits and pick up a black flag, which Louise Michel identified as the one she carried on March 9.

Question: You came to the boulevard Saint-Germain. Why did you stop in front of Bouché's bakery?

MICHEL: I kept on walking. The kids told me that someone was giving them bread. I didn't bother with the details.

Question: You claim that the bakers were voluntarily giving bread away?

MICHEL: Yes, monsieur. The kids told me they were being given bread and some small change. I was very humbled by that.

Question: And the men who were armed with clubs. Was anyone giving them bread voluntarily?

MICHEL: We didn't have anyone with us armed with a club. They are not among the accused.

Question: You can't challenge the facts. The witness Bouché saw you arriving at the head of a mob, and fifteen or twenty individuals moved away from it to pillage his shop. They were chanting, "Bread and work or lead."

MICHEL: They weren't with us. That was something the police staged.

Question: You said during one interrogation that you didn't look on taking bread as a crime.

MICHEL: Yes, I said that, but I have never taken any, and I never shall take any, even if I were dying of hunger.

Question: When you were stopped on the place Maubert, did you say to the police officer, "Don't hurt me. We are only asking for bread"?

MICHEL: I didn't say, "Don't hurt me." Perhaps I said, "We are only asking for bread. You won't be hurt."

Question: In short, M. Bouché's bakery was completely looted.

MICHEL: I did not see the bakery, nor do I know M. Bouché.

Question: The shop sticks out into the street and stares you in the face.

MICHEL: I was thinking only about poverty; I wasn't thinking about bakers' shops.

Question: You then arrived in front of M. Augereau's shop?

MICHEL: I don't know M. Augereau.

Question: Did you raise your flag in front of that shop?

MICHEL: I could have raised and lowered it many times.

Question: Did you say "Go"?

MICHEL: I could have said it. I must have said "Let's go": or "Let's move" many times. I don't remember it.

Question: How many persons did you see around you?

MICHEL: I don't know.

Question: To be brief, the shop of M. Augereau was completely wrecked.

MICHEL: I didn't know that, and I am astonished that M. Augereau is concerned with trifles like that. I have seen something else plundered and killed.

Question: Then you are absolutely indifferent to the looting of his shop?

MICHEL: Yes, absolutely indifferent.

Question: Then you moved out into the boulevard Saint-Germain and stopped in front of Moricet's shop?

MICHEL: I don't know, and I don't understand why you're asking me such a question.

Question: Did you start to laugh in front of Moricet's shop?

MICHEL: What could have made me laugh? Would it have been the distress of the people around me? Would it have been the sad state of things which takes us back before 1789?

Question: In short, you claim to be unacquainted with all those events I've mentioned.

MICHEL: Yes, monsieur.

Question: But those three merchants who were robbed assert that the crowd was obeying a signal.

MICHEL: That's absurd. To obey a signal, it would have to be agreed upon in advance. Therefore, it would have been necessary to make it known throughout Paris that I would raise or lower a flag in front of the bakeries.

Question: Then the looting was an instinctive movement of the populace?

MICHEL: It was the work of a few children. The reasonable people around me did not bother with it.

Question: You left the demonstration at the Place Maubert, leaving Pouget and Mareuil, who had gotten themselves arrested to save you, in the hands of the police. Then you disappeared.

MICHEL: My friends demanded that I not let myself be arrested at that time.

Question: Did you know about Pouget's having distributed a brochure entitled *To the People's Army* in the provinces?

MICHEL: At the time when the Orleanists were openly inciting people against the Republic, I wanted to incite people to support the Republic, and that brochure was distributed at my suggestion. It was a cry of anguish.

Question: Did you know about the special studies of incendiary materials to which Pouget devoted himself?

MICHEL: Today, everybody is interested in science. Everybody reads the *Revue scientifique* and tries to better the lot of the workers through the information there.

Question: We aren't here to make theories. Were you informed about the studies Pouget was making?

MICHEL: I do not pay any attention to whether someone reads or does not read scientific journals.

The court then proceeded to question M. Pouget. [The account of his questioning is not included in the *Gazette des tribunaux*. The other witnesses were examined next.]

THE WITNESSES

JULES BOUCHÉ, baker, rue de Canettes: On March 9, around one o'clock in the afternoon, a score of people invaded my bakery. They were armed with leaded canes and demanded "bread or work." I told them, "If you want bread, take some, but don't break anything."

Question: Do you recognize the accused?

BOUCHÉ: No, monsieur.

Question: Did you let them take your bread because you couldn't do otherwise?

BOUCHÉ: There was no way to do anything; any resistance was impossible.

Question: Was it children who came into your shop?

BOUCHÉ: No, sir. They were of the age of reason. (Laughter)

LOUISE MICHEL: The persons armed with leaded canes weren't ours. I know where they came from.

Question: Where?

MICHEL: The police. (Laughter)

MME AUGEREAU, wife, baker, rue du Four-Saint-Germain: During the afternoon of March 9 Mme Louise Michel stopped in front of my door. Someone yelled, "Bread, bread!" These men entered my store and stole some bread and baked goods. They broke a platter and two window panes.

Question: Was it youngsters who plundered your shop?

MME AUGEREAU: Oh, there were more grown-ups than youngsters.

Question: Where was Louise Michel while they were plundering your shop?

MME AUGEREAU: She was stationed exactly in the middle of the street.

Question: Did you give your bread away voluntarily?

MME AUGEREAU: Oh, no, monsieur.

....

THE WIFE OF MORICET, baker, 125, boulevard Saint Germain: Last March 9, a crowd gathered in front of my shop. At its head was Louise Michel. She stopped in front of my shop, struck the ground with her flag, and started to laugh. The crowd was asking for bread or work. I began to give them bread, but they didn't wait for it. They took it themselves and broke up everything.

Question (to Louise Michel): What do you think of that testimony? Is it clear enough?

LOUISE MICHEL: So clear I have never seen anything like it. (Laughter) How was I able to laugh in front of her store? She dreamed all of it.

MME MORICET: I'm here to say what I saw.

LOUISE MICHEL: You are free to say what you want, but I'm free to say that you dreamed it.

Question (to the witness): You didn't give your bread to those people freely?

MME MORICET: No, monsieur, I did it because they were making such frightful gestures when they came in; they were yelling, "Work and bread!"

LOUISE MICHEL: Oh, they were very frightful. I, too, was frightful. These women were hallucinating from fear. They saw Louise Michel as a monster.

CORNAT, a municipal police officer of the VIe Arrondissement: On last March 9 when I learned that a gang was crossing the arrondissement yelling out seditious slogans, I went in pursuit and caught up with it at the Place Maubert. The gang was led by Louise Michel, with Pouget and Mareuil at her side. I arrested the latter two, and Pouget called me a coward and a scoundrel. As for Louise Michel, she was able to slip away. All those people were yelling, "Long live the Revolution! Down with the police!"

Question: Did not Louise Michel say something to you?

POLICEMAN CORNAT: She said to me: "Don't hurt me."

BLANC, a policeman in the VIe Arrondissement: Last March 9 a policeman came to inform the municipal police officer that a bakery on the rue de Canettes was being plundered. We set off in pursuit of the gang, and we caught up with it at the Place Maubert. The municipal police officer stopped Louise Michel, who said to him, "Don't hurt us; we're only asking for bread." Pouget called the municipal police officer a coward and a scoundrel. Mareuil yelled out, "Down with the police! Down with Vidocq! Long live the Social Revolution!" The assailants had leaded canes, revolvers, and knives.

LOUISE MICHEL: I never said, "Don't hurt us," but only, "You won't be hurt." Both those men were very disturbed.

Question (to Louise Michel): No one but you was showing any self-control?

LOUISE MICHEL: We have seen so much of it! For the sake of the honor of the Revolution, I protest. I surely have the right to point out discrepancies in the witnesses' testimony. I have never prostrated myself in front of anyone, and I have never asked for mercy. You can say anything you want to about us, you can sentence us to prison, but I do not want you to dishonor us.

SESSION OF JUNE 22
WITNESSES FOR THE PROSECUTION (CONTINUED)

YOUNG MLLE MORICET: Last March 9, I was in the shop with my sister and mother when I saw a gang stop in front. They were led by a woman armed with a black flag. That woman stopped in front of the shop, struck the ground with her flag, and *began to laugh.*

Immediately the gang rushed into the shop, and took all the bread and cakes there; then they broke the platters and windows. I went quickly to get my father.

Question: You are very sure you saw Louise Michel stop in front of the shop and laugh while she struck the ground with her flag?

YOUNG MLLE MORICET: Yes, monsieur.

LOUISE MICHEL: I would be ashamed to respond to testimony like that. If little Mlle Moricet brings in her sister, her cousin, her little brother—whomever she wants—I will not hold matters up to answer charges as frivolous as those. I shall wait for the prosecution's summation before I answer them.

YOUNG MLLE MORICET, the sister of the preceding one: I was in the shop with my mother. Suddenly I saw a whole gang headed by a woman. It was madame. She *began to laugh* as she looked at the shop, and I even said to my mother, "Hey, she knows you?" At that moment all those people rushed into the shop and started to take everything.

LOUISE MICHEL: I will repeat what I said a moment ago: It is shameful to see children reciting in this court the lessons that their parents have taught them.

[WITNESSES FOR THE DEFENSE]

CHAUSSADAT, a painter, quai de Louvre, was heard at the request of the defense: On March 9, I was at the corner of the rue de Seine opposite the Moricet bakery. From a distance I saw the crowd arrive. Mlle Louise Michel went by without stopping. Later I heard talk about the looting of the bakery, or rather I saw bread thrown about.

Question: You don't call that plundering?

CHAUSSADAT: I saw that bread was being thrown about, and some poor people were gathering it up.

LOUISE MICHEL: I must thank the witness for rendering homage to the truth.

....

[Three witnesses, Rochefort, Vaughan, and Meusy, testified concerning a sum of money in Pouget's possession, declaring that it came from a collection taken up at the demonstration. That testimony is irrelevant to Louise Michel's trial, and it has been omitted.]

ROUILLON, a neighbor of Louise Michel's mother: Citizen Louise Michel had absolutely no faith in the result of the demonstration. She told me that before she went to it. The citizen went only out of duty.

The witness Rouillon then went into lengthy details about the violence and threats to which Louise Michel and her family have been subjected.

LOUISE MICHEL: You can see very clearly that our families are being murdered in our homes, and the authorities are allowing it to happen.

That was the last witness for the defense. Then Avocat-général Quesnay de Beaurepaire was called on. Then Maître Balandreau, the counsel appointed for Louise Michel, declared that she intended to defend herself.

LOUISE MICHEL'S STATEMENT

What is being done to us here is a political proceeding. It isn't we who are being prosecuted, but the anarchist party through us. For that reason I had to refuse Maître Balandreau's offer to defend me and also the offer made by our friend Laguerre, who, not long ago, undertook to defend our comrades at Lyon so warmly.

M. l'Avocat-général has invoked the Law of 1871 against us. I won't bother to find out whether this Law of 1871 wasn't made by the victors against the vanquished, made against those whom they were crushing as a millstone crushed grain. Eighteen seventy-one was the time when the National Guard was being hunted on the plains, when Gallifet was pursuing us in the catacombs, when the streets of Paris had heaps of corpses piled on either side.

What is surprising you, what is appalling you, is that a woman is daring to defend herself. People aren't accustomed to seeing a woman who dares to think. People would rather, as Proudhon put it, see a woman as either a housewife or a courtesan.

We carried the black flag because the demonstration was to be absolutely peaceful, and the black flag is the flag of strikes and the flag of those who are hungry. Could we have carried any other flag? The red flag is nailed up in the cemeteries, and we should take it up only when we can protect it. Well, we couldn't do that. I have told you before and now I repeat: It was an essentially peaceful demonstration.

I went to the demonstration. I had to go. Why was I arrested?

I've gone throughout Europe saying that I recognize no frontiers, saying that all humanity has the right to the heritage of humanity. That inheritance will not belong to us, because we are accustomed to living in slavery; it will belong to those persons in the future who will have liberty and who will know how to enjoy it.

When we are told that we are the enemies of the Republic, we have only one answer: We founded it upon thirty-five thousand of our corpses. That is how we defended the Republic.

You speak of discipline, of soldiers who fired on their officers. Do you believe, M. l'Avocat-général, that if at Sedan the soldiers had fired at their leaders, who were betraying them, they would not have been doing the right thing? If they had done that, we wouldn't have had the filth of Sedan.

M. l'Avocat-général has talked a lot about soldiers. He has boasted about those who carried the anarchist manifestos to their superiors. How many officers, how many generals reported back the bribes of Chantilly and the manifestos of M. Bonaparte? I'm not putting [the Duc d'] Orléans or M. Bonaparte on trial; we're putting their ideas on trial. M. Bonaparte has been acquitted, and we are being prosecuted. I pardon those who commit the crime, although I do not pardon the crime. Isn't it simply a law of might makes right which is dominating us? We want to replace it with the idea that right makes right. That is the extent of our crime.

Above the courts, beyond the twenty years in prison you can sentence us to—beyond even a life sentence—I see the dawn of liberty and equality breaking.

Knowing what is going on around you, you too are tired of it, disgusted by it. How can you remain calm when you see the proletariat constantly suffering from hunger while others are gorging themselves?

We knew that the demonstration at les Invalides would come to nothing, and yet it was necessary to go there. At this time in history we are very badly off. We do not call the regime that rules us a republic. A republic is a form of government which makes progress, where there is justice, where there is bread for all. How does the republic you have made differ from the Empire? What is this talk about liberty in the courts when five years of prison waits at the end?

I do not want the cry of the workers to be lost. You will do with me what you wish, but it's a question of more than me alone. It's a matter that concerns a large part of France, a large part of the world, for people are becoming more and more anarchistic. People are sickened when they see power used the way it was under M. Bonaparte. The people have already led many revolutions. Sedan relieved us of M. Bonaparte and the people revolted again on the eighteenth of March.

There is no doubt that you will see still more revolutions, and for that we will march confidently toward the future.

When one person alone no longer has authority, there will be light, truth, and justice. Authority vested in one person is a crime. What we want is authority vested in everyone. M. l'Advocat-général has accused me of wanting to be a leader; I have too much pride for that, for to be a leader is to lower oneself, and I do not know how to lower myself that way.

Here we are very far from M. Moricet's bakery, and it is difficult for me to return to those details. Do we have to talk about the breadcrumbs distributed to children? It wasn't bread that we needed; it was work that we were asking for. How can you think that reasonable men trifled by taking a few loaves of bread? Some youngsters were gathering up crumbs, yes, but it is difficult for me to discuss things that are so trivial. I would prefer to return to serious ideas. Young persons should work instead of going to cafés, and they will learn to fight to ease the plight of the unfortunate and to prepare for the future.

People recognize homelands only to make them a foyer for war. People recognize frontiers only to make them an object of intrigue. We conceive homelands and family in a much broader sense. There are our crimes.

We live in an age of anxiety. Everybody is trying to find his own way, but we say anyhow that whatever happens, if liberty is realized and equality achieved, we shall be happy.

The session adjourned at five o'clock and the proceedings were continued the next day.

SESSION OF JUNE 23

The presiding judge asked the accused if they had anything to add in their defense.

Louise Michel spoke as follows:

I wish to say only a word. This trial is a political trial. It is a political trial you are going to have to judge.

As for me, you have given me the role of the primary person accused. I accept it. Yes, I am the only person responsible. I sacrificed myself a long time ago, and what is pleasant or unpleasant to me is no longer a standard to judge by. I see nothing more than the Revolution, and it is the ideal I shall always serve. It is the Revolution I salute. May it rise up over men instead of rising up over ruins.

At two forty-five, the jury withdrew into a room for its deliberations. It came back at four-fifteen.

The foreman of the jury read the verdict. It was 'guilty,' but mitigated by extenuating circumstances as far as Louise Michel, Pouget, and Moreau (alias Gareau) were concerned. The other accused were found 'not guilty.'

After deliberating half an hour, the court passed a sentence by which the two accused who had been tried in absentia, Gourget and Thierry, were condemned to two years in prison. Louise Michel was sentenced to six years of solitary confinement, Pouget to eight years of solitary confinement, and Moreau (alias Gareau) to one year in prison.

Louise Michel and Pouget were also to be placed under police supervision for ten years.

THE JUDGE: Those of you found guilty have three days to petition for reversal of the sentences just passed.
LOUISE MICHEL: Never! You are too good an imitator of the Empire's magistrates.

From the back of the room violent protests greeted the sentencing of the accused. A few cries of "Long live Louise Michel!" were heard, and the session was adjourned in the midst of noise and the most varied outcries.

The tumult continued outside the courtroom and citizen Lisbonne, who called attention to himself by the vehemence of his protests, was expelled from the Palais de Justice. The crowd continued to stand for some time on the Place Dauphine. [Here ends the account taken from the *Gazette des tribunaux*.]

NOTE

Since I am speaking to the crowd today, I shall say what I did not think was necessary to say in front of the prosecutor because we were not trying to move our judges. It would have been a useless effort because we were judged in advance.

I did not start laughing stupidly in front of some door—and having just left my mother who was begging me to wait until she was no longer alive before going to demonstrations, I did not feel much like laughing.

As for choosing Moricet's bakery to be the target of a revolutionary movement, I do not need to defend myself against such an absurdity.

It is not a question of breadcrumbs. What is at stake is the harvest of an entire world, a harvest necessary to the whole future human race, one without exploiters and without exploited.

Chapter 22

Prison

There's no party without a morning after. Two years ago on July 14, I was taken to the Centrale Prison at Clermont. Women's prisons are less harsh than men's. I did not suffer from cold or hunger or any of the vexations our male friends underwent.

As far as I am concerned, my stay in prison was as easy as it would be for any other schoolmistress. Solitude is restful, especially for a person who has spent a great part of her life always needing an hour of silence and never finding it, except at night. That is the case with a great number of schoolmistresses.

In those silent hours of the night, she hurries to think, to feel alive, to read, to write, to be just a little free. At the end of the day, at the last lesson, she feels herself becoming an overworked beast of the fields, but a beast that is still proud, still lifting its head to go to the end of the hour without breaking down. When the hour is ended, silence surrounds her, fatigue has disappeared, and she lives and thinks and is free. In prison, I found those few hours of rest laboriously paid for over long years.

I'm going to write a book on prisons. I have a lot of pages for it already, and all I have to do is gather them up. The first pages will be dedicated to the poor gallant ambulance attendants of the Commune, the women condemned to death who instead were sent to Cayenne, where the climate is the murderer. They were convicted because they had cared for the wounded of the Commune and, in passing, for wounded men of the Versailles forces. Wounded men belonged to neither side, and those brave women dressed the wounds of anyone they found, whereas the leaders of the Versailles forces often opportunistically abandoned their wounded soldiers so they could snipe at us better.

Victor Hugo got pardons for those unpretentious and gallant women, Retif and Marchais. Following them were Suétens, Papavoine, and Lachaise, who had been condemned to forced labor for the same deeds.

After my first pages on the ambulance attendants, the chapters that followed would belong to the friends met in prison. I would begin with my own. At Satory the wives of my prisoner friends were not afraid to embrace me, although I warned them that the authorities were going to "treat me as I deserved." By embracing me they risked their lives. At Chantiers in the great morgue of the living, it was the same, under the rags hung at night along the walls. I must thank those brave souls for their friendship.

Many, alas, are now dead. The first to die was Mme Dereure; already ill, she could not survive the harsh ordeals to which she had to submit. In the full view of conquered Paris, the colors of the Commune followed her coffin. Without doubt, others are dead; we have not seen them again.

How many prisons! Have I said that already? Yes, how many prisons. From Bastion 37 to New Caledonia, stopping at Satory, Chantiers, la Rochelle, Clermont, Saint-Lazare . . .

When my book on prisons appears, grass will have grown up over still more unknown corpses, but the idea will remain the same. It will still be on the same subject: that human beings suffering through destitution, poverty, and ignorance are not responsible for acts against each other. The old nations are the murderers, the old nations, where the struggle for existence is so terrible that people turn on each other incessantly, clamoring for their prey. The only noise that can be heard is the cries of crows and the flapping of their wings above people who have been beaten to the earth.

A trap is set all around us, and poor, wretched women get caught in it. Is it the fault of those poor women that there is a place for some of them only in the streets or on display? Is it their fault if they have stolen a few sous to live on or to keep their children alive? Rich people can spend millions of francs and thousands of living beings on their whims. I can't stop myself from speaking about those things with such bitterness.

Everything weighs so heavily on women. I'm well placed to judge that here at Saint-Lazare prison, this general warehouse from which women leave in all directions—even to liberty. Someone who stays here only a few days cannot see things clearly, but after being here for a long time, a person can sense how many generous hearts beat under the shame that stifles them.

You know the lines from Hugo:

Lazarus, Lazarus, Lazarus
Rise up.

Yes, like Lazarus, rise up, you poor women. You have fought so long and you are crying over your shame, and it isn't you who are guilty. Was it you who gave the fat, scrofulous, swollen bourgeois their hunger for fresh flesh? Was it you who gave pretty girls, who owned nothing, the idea of making themselves into merchandise?

And the others, the female thieves, how guilty are they? When women are thrown into the street, it is certain that they will go wherever the man they call their pimp sends them, because he beats them and exploits them. They will also go into the streets alone. People keep walking when they are lost. There are also seamstresses who steal. They have kept little remnants of the cloth they were stitching. Do the great dress designers carry those remnants home? Other women deceive their husbands. Haven't their husbands ever deceived them? If only we let people choose each other instead of making marriages by matching up fortunes, that would happen less often.

Still other people, old women most often, when they are dying of hunger and want to live a little longer, insult a policeman to get some bread in prison. I saw one old woman who had eaten nothing for such a long time that after she had a little soup she sank down as if she were drunk. A few days later she died. Her stomach could no longer accustom itself to receiving nourishment.

When I was in my cell at Clermont, I was unable to see anybody, but I heard some scraps of conversations. From a cell you can understand everything best. Every cell looks out on some kind of courtyard and voices rise up to it. All you have to do is follow a few of the parts of this horrible choir of misery. Here are some fragments. I am choosing ones that tell the sadness at the bottom of misery. Listen to them.

"You're getting out tomorrow. You're lucky."
"Hell, no. It's too cold and hungry outside."
"But your mother has a nice place."
"She was thrown out because I was in prison."
"Where is she?"
"In the street."
"Where are you going to go?"
"Big Chiffe made me ask to go back to tricking on the streets. I'll give my mother however much the prison sends me out with, and I'll go back to Big Chiffe."
"You'll be back here again, I bet."
"What could I do so I wouldn't be? There's no work for girls who have worn-out work permits. People with prison numbers can't get one."

Here are some others.

"Where are you from?"
"From Saint-Lazare, naturally, because I'm from Paris."
"What did you do?"
"How should I know? My pimp stole somebody's stash, and it looked like I was his partner."
"You didn't know anything about it?"
"Do you think he tells *me* where he's going to work his fingers to the bone?"
"Maybe he gives you something."

"Him? Give to me? He takes my stuff. He has to get fifteen francs a day off me."

"What does he do with it?"

"Lady, he isn't rich. He's got to pay off a buddy who knows what he does. If he doesn't pay him off, his buddy will split on him to the cops."

"What do you do to make him his fifteen francs?"

"I did the window bit. That's better than tricking on the streets. You've got to live. When I went looking for real work, I got sent away from the stores because I wasn't dressed well enough. One time somebody lent me a dress, and then it was the other side: I was too well dressed. Then this john picked me up, and that was that. I had to get a card, and on top of that, a pimp."

"Where'd you do the window?"

"At Relingue's place—you know her, the one that gets herself arrested so she can recruit for her crib in the prison."

"That Relingue woman! If you ask me, I'll take this crib over hers. She makes too many francs out of our poor carcasses."

"So where else would I go? Prison grain takes root only on sidewalks."

And here are some others.

"Hey, you look sad, snub-nose."

"That's because I'm just going out to meet up with my bad luck."

"What's your bad luck?"

"He's the father of my children."

"Are you married?"

"No."

"Why don't you leave him?"

"Because he's the father of my children. The poor dog got upset about the first ones, but men stand pain less easily than women. When ill winds blow, they have to lie down."

And after women prisoners are released, there isn't any place for them to seek refuge. There are some asylums for women who get out of prison, but they don't have room for everybody. It's only holding out a cup to catch a waterfall.

If the women in prisons horrify you, it is society that disgusts me. Let's take away the sewer first. When the place is clean with the sunlight shining on it, then nobody will have to roll around in the sewer any more. You young girls with sweet, pure voices, here are some girls your own age with rough, broken voices. Your voices are clear because you do not live the way they do, drinking to divert your mind, drinking to forget that you're alive.

Saint-Lazare. Listen, you young girls who have never left your mothers, there are some children here like you, children sixteen years old. But the ones here either don't have mothers, or their mothers didn't have the spare time to watch over them. The poor cannot watch over their little ones; they cannot even take the time to watch over their dead.

The young girls in Saint-Lazare are pale and blighted. Idiots claim it has to be that way to protect you nice girls from men hungering for fresh flesh. If they weren't able to glut themselves on the daughters of the people, they would attack you. We no longer eat each other's flesh the way our cave-dwelling ancestors did—we aren't strong enough—but we eat each other's lives.

That is equality and justice.

Let's glance at one of the most terrible human misfortunes. I want the reader to revolt against the crimes of society instead of only having him lament the woes of one person.

Bordello-keepers trade women with each other, just as farmers trade horses or cattle. Women are just herds of livestock, and this human livestock makes more profit.

When the johns of some city in the provinces decide that some weak woman is too worn out or they get tired of her, the bordello-keeper arranges it so the girl owes the house a sum she can never pay off. That makes her a slave. Then she can be swapped in any horse-trade possible. The animal has to go into whatever stable will make the most profit for the swappers.

For other girls it is an enlistment. They come from their provinces too naive to know any better, or if they are Parisians and aware that there are ogres for fresh flesh and appetites to feed, poverty makes them tractable. Then, too, there is false finery to lure them; when they are once in the lion's den, they will be charged six times its worth to get them in debt.

There is also recruiting. Despicable old women find ways to get themselves imprisoned for a few months, and then they recruit and entice all the pretty girls who are stranded in prison. They tell the girls they don't have to fear being hungry. When they leave there will be a drinking spree—enough of a spree for the girls to die from it. Their voices will get hoarse, and their bodies will fall to pieces. It'll be a spree—a spree for the hungry bourgeois.

The women on the street are still the least unhappy; those in closed houses have a life so horrible that it would surprise people who no longer feel surprise. What I know about it I will write sometime, because it is so terrible, so shameful, that people must learn about it.

But for the moment I'll stay with the pathetic stories of the streetwalkers. Won't anyone ever understand that to allow prostitution is to support every crime? Once a woman becomes a prostitute, she becomes numb while she obtains money from idiots; and men thereby become murderers. Everybody should know that, so why does prostitution continue to exist?

If the great merchants of the trade in women who crisscross Europe canvassing orders for their business were each hanging on the end of a hangman's rope, I wouldn't go cut it.

And when a poor girl who believes she has entered an honest house (there are some) realizes where she is and finds it impossible to leave, and then with her own hands she strangles one of the despicable persons who keeps her there, or she sets the cursed place on fire, I believe it is better to do those things than to wait for court action. So long as circumstances are as they are, there will be no change.

Will the owls who bite the paws off mice to keep them in their nests ever stop acting so cruelly? If the captive mouse, instead of uttering his little plaintive cry from the owl's nest between earth and heaven, which are equally deaf, tried to gnaw the throat of the owl that was eating him, the first mouse to do so would certainly die. But eventually the owl would become fearful, and as every being wishes to continue living, the owl would end up keeping itself alive on grain rather than risking death.

That's the way the poor human livestock must proceed. A woman should not waste her time demanding illusory rights. The people who promise them to her have no such rights themselves. She ought to take her place at the head of the group which is struggling and at the same time free herself from prostitution. No other person can free her from it. When she no longer wants to be the prey of appetites and lusts, she will know that death is preferable to that life, and she will not be so stupid as to die uselessly.

Here is what I am hearing while I am writing this. It is the story of a sale.

"There was a fellow who made me sell it on the boul' de Batignolles. He wanted to give me only twenty sous, but I was hungry, and then I had a pimp who had a deal with the cops. I had to pay him or he would have beaten me up, and I sure didn't want that."

"What did you do with the forty sous from the old goat who was so drunk?"

"I gave twenty to my pimp and twenty to a poor little kid."

"Why didn't you try to get away when the cops grabbed you?"

"Because, I told you, I had nothing to drink. Might as well be in prison. Shit, might as well be dead."

Yes, those poor girls speaking from the bottom of the pit are right. It would be better to die than to continue a life where you have to drink so as not to feel being alive.

I don't want to believe that a man has to feed himself by gorging himself with all sorts of orgies. Even if he does, however, a woman, whoever she is, must not be dirtied by these indecent brutalities.

But let's look forward, because in the midst of these tortures, the new humanity will be born. Ferré at the execution post at Satory, the nihilists from the czar's gallows, the German socialists with their heads under the axe salute that newborn humanity as I salute it while I look at life, which now is more horrible than death.

Chapter 23

My Mother's Death

For a while during my deportation my mother lived with a relative she had always been very fond of, at a little woolens shop opposite the Louvre stores in Paris. After a time she went to live with other relatives in Lagny, and she was living there when I returned from New Caledonia. Four months after my return she moved back to Paris where we lived at 24 [*sic:* 36], rue Polonceau, and at that place we had fleeting moments of joy. With my mother and Marie near me, I was almost afraid, because happiness is such a fragile branch, and we break it when we rest on it. Two old women, friends of my mother, came to see her every day, and they gave her those little attentions old people love so much; my dear Marie stayed with her while I was away at meetings.

My mother's last home was at 45, boulevard Ornano on the fifth floor. There she underwent the long torture of two years without me before her death. In the middle room her bed was placed parallel to the hall, and above the chest of drawers hung a large portrait of me that Mme Jacqueline had painted. How many times my poor mother must have had her eyes on it during those two years! In her last moments when it was difficult for her to speak, it seemed to me that she wanted me to give that painting to Rochefort, and he has kept it for me ever since.

On sunny days, so long as we could make her believe that I would be in prison for only one year, she stayed at her window for hours at a time. It was there where she had waited for me so often, Mme Bias waiting with her, when I was expected home from my last lecture tours. Each time a group of prisoners was released my mother would rally because of the hope I would be among them. Finally it was necessary to admit that instead of my being sentenced to only one year, I had been sentenced to six years, and instead of being near her at Saint-Lazare, I was at Clermont. Personal hatreds unleashed by unscrupulous persons had contributed to my being sentenced to six years in prison, and from Bastille Day of 1884 on, when my mother had to be told the truth, she no longer went to the window. From the moment she learned that news, she got up from her easy chair only to lie down on her bed, and from her bed she went only to her coffin.

I could have fled abroad and taken her with me instead of submitting to trial, but I allowed myself to be put on trial because that is our custom. I could also have baffled the people who questioned me. They were trying to find out if I was responsible, and I could have made fun of their heavy-handed tricks, but we revolutionaries do not avoid responsibility. I answered the worthy investigators as if I suspected nothing, though I knew very well where their vengeance came from.

In prison I was well treated. Anybody who believes that simply being well nourished is enough to make a person happy would have believed me far happier than I was. Even if I had been poorly treated, I would have felt nothing but my mother's affliction.

From prison I wrote several letters to the authorities, some at the moment when cholera was rife in Paris, and then I had a twofold right: to be near my mother and to be in the city that I had never deserted in its days of trial. I wrote other letters when my mother was in her last days, and I asked to be taken to her. These letters should be in a Book of Memorial, for they contain two death agonies—my mother's and my own.

Here is one letter:

> Prison of Clermont (Oise)
> Number 1327
> Sunday, 15 November 1884
> (Personal)

Monsieur le président de la République

Here is the truth. If no man's heart understands it, may it stand alone as my witness.

For eighteen months I haven't read one line from a newspaper. But across the prison wall which separates us from the world a scrap of a sentence has reached me. Cholera is in Paris. It has been going on for a long time, and all the denials in the world won't convince me otherwise.

Not one person has called to mind that in those circumstances my place is in Paris, even if it be in an underground cell. It is to you, therefore, that I say: If I am treated like a criminal of the State, remember that I came forward openly to place myself in the hands of my judges. May they act similarly towards me.

Louise Michel

A week later I wrote:

> Prison of Clermont (Oise)
> Number 1327
> 21 November 1884

Monsieur le ministre de l'Intérieur

I have only my mother left in this world. My cruelest enemies would ask for my immediate transfer to a prison in Paris if I could speak out, because under the present circumstances either her illness or cholera could take my mother from me.

I am not asking for visits or letters in the prison you might put me in. If you want, I won't be eligible for release. But I shall be in Paris breathing the same air that my mother breathes, and my mother will know that I am there. She can experience that happiness while she is alive and not after she is dead.

> Sincerely,
> Louise Michel

Here are some fragments of letters I wrote asking to be brought near my mother:

> I shall be absolutely straightforward. In exchange for a release or transfer to another prison, just so it be in Paris near my mother, I will go to New Caledonia when she is no longer with us. I have already been useful there, and I can be so again by founding schools in the midst of the tribes.

The beginning of that letter is missing, but undoubtedly it also was sent to the Minister of the Interior. Still another fragment contains these words:

> I have not had an answer to my letters and shall probably never have one. But considering the times we live in, who knows whether one of your grandsons caught in the same situation won't be sorry you didn't answer me.
>
> It is not a political question. It is a question concerning mothers, and unfortunately, I shall not be the last prisoner.
>
> Louise Michel

I do not believe that this sorrow inflicted on my poor old mother increased anyone's happiness very much, but no one can do anything about it any longer. You cannot awaken the dead.

For a long time I had no response to the letters I had written to all those officials. Finally, I was transferred to Saint-Lazare. If the authorities had only brought me near my mother sooner! Her powerful constitution immediately rallied at each of my visits, and she would not be dead.

Even at this point my anonymous enemies threatened to trouble her last days by claiming that her paralysis was some contagious disease. Although the public is always credulous in times of cholera, my enemies failed. Those vipers are consoling themselves now by writing false letters over my name. I envy the happiness of people who bother with this sort of thing. I no longer feel them. All the venom in the world could fall on my head without my noticing it, and those letters are only a few drops of water where a whole ocean has passed.

The authorities acted very well at the last, and allowed me to go to my dying mother's bedside. As always, the rulers were less evil than their laws, and they allowed me several days near her. Policemen, instead of tormenting me, helped me move my mother smoothly from one bed to another each time she wanted. Those policemen were not like the ones who take care of politicians, and they weren't among the ones who savagely beat down the people on May 24 this year at the Père Lachaise cemetery. My mother thanked the policemen who helped me to move her, and I remember it, too.

At 4:57 in the morning of 3 January 1885 my mother died. When I came down the stairs at 45, boulevard Ornano on the morning of her burial, I left her lying in her coffin, which had not yet been nailed shut, and I thought of all her sorrow during the past two years. In my heart I felt everything she had suffered. Poor mother! How happy she would have been to spend a few days with me.

I must say that the authorities acted well here, for I had been able to stay with her until the end. Then, before I left her house forever, I was able to lay her out on her bed as she used to like to lie down. She no longer suffered. Let justice be done to everyone in the world, even the least important person.

Because my mother was no longer suffering, I didn't ask the authorities for permission to attend the funeral; with her death I had nothing more to ask for. Her funeral on 5 January 1885 became the occasion for a massive outpouring of public sentiment. Here is how it was reported:

At the Home of the Deceased

The working-class districts of the city emptied their dark alleys as they had done during the great days of the popular awakening. From every direction came the great mass of the people, the true people, from their dank dens and from their workshops.

In front of 45, boulevard Ornano in the XVIIIe Arrondissement the crowd was such that no traffic could move.

The coffin was placed on the hearse at 11:00 A.M. precisely—too precisely, because thousands of people arrived in the half hour that followed the departure of the hearse.

Louise Michel, before her return to Saint-Lazare prison, had placed a few mementos near the body of her mother: a red-framed photograph of herself leaning on a rock; a lock of her hair tied with a black ribbon; a bouquet of red immortelles which she had brought back from the burial of her friend, Marie Ferré; a portrait of Marie; and finally, some of the flowers which had been brought to her sick mother during her last days.

Citizen Clemenceau had come to offer his condolences to the family and to apologize for not being able to be in the funeral procession.

Numerous wreaths had been placed on the coffin and at the rear of the hearse. Many bouquets of real flowers were mingled with the wreaths.

There was one wreath inscribed: "To the mother of Louise Michel from *L'Intransigeant* staff"; one from the *Libre-Pensée;* one from the *Bataille;* and many others. Louise Michel placed a wreath made of black beads; it bore only the words, "To my mother."

The funeral procession began. Immediately after the hearse came an old man with white hair. He was M. Michel, the nearest relative of the deceased, and he was accompanied by his two daughters, the cousins of the imprisoned Louise.

Behind them Citizen Henri Rochefort walked with his eldest son, Vaughn, and the entire staff of *L'Intransigeant.*

Then came Citizen Louise Michel's comrades in the struggle, those who followed her in becoming enemies of the state and who were continuing the revolutionary fight in the press or in the courts. Notable among them were: Alphonse Humbert; Joffrin; Eudes; Vaillant; Granger; Lissagaray; Champy; Henri Maret; Lucipia; Odysse Barot; S. Pichon, who is a municipal counsellor of Paris; Antonio de la Calle, a former member of the revolutionary government of Cartagena; Moïse, a councilman in his arrondissement; Frédéric Cournet; Victor Simond and Titard of the *Radical;* and still more—many former deportees from the Ducos Peninsula and convicts from Nou Island.

We must note also the presence of Citizen Deneuvillers, a former exile of 1871 and now *L'Intransigeant* correspondent at Brussels; Citizen Théleni, the representative of the *Radical des Alpes;* Bariol, the delegate from the Club of the Rights of Man in Vaucluse; P. Arnal, the delegate from the Fraternal Association of Republicans of the Basses-Alpes, Vaucluse, and Var; and many delegates representing groups in the provinces and Paris, but we regret we are not able to give all their names.

Mingled with this funeral procession of persons who had fought in 1871 and persons who had been tested at other times were fervent young people from recently founded revolutionary groups. Among them were a hundred anarchists. As soon as the funeral procession began to move, these young people unfurled three red flags, one of which bore the inscription: "The Revolutionary Sentinel of the XVIIIe Arrondissement."

Behind, filling the entire width of the street, came an immense crowd bringing the tribute of its respect and gratitude to Louise Michel in these sorrowful circumstances.

On the Way

Not since the burial of Blanqui has such an imposing spectacle of a popular demonstration occurred—nothing so grand and majestic as yesterday.

The funeral procession headed towards the cemetery of Levallois-Perret by way of the boulevards of Ornano, Ney, Bessières, Berthier, and the Porte de Courcelles. The slope of the ramparts on the right of the procession was occupied by numerous spectators who rose in tiers up the incline. On the other side, the walls, roofs, and windows were also filled with the curious.

From every street opening on the main road, a new crowd of workers and the poor either lined up respectfully for the passing of the cortège or joined it, making the procession even larger.

The police remained hidden, and thus calm continued to reign and no clashes occurred. Order was kept by only two constables under the direction of a corporal, but the authorities had taken extraordinary measures to throw a hidden army against the demonstrators if the need arose. The Garde républicaine was to the left of the marchers on the rue Ordone, and policemen had been put inside all the police stations along the route. In the courtyard of the La Pépinière Barracks in the Place Saint-Augustine near the Etoile a battalion of infantry was drawn up with their packs ready to march.

When the funeral procession reached the Porte Ornano, it was estimated at over twelve thousand persons. From time to time the cry of "Long live the Commune!" or "Long live the Social Revolution!" came from the midst of that immense crowd.

As the cortège crossed the bridge over the Western Line Railroad, two despatch riders appeared. Because the going and coming of official messengers is never a good omen, shouts of "Long live the Revolution!" multiplied. The two riders hurried to withdraw as soon as their task was done.

At the boulevard Berthier, in front of Bastion 49, a couple of dozen policemen were drawn up. They were under the command of Florentin, the municipal police chief of the XVIIIᵉ Arrondissement, who had just been given a medal for having protected the police spy and agitator, Pottery. This Florentin was doubtless looking forward to working wonders here and winning new stripes and new medals.

The moment the hearse passed in front of the police station, Florentin, followed by his men, blocked the boulevard and ordered the red flag to be taken down.

Resounding cries of "Long live the Revolution!" and "Long live the Commune!" answered him. The demonstrators, keeping a close watch on their flags, seemed ready to defy this savior of informers. At this tense moment Citizen Rochefort moved towards the police officer and said to him: "Your attitude is the real provocation. Up to now, everything has happened in the most perfect order, and your intervention is completely improper."

Visibly intimidated, Florentin answered, "M. Caubet sent me the express order to stop the parading of the red flag."

"Those red flags you are speaking of," Rochefort said, "are the banners of societies which have the perfect right to choose whatever color suits them. There were also red banners following Gambetta's coffin, and no one dared to oppose their being unfurled."

These words and the forceful attitude of the citizens present made Florentin pause. He relented and went with his two dozen men to the head of the funeral procession in front of the hearse.

But when the police are not ferocious, they are treacherous. They planned their actions, and at the Porte d'Asnières, as soon as the hearse crossed the iron bars in front of the tollbooth, they tried to close the gates quickly. The police intended to cut the hearse off from the funeral procession and thus prevent the exhibition of red flags, which they had their hearts set on doing.

They failed to count on the determination of the revolutionaries. The gates gave way before the pressure of the crowd. A few carriages returning to Paris while this was happening owed their not being inspected at the tollbooth to these events.

One last incident occurred while the funeral procession was going along beside the tracks of the Inner Circle Railroad. A train passed by with all the passengers at the side doors. Recognizing the funeral procession of Louise Michel's mother, a great number of them began to wave their hats and hankerchiefs.

So the funeral procession arrived at Levallois-Perret, just outside the city walls.

At the Cemetery

The little city of Levallois-Perret was in a state of great excitement; so many people had not been seen for a long time. Many carriages were parked at the approaches to the cemetery, and all the residents of Levallois-Perret were standing, forming a hedge along the road where the funeral cortège was to pass.

The little cemetery had been tidied up. The gates were wide open, and the more eager citizens had already taken their places around the spot chosen for the burial.

It was Ferré's tomb, Théophile Ferré, whom the Versailles forces had murdered at Satory. He is buried there with his sister Marie Ferré, who was the close friend and devoted companion of Louise Michel. The memorial statue is modest. The plot is surrounded by an iron fence, and the graves are covered by a large flat stone. A marker bears the name of the martyr and his sister.

The bell at the cemetery rang to announce the arrival of the funeral procession. In a second, the crowd had invaded the field of the dead. It was only with great difficulty that the pallbearers brought the body to the tomb, and the only way the wreaths could be gotten from the hearse to the coffin was to pass them from hand to hand.

The red flags were unfurled, and the tombs disappeared under a living tide that rose over them from the ground up to the top of the memorial statues. The spectacle was one of grandeur and majesty.

The Speeches

After a moment of silence and contemplation, the first speaker was our contributor, Ernest Roche. Here is a summary of his speech, which was interrupted frequently with cheers and applause from the crowd.

"Who are we, standing here around the coffin of this simple and good woman who never dreamed of being famous?

"Why is there such a mixture here of so many different sorts of republicans and socialists?

"What feeling moves all of us?

"What attraction draws us here?

"What unity of spirit inspires in each of us the same respect and gives each of us the same feeling of indignation in front of this dead woman?

"Let me tell you.

"There is one flag sacred to all of us, the flag that people fly only at certain solemn times, the flag that inflames us more than any gorgeous fabric. It is the flag of our martyrs, the flag of our heroes.

"The corpse of Lucrecia overturned the Tarquins and founded the Roman Republic. The bodies of unknown men who were struck down on 23 February 1848 by Louis Philippe's soldiers brought on the collapse of his throne. The corpse of Victor Noir in the spring of 1870 caused the weakening of Louis Napoleon's Empire and precipitated its fall.

"The body of Louise Michel's poor mother is our common bond, for in each of our spirits it causes the same feeling of horror against the criminals who have murdered her.

"Don't take shelter behind the age of your victim, you hypocrites. Her age doesn't mitigate the odiousness of your terrible crime.

"Certainly, we know very well it wasn't she you meant to reach, any more than the Empire had any particular hatred for Victor Noir. What difference does it make to us whether your ferocity strikes down a simple person, or an unknown one, or a famous one from our ranks? The martyrdom with which you crown the person is enough to ignite our anger and is enough to explain it.

"Those two poor women, Louise Michel and her mother! Those who have known them know how indispensible they were to each other. The mother survived on the atmosphere of filial love with which her daughter surrounded her. By taking away her daughter, you killed her, and her death, perhaps, will drag along a second victim.

"After her, it will be Peter Kropotkin's turn; he is dying in prison. Then will come others, more obscure, but no less unfortunate.

"And you don't want us to get hold of these corpses, nor for us to rally around them with the idea of legitimate defense against those thieves who are stealing billions of francs and ruining our country until they can auction it off.

"We have come here to sign a compact for danger, vengeance, and justice. We have come to sign it in front of the tomb of Ferré, who was assassinated by the bullets of Versailles, and in front of the coffin of this woman poisoned by sorrow.

"I have one last thing to say: On behalf of our friends and colleagues at *L'Intransigeant* in whose name I am speaking, on behalf of those who fought beside our valiant citizen, Louise, on behalf of those who shared her agonies at being exiled and her joys upon returning—on behalf of all these, I must say how much we are moved by the sorrow that afflicts our friend Louise Michel and how much we would like to lighten its weight, if friendship and esteem can be any compensation for such a loss."

All or nothing.

I don't want them to pay me for the corpse of my mother. May the friends who warned me in time be thanked also.

I accept completely the responsibility for refusing the pardon. If my friends think about it, they will come to feel that if they can't do anything more for me, at least they shouldn't insult me.

My adversaries felt that way.

I clasp your hand.

Louise Michel

P.S. If the government hadn't listened to me and refused the pardon, I would have left France immediately and gone to Russia or Germany. In those countries they kill revolutionaries; they don't besmirch them.

May I just be left alone.

L.M.

"All or nothing." That's the way I hope I always feel. I also hope that they won't repeat the insult that I didn't merit and which they were kind enough to take away.

A man who is a prisoner has to fight only against the situation which his adversaries make for him. A woman who is a prisoner has not only that same struggle but also the complications caused by her friends intervening in her behalf. They come to aid her because they attribute to her every weakness, every stupidity, every folly.

A woman must be a thousand times calmer than a man, even facing the most horrible events. Although pain may be digging into her heart, she cannot let one word that is not "normal" escape her. If she does, her friends, fooled by pity, and her enemies, motivated by hate, will push her into a mental institution where, with all her faculties intact, she will be buried near madwomen, madwomen who perhaps weren't mad when they were locked up.

Comrades, you have been very good to my poor mother and me. My dear friends, you have to get used to not passing it off as madness if the thought of my mother's death rushes up in front of me and bewilders me. Remember that once the poor woman was no longer suffering, I buried her without shedding a tear. Returning to Saint-Lazare, I started back to work the day after her death without anyone ever seeing me cry or stop being calm, even for an instant. What more does anyone want? I shall live for the fight, but I do not wish to live under shameful circumstances.

During the May Days of 1885 the dead went quickly: Hugo, Cournet, Amouroux. All three remind us of 1871. Amouroux dragged the ball of penal servitude in New Caledonia. Cournet was exiled, and exile was the unhappiest fate of the vanquished. Victor Hugo offered his house at Brussels to the fugitives from the slaughterhouse.

Three others were mowed down along with the century that is ending—Louis Blanc, Père Malézieux, and Louis Auguste Blanqui. I remember Blanqui's last speech. The hall was bedecked with the Tricolor. The brave old man stood up to curse the colors of Sedan and Versailles waving in front of him, the symbols of surrender and murder. The howls of the reactionaries often covered the words of the old man, but then his dying chest filled up with the immense breath of the future and dominated the hall in its turn. After the meeting he went to bed and never got up again.

Malézieux was a man of both June and of Seventy-one, and when, upon his return from exile, the bosses found him too old to work, he lost the will to live. The facial resemblance between him and Victor Hugo was striking and complete. Their faces had the same nobility, proud in the old fighter's, gentle in the poet's. Their nobility lit up those two old Homers, and they looked like two old lions lying down observing you.

Hugo was the last of the old bards who sang alone, like Homer. The new bards will sing from one end of the earth to the other when we finally drag down the wreck of the old world, and they will have us as their chorus.

In New Caledonia on an enormous rock that opened its petals of granite like a rose, a granite rose that was spotted with little black streams of cold lava like trickles of black blood, I engraved one of Hugo's poems for the cyclones:

To the People

Paris bleeding by moonlight
Dreams over the common grave.
Give honor to mass murderers.
More conscription, more tribunes:
Eighty-nine is wearing a gag.

The Revolution, terrible to those it touches,
Is buried, a robber-chief doing
What no Titan could do,
And a Jesuit logician laughs crookedly.

Unsheathed against the great Republic
Are all the Lilliputian sabers.
The judge, a merchant clothed
In legal vestments, sells the law.

Lazarus, Lazarus, Lazarus
Rise up.
                              —Victor Hugo

As a child and all through my later life I kept sending poetry to Victor Hugo. But I sent him none after I returned from New Caledonia, because then it was unnecessary to do anything more to honor him. Everyone was celebrating the master, even those who had been far from fêting him in the past, and there was no need for me to assist in those joyful days. That is why I was so horrified to learn that Maxime du Camp planned to speak to the crowd from the top of Hugo's tomb.

It was Maxime du Camp—du Camp of Satory—who betrayed himself and us to the Versailles criminals. He was a purveyor of hot and cold massacres, besliming all those he pointed out. His forehead is marked with blood from the six years he spent flushing out citizens for the courts-martial, and he did it for pleasure. For him to speak under the blooming trees on the red anniversary would insult our sleeping dead. Master Hugo, on you shall fall no single word of his voice, nor any noise of his steps.

We revolutionaries aren't just chasing a scarlet flag. What we pursue is an awakening of liberty, old or new. It is the ancient communes of France; it is 1793; it is June 1848; it is 1871. Most especially it is the next revolution, which is advancing under this dawn. That is all that we are defending.

We wish that all the people of the world might be revenged for all the Sedans to which despots and fools have dragged humanity. Revenge is the Revolution, which will sow liberty and peace over the entire earth. When the people gain their full vigor, every person will have to line up on one side or the other. People will have to choose either to crowd with their castes into the ruts that moving wheels have left behind or to shake off the absurd limitations of class and take their places on the human stage under the light of the rising sun.

At the burial of Vallès there was an emotional multitude over which the red and black banners waved. Was that the whole revolutionary army? The advance guard? It was hardly a battalion. When the hour comes, which ferocious and stupid governments are pushing forward, it will not be a boulevard that quivers under the steps of a crowd. It will be the entire earth trembling under the march of the human race.

In the meantime, the wider the river of blood flowing from the scaffold where our people are being assassinated, the more crowded the prisons, the greater the poverty, the more tyrannical the governments, the more quickly the hour will come and the more numerous the combatants will be. How many wrathful people, young people, will be with us when the red and black banners wave in the wind of anger! What a tidal wave it will be when the red and black banners rise around the old wreck!

The red banner, which has always stood for liberty, frightens the executioners because it is so red with our blood. The black flag, with layers of blood upon it from those who wanted to live by working or die by fighting, frightens those who want to live off the work of others. Those red and black banners wave over us mourning our dead and wave over our hopes for the dawn that is breaking.

If we were free to fly our banners wherever we wanted in some country, it would show better than any vote can show on which side the crowd was lining up. No longer could men be put in the pockets of the authorities the way fistfuls of bulletins are stuffed there now. It would be a good way to assure each other of our unfalsified true majority, which this time would be that of the people. But we are allowed to fly our flags only over our dead.

People must continue to fight against the masters who oppress them. In England, the gallows will probably greet them, but that does not spoil the vision. They should fight anyway. There was a time when I found the idea of some poor person grimacing at the end of a rope disagreeable. Since than I have learned that in Russia they put you in a sack first. Germany had the headsman's block, as Reinsdorff and others saw. These various techniques are only different forms of the same death, and the more mournful the setting, the more it is wrapped in the red light of dawn.

At the time when I had a preference, I imagined a scaffold from which I could address the crowd. Then I saw the execution post on the plain of Satory, and as far as the manner of my execution was concerned, the white wall of Père Lachaise cemetery or even some angle of the walls of Paris would have suited me. Today I don't care. I don't care how, and I don't care where. What does it matter to me whether I'm killed in broad daylight or in a woods at night?

A decade and a half have elapsed since the struggle of the Commune. Of the living I say nothing. They are fighting hard in the struggle for life. They have days without work, which means days without food. When I speak of the survivors of the battle and the exile and the deportation to New Caledonia, I must speak of the courage of Mme Nathalie Lemel during all those events. It won't hurt her, for where she is working now, all the employees are criminals of the Commune and convicts returned from the "justice" of Versailles. I shall name only those to whom an employer won't say: "Ah, you come from being imprisoned for the Commune. Well, get out of here. There is no longer any work in my place for you." That happened and still happens often.

The court, just for the sake of variety, had sentenced some of us to hard labor. Some were deemed too weak to stand the trip to New Caledonia, and several of them are now dead: Poirier, so courageous during the Siege and the Commune; Marie Boire; and many others who were no longer alive when we returned from New Caledonia. Mme Louise was sent to New Caledonia in spite of her age, and she died there calling for her children, whom she could not see one more time in he last hours. Of those who were sent to Cayenne, two are dead. One was Elisabeth Retif, a poor and simple girl, who did a magnificent job of carrying out the wounded under fire and who never understood how anyone could find her actions evil. Elisabeth de Ghi, who had married and become Mme Langlais, died on the ship during the voyage home from New Caledonia. She would have loved to see Paris again, but we were still far away from it when, between two cannon shots, her body was slid through a cargo port into the depths of the sea. Marie Schmidt, one of the bravest, died last year in the home for the destitute on the rue de Sèvres. In 1871 she had been a stretcher bearer and a soldier, but work was hard to find upon our return and poverty kills quickly.

Sleep in peace, valiant ones, whether you be under the storms and waves, or lying in a common grave. You are the happy ones. Let us honor the obscure dead who suffered to aid those who will come after us. Let us honor the obscure dead who sensed only indistinctly the far-off horizon that will raise up their shades in sprays of stars and let them see the dazzling light of dawn.

As for the executioners, retribution wasn't long in coming. The prosecutor, Major Gaveau, whose passionate indictments were known to everyone, died insane. It had been necessary to lock him up for some time before his death, and according to the newspapers of the time, he had the most terrible death agonies imaginable. During the whole day before his death he believed that he saw fantastic creatures tumble around in front of his eyes, and it seemed to him that someone was beating a hammer on his skull. The expert Delarue, who had testified to a falsehood against Ferré, was himself later condemned for giving false expert testimony that sent a man to prison for five years. The cost of sending one of our comrades to the execution post at Satory wasn't as great. The farm of Donjeu, which belonged to M. Feltereau of Villeneuve, was burned by accident. I don't know if any accident befell Colonel Merlin, who had been a judge in the trial of the members of the Commune and who had commanded the troops which oversaw the assassinations of November 28. Why do criminals escape the consequences of their acts more easily than other people? Doesn't each act prepare its own destiny?

After the amnesty, I came home from ten years of exile in New Caledonia only to see my poor mother die. With my own hands I laid my mother down in her coffin, as I did Marie Ferré, the one in my red shawl, the other in a soft red coverlet which she liked. So they are for the eternal winter of the tomb, and people ask me if now I am turning my attention to liberty and the spring which makes the branches blossom out again. Am I giving up, now that I have shut my heart under the earth? No! I shall remain standing until the last moment. I returned from deportation faithful to the principles for which I shall die.

Yesterday was May 24. From a distance, I heard some kind of rapid bugle call whose brazen notes sent a chill through my heart. That call was like an echo of the May Days of 1871. Do they still lead soldiers against the people?

See the grains of sand and the piled-up hay and in the highest heavens the crowded stars. Where all that is seen is where we're going. And here comes the great harvest, grown in the blood of our hearts. The heads of the wheat will be heavier because of that, and the harvest will be greater.

In this somber life, cradling sad days, some refrains come back again and again. They catch at your emotions and rip you apart at the same time.

Flow, flow, blood of the captive.

The Baguades, the Jacques, all of you who wear an iron collar, let's talk while we wait for the hour to strike. The dream emerges from the scents of spring. It is the morning come of the new legend. Do you hear, peasant, the winds that pass in the air? They are the songs of your fathers, the old Gallic songs.

Flow, flow, blood of the captive.

See this red dew on the earth. It's blood. The grass over the dead grows higher and greener. On this earth, the charnel house of the people's dreams, the grass ought to grow thickly. As long as it pleases you to be the beef of the slaughterhouse, to be the ox that pulls the plow or the one dragged to the carnival, people will repeat the terrible refrain:

Flow, flow, blood of the captive.

I don't know where the final struggle between the old world and the new will take place, but it doesn't matter, because wherever it is—Rome, Berlin, Moscow—I'll be there. And other revolutionaries will be there, too. Wherever it begins, the spark will unite the whole world. Everywhere the crowds will rise up. Meanwhile we wait and while we wait, speeches continue. Those speeches are the rumblings of a volcano, and when everybody least expects it, the lava will spill out.

The evening will come. They will still be dancing in the palace. Parliaments will say that discontent has been building up for a long time, but that the grumbling will go on without anyone being able to do anything about it.

Then the great uprising will come. The rising of the people will happen at its appointed moment, the same way that continents develop. It will happen because the human race is ready for it.

That uprising will come, and those whom I have loved will see it. O my beloved dead. I began this book when one of you was still living. Now I end it bent over the ground where you both are sleeping.

Dead, both of them. The stones of my home overturned. I'm alone in the room where my mother spent her last years. Friends have arranged my mother's furniture and bed as it was when she was still alive. A little bird has slipped between the slats of the blinds to make its nest in the window, and the room is less forlorn because of it. My mother's poor old furniture, which was like part of her clothing, has the wings of an innocent bird beating over it, and that bird alone hears the ticking of the old clock which marked her death.

Soon, my beloved mother, Myriam!

If she had lived a few more years, even a few more months, I would have spent all that time near her. Today, what do prisons, lies, all the rest matter? What could death do to me? It would be a deliverance because I'm already dead. Why do people speak of courage? I'm in a hurry to join Marie and my mother.

Memory crowds in on me. The cemetery at Vroncourt in the upper turning of the road under the pines. Audeloncourt. Clefmont. And my uncles' little, low, dark houses. The little house of Aunt Apolline, dug into the ground. Uncle Georges's up on top of the hill. The schoolhouse. Who hears the noise of the brook there now? Through the open window comes the smell of roses, of stubble, of hay in the summer sunlight. They all come to me now more than ever. I smell the bitter odor of the niaoulis mixed with the sharp freshness of the Pacific waves. Everything reappears in front of my eyes. Everything lives again, the dead and all those things that have vanished.

Who am I, Louise Michel? Don't make me out to be better than I am—or than you are. I am capable of anything, love or hate, as you are. When the Revolution comes, you and I and all humanity will be transformed. Everything will be changed and better times will have joys that the people of today aren't able to understand. Feeling for the arts and for liberty will surely become greater, and the harvest of that development will be marvelous. Beyond this cursed time will come a day when humanity, free and conscious of its powers, will no longer torture either man or beast. That hope is worth all the suffering we undergo as we move through the horrors of life.

Epilogue

Much against her wishes, Louise Michel was pardoned and expelled—there is no other word for it—from prison in January 1886. By now, she was legendary. Or as Paul Verlaine put it in his "Ballade en l'honneur de Louise Michel," she was "nearly Joan of Arc." She was "Saint Cecilia / And the harsh and slender Muse / Of the Poor, as well as their guardian angel." Now in her late fifties, Michel was indefatigable; she produced poetry, wrote several involuted novels, and marched incessantly to the speaker's platform. And the summer following her release she was indicted once again, this time in company with Jules Guesde, Paul Lafargue, and Susini, for "instigating murder and looting."

She was accused of saying that the government was composed of "thieves and murderers. Thieves are arrested and murderers are killed. Throw them in the water!" Although Michel denied saying those exact words, she admitted that the tone was correct—which seems likely. The jury found her guilty, but despite their convicting her, it would have caused the government grave embarrassment to send her to jail again, and ultimately she was pardoned without going back to prison.

In January 1888, while Michel was delivering a speech at Le Havre, a fanatical Catholic Breton shot her. Her injury, a bullet that lodged behind her left ear, did not heal well, and for a time her health was precarious. True to her principles, however, Michel entered the trial of her assailant to plead for him, arguing that he was misled by an evil society, and he was acquitted.

This period of Michel's life coincided with the peak of the Boulangist movement, a political phenomenon that began on the left and moved over the years to the right, uniting at one time or another all those who opposed the Third Republic and particularly, at the end, those who wanted revenge against Germany. Although Michel's general principles would seem to dictate her opposing the final stages of the movement, she avoided involvement, perhaps because her friend Henri Rochefort was a staunch Boulangist. It is also possible that Michel, like the Marxist Guesde, saw Boulangism as only a bourgeois struggle and, as such, irrelevant.

Michel did take the lead in a temporary alliance of anarchists and monarchists who found a common enemy in the Third Republic. Through her, the royalists funneled funds to support anarchist activities. Some of the monarchists certainly were using Michel as the Germans would use Lenin in 1917; any trouble the anarchists fomented would serve the monarchist cause. But Michel, if she was aware she was being used, was entirely happy with the situation. Her main enemies now were not monarchists but "Possibilist" socialists, who in her eyes were no better than the "Opportunist" republicans she loathed.

The Possibilists, usually classified today as evolutionary socialists, hoped to alleviate the misery of the poor through small reforms and to work within the system to win power. Michel believed that, in fact, the Possibilists had no greater aim than to replace the bourgeoisie with themselves. Moreover, the minor reforms they supported would only postpone the Social Revolution.

In 1889 the problems in founding the Second International illustrated these theoretical distinctions. The First International had perished officially in 1876, although it had been moribund for several years prior to that date, the victim of repression from without and schism from within. Posthumously, the First International was gaining a reputation for effectiveness it had not earned during its life, and in 1889, the centenary of the first French Revolution, there were two international meetings held simultaneously in Paris to revive it, one of Possibilists and the other of Marxists, with delegates drifting from one meeting to the other. Michel played little role in either of those meetings, perhaps because of her lack of interest in organizations and organizational politics.

But from that chaotic founding of the Second International came the idea of using May Day demonstrations to show solidarity. By the late 1880s Michel had come to focus on the general strike, *la grande grève,* as the means by which the poor would achieve the Social Revolution. It would "interrupt . . . all industries and all branches of commerce and would finally carry the Social Revolution along." Despite Michel's dreams of *la grande grève,* her enthusiasm for the May Day demonstrations was limited; the demonstrations were not intended to incite the people to rebel but only to publicize the Left. Perhaps Michel was no longer so sure of crowds, and clearly she was inclining more and more simply to belief in "propaganda by the deed" and faith in direct action inspired and led by a small elite.

But Michel believed, as she always had, that it was her duty to participate in demonstrations, and she was preparing to participate in the 1890 May Day demonstration when she was arrested the day before its scheduled occurrence. In a fit of rage and frustration she destroyed the furnishings of her cell, and officials rushed to use that behavior to have her certified insane. For reasons that remain unclear, the Minister of the Interior, Constans, intervened directly to stop the committal proceedings and to have her released.

Michel immediately left for England, and from 1890 until her death she spent the greater part of her time there. Perhaps the near-successful committal proceeding had frightened her; being committed was a fear she had carried for years. Perhaps she was simply tired. In any event, England was the traditional home of foreign exiles, and Rochefort, himself a refugee after the collapse of Boulangism, was there. Rochefort gave her money to live on, and Prince Kropotkin gave her what aid he could. During the following years she tried through personal contact to help the English poor—as always, whatever money she had at any moment she gave away on request—and she became known in the worst slums of London as "the good woman."

She returned to France only once, briefly, during the five years from 1890 to 1895, which were the years of anarchism's greatest notoriety in France. It was during those years that France lived in daily fear of bombings, the most savage period being the months from Ravachol's bombings in the spring of 1892 to the explosions in the Chamber of Deputies in December 1893 and the Café Terminus in February 1894. Although Michel objected to bombs because they indiscriminately killed women and children, she continued to approve the use of force. Ravachol was, she said, "the hero of modern legend," and later she approved the bombing of the Chamber of Deputies.

In 1895 Michel returned to France and for the next seven months made speeches and wrote poetry. The following summer she returned to England, presumably so she could attend the scheduled meeting of the International, the one which confirmed the expulsion of the anarchists. Michel was horrified at the proceedings and the enforcement of Marxist orthodoxy. The meeting proved, she said, that even the best, most intelligent, and most devoted Marxist revolutionary "will be worse than anyone he replaces because the Marxists claim infallibility and practice excommunication." The rupture between Michel and the Marxist socialists, like the one with the Possibilists before them, was complete.

In the spring of 1897 Michel, now in her sixty-seventh year, made an extensive speaking tour throughout France. In France, the Dreyfus Affair was reaching its height, but Michel took no active part in it, although she did speak out against secret trials and anti-Semitism. Maybe her faith temporarily was burning low. She had, after all, been preaching revolution, or been imprisoned for preaching it, for forty years. Moreover, her audiences were dwindling.

In spite of her increasingly frail health she began a new series of speeches in France in May 1902, which continued into 1903 with one break in London. By then, Russia, which had fascinated her for years, seemed on the verge of revolution, and events there were rekindling her enthusiasm, particularly after the outbreak of war in 1904 between Russia and Japan. A determined antimilitarist, Michel was nonetheless delighted at the opportunity an unpopular war provided for the onset of the Social Revolution. She made more speeches in France during February and early March 1904, but then fell gravely ill.

She recovered, and after her well-publicized illness, which the public had supposed would be mortal, the enormous crowds as of old came to hear her speak. Perhaps now people were only coming to view a legend, but come they did in great numbers, and they applauded her. At the end of the year she went to Algeria; upon her return to France she fell ill in Marseille. This illness was her last. On 9 January 1905 she died in that city at the Hôtel de l'Oasis.

Her death became the occasion of one of those spectacles she would have loved. With red flags, masses of flowers, and two thousand mourners—representatives of labor unions, socialist groups, anarchists, and antireligious organizations—the funeral procession was a kilometer long as it wound through Marseille to the cemetery. Memorial services took place throughout France and in London and elsewhere. On January 20 her body was disinterred, taken to Paris, and two days later buried at her mother's side in Levallois-Perret to the accompaniment of another spectacle, the largest, said the press, since the death of Victor Hugo. Not only would Michel have approved the spectacle, she would have noted how strange it was that on that very day a crowd of Russians in St. Petersburg attempted to deliver a petition to their czar, and the ensuing massacre marked the day forever as Bloody Sunday.

Today, Michel's birthplace of Vroncourt has a statue to her, and the street going through town bears her name. Her grave in Levallois-Perret—not the one in which she was buried in 1905, but a new one to which she was moved during the Popular Front days of 1936—still has flowers placed on it by anonymous hands. The authorities have even named a metro station and a street for her, but both are just barely outside the city limits of Paris.

She is now a legend. That she invented part of it herself is irrelevant. Louise Michel was heroic, but as she herself said: "There is no heroism; people are simply entranced by events."

Bibliography

Louise Michel discussed her own writings briefly in her memoirs.

Let me record a balance sheet of my writings. I have spoken of the various bits of poetry from the years before the events of 1870–71 inserted in different newspapers, in the *Journal de la jeunesse*, in the *Union des poètes*, in Adèle Esquiros' newspaper, in Adèle Caldelar's *La Raison*, and other places. Of the verses I sent to Victor Hugo in my childhood and youth, of which I have cited a few here and there, two or three pieces which were in the papers that Marie Ferré and my mother arranged during my deportation will be found in my volume of verse. I used the name Enjolras on a certain number of pieces of verse, *Louis* Michel on others, and my own name on still more. I don't know what has become of them. I've mentioned an article signed Louis Michel in *Le Progrès musical* in which I discussed an instrument I dreamed up, a piano with bows instead of mallets. They make them now in Germany.

There are a large number of signed articles in the *Révolution sociale*, the *Etendard*, and a number of other signed articles are scattered. The first part of my *Encyclopédie enfantine*, which I wrote in New Caledonia, appeared in Mlle Cheminat's *Journal d'éducation*.

During my last trip to Lyon I left a drama, *Le Coq rouge*, at the *Nouvelliste*. The masses of drama for children have all vanished after each awarding of prizes during so many years.

All my life I have kept working on *La Légende du barde;* there are fragments of it everywhere. I have some fragments of other prose manuscripts, the *Livre d'Hermann*, the *Sagesse d'un fou*, *Littérature au crochet*, the *Diableries de Chaumont*, and so forth. Perhaps I will put them together some day to search in them, as in my poetry, for the changes of my ideas across life.

Of the works done at Auberive I have a few pages remaining from the book *Le Bagne. La Conscience* and *Le Livre des morts* are completely lost. The first part of *La Femme à travers les âges* was published in H. Place's *L'Excommunié*. That newspaper had announced it would publish *Mémoires d'Hanna la nihiliste*, but the paper died. Under that title I had gathered a great many episodes of my life, along with Russian episodes. The *Océaniennes* and the *Légendes canaques* have appeared in fragments in Nouméa and here upon my return.

When I collaborate with someone, I keep the papers which establish the facts of my collaboration so as to be free not to take part in the profits or losses in any lawsuits my collaborators attempt. They are at liberty to do as they wish. I collaborated with Grippa de Winter in a novel, *Le Bâtard impérial*, and took a play, *Nadine*, from it. Since my return from New Caledonia I have had two collaborators, one of whom was Mme Tynaire, Jean Guetré. She wrote almost all the first part of *La Misère*, while the second part, from the chapter on Toulon on, is completely mine. In a Lille magazine, *Le Forçat*, I had begun to publish this second part in installments which would form a complete work with the addition of a few lines of introduction. Mme Tynaire could also make a complete work out of the first part by adding a few pages.

Mme Tynaire can be my friend, but it turned out that she could not be my collaborator because we see things differently. Those differences are perfectly visible in *La Misère,* and the two distinct parts are easily discernible. Mme Tynaire expects to promote general well-being through means in which I see no effectiveness. I see general well-being promoted only by successive revolutions cutting through the series of social transformations.

To remain good friends with Mme Tynaire instead of quarreling with our pens, I gave up a second collaboration with her, the second part of *Les Méprisées.* If I had taken it on, I would have been obliged to make the remaining characters undergo changes in character and circumstances which would have been incompatible with the way they were introduced to the reader in the first part. The novel *Les Méprisées* thus contains only one line I wrote.

I can't list the sketches in progress, novels begun everywhere which I never had the time to finish owing to events. Let me end by noting that the complete text of the *Encyclopédie enfantine* will be published at Mme Keva's and that the *Légendes canaques* has already been published by the same publisher.

Translators' Note

The debts that Louise Michel's translators owe are legion. First and foremost is their great debt to the painstaking biography of Louise Michel prepared by the late Edith Thomas, *Louise Michel ou la Velléda de l'anarchie* (Paris, Gallimard, 1971).

Other biographies of Michel include: Irma Boyer, *Louise Michel* (Paris: André Delpeuch, 1927); Charles Chincholle, *Les Survivants de la Commune* (Paris: L. Boulanger, 1885); Dominique Desanti, *Visages de femmes* (Paris: Editions Sociales, 1955); Ernest Girault, *La bonne Louise: Psychologie de Louise Michel* (Paris: Bibliothèque des auteurs modernes, 1906); and Carl, Freiherr von Letetzow, *Louise Michel (la Vierge Rouge): eine Charakterskisse* (Leipzig: F. Rothbarth, 1906).

Louise Michel wrote a later work specifically on the Commune, *La Commune* (Paris: P.-V. Stock, 1898), and although we have resisted the temptation to add material to the text of her memoirs from that source, it was helpful in establishing the sequence of events, which is unclear in the memoirs. In addition, for the period of the Siege and the Commune, Alistaire Horne's *The Fall of Paris* (New York: St. Martin's Press, 1965), Michael Howard's *The Franco-Prussian War* (New York: Macmillan, 1962), and Stewart Edward's *The Paris Commune, 1871* (London: Eyre and Spottiswoode, 1971) were useful. The work of the Association pour la Conservation et Reproduction Photographique de la Presse in preserving Communard newspapers was invaluable.

Michel's account of her trials was checked against the *Gazette des tribunaux;* she was accurate. The *Gazette des tribunaux* also furnished the account of the trial of 1886 referred to in the Epilogue (13 August 1886, pp. 764–65).

On New Caledonia, we found a school text by Jean le Borgne, *Géographie de la Nouvelle-Calédonie et des Iles Loyauté* (Nouméa: Ministère de l'éducation, de la jeunesse et des sports, 1964), most useful for its descriptions of the flora and fauna of that island. On the Kanaka rebellion we found Roselene Dousset, *Colonialisme et Contradictions: Etude sur les causes socio-historiques de l'Insurrection de 1878 en Nouvelle-Calédonie* (Paris: Mouton, 1970), instructive.

Her voyage out, her early years in New Caledonia and her relationship with Henri Rochefort were made more comprehensible by Rochefort's memoirs, *Les Aventures de ma vie* (5 vols.; Paris: Paul Dupont, 1896); and his *L'Evadé* (2d ed.; Paris: Bibliothèque Charpentier, 1895); see also Roger L. Williams, *Henri Rochefort: Prince of the Gutter Press* (New York: Charles Scribner's Sons, 1966).

The memoirs of L. Andrieux, *Souvenirs d'un Préfet de Police* (2 vols.; Paris: Jules Rouff, 1885) allowed us to comprehend Louise Michel's comments about police involvement in *La Révolution sociale*.

Standard works on the Third Republic, including Brogan, Chastenet, Thomson, and Cobban, were all useful, as were standard studies of anarchism, particularly George Woodcock's. Our translation of the Anarchist Manifesto of Lyon differs from the usual translation; Michel attributes it to Gautier, not Kropotkin. Daniel Ligou's *Histoire du Socialisme en France: 1871–1961* (Paris: Presses Universitaires de France, 1962) was useful.

We must also note our debt to the French Ministry of Marine, which found for us the manuscript report of the *Virginie*'s voyage to New Caledonia. In France the staffs of the Bibliothèque Nationale and the Archives Nationales both sought exotic publications for us with customary courtesy.

The Public Record Office in London furnished the Admiralty charts of the vicinity of Nouméa which enabled us to untangle Michel's description of the convict encampment on the Ducos Peninsula. The Library of Congress provided charts of the harbor of Las Palmas, Gran Canaria.

For a list of some of Louise Michel's published writings, an extraordinarily varied assortment, see Edith Thomas, *Louise Michel,* pp. 459–60.

Finally, the translators wish to express their gratitude to Hilde L. Robinson for her extraordinarily thorough job of copyediting; she saved us from ourselves many times. We also owe thanks to Eloise Green, Cindy Carrell, Karen Yount, and Beth Broyles for their assistance in typing the final manuscript.

Appendix I

Chapter List Showing Source in Original Text

Chapter 1, "Introduction," Part 1, Chapter 1; with minor additions from Part 2, Chapters 11, 13.

Chapter 2, "Vroncourt," Part 1, Chapters 2, 3, 4, 5, 6, 7, 11; Part 2, Chapter 1.

Chapter 3, "The End of Childhood," Part 1, Chapters 2, 3, 4, 6, 7, 10; Part 2, Chapter 1; with minor additions from Part 1, Chapter 5.

Chapter 4, "The Making of a Revolutionary," Part 1, Chapter 11; Part 2, Chapter 1; with minor additions from Part 1, Chapter 6; Part 2, Chapter 2.

Chapter 5, "Schoolmistress in the Haute Marne," Part 1, Chapters 6, 7.

Chapter 6, "Schoolmistress in Paris," Part 1, Chapters 7, 8; with minor additions from Part 1, Chapter 4.

Chapter 7, "The Decaying Empire," Part 1, Chapters 7, 8, 9, 12, 13.

Chapter 8, "The Siege of Paris," Part 1, Chapters 12, 13, 14, 15; with minor additions from Part 1, Chapter 10.

Chapter 9, "The Commune," Part 1, Chapters 12, 14, 15; Part 2, Chapter 2.

Chapter 10, "After the Commune," Part 1, Chapters 15, 16; Part 2, Chapters 2, 4, 15.

Chapter 11, "The Trial of 1871," Appendix.

Chapter 12, "Voyage to Exile," Part 1, Chapter 16; Part 2, Chapter 6; with minor additions from Part 1, Chapters 1, 6.

Chapter 13, "Numbo, New Caledonia," Part 1, Chapter 16; Part 2, Chapter 6.

Chapter 14, "The Bay of the West," Part 1, Chapters 10, 16; Part 2, Chapters 6, 8, 9.

Chapter 15, "Nouméa and the Return," Part 2, Chapters 6, 10, 11; with minor additions from Part 2, Chapter 8.

Chapter 16, "Speeches and Journalism, November 1880–January 1882," Part 1, Chapter 17; Part 2, Chapters 5, 6, 11, 12; Appendix; with minor additions from Part 1, Chapter 16; Part 2, Chapter 3.

Chapter 17, "The Death of Marie Ferré," Part 2, Chapters 11, 15.

Chapter 18, "Women's Rights," Part 1, Chapter 9; Part 2, Chapter 13.

Chapter 19, "Speeches Abroad, 1882–1883," Part 2, Chapters 2, 3, 11; with minor additions from Part 2, Chapter 12.

Chapter 20, "Speeches in France, 1882–1883," Part 2, Chapters 11, 12, 13.

Chapter 21, "The Trial of 1883," Part 2, Chapter 13; Appendix.

Chapter 22, "Prison," Part 2, Chapters 6, 14.

Chapter 23, "My Mother's Death," Part 2, Chapters 5, 15, 16.

Chapter 24, "Final Thoughts," Part 1, Chapters 14, 16, 17; Part 2, Chapters 3, 4, 6, 9, 13, 15, 16; with minor additions from Part 1, Chapter 15; Part 2, Chapters 10, 12.

"Bibliography," Part 2, Chapter 7.

Appendix II

Table of Poems in Original Text

Poems by Louise Michel

"A bord de la *Virginie*," Part 2, Chapter 6

"Adieux à ma tourelle," Part 1, Chapter 2. Translated as "Farewell, my dreaming retreat in the manor," p. 23.

"A Th. Ferré," Part 1, Chapter 13.

"A mes frères," Part 2, Chapter 4.

"Au bord des flots," Part 1, Chapter 4.

"Au 3ᵉ Conseil de Guerre," Part 2, Chapter 4.

"Aux manes de Victor Hugo," Part 2, Chapter 9.

"Ballade du squelette," Part 1, Chapter 8. Translated as "Ballad of the Skeleton," p. 41.

"La Chanson des poires," Part 1, Chapter 3.

"Chanson du chanvre," Part 1, Chapter 15.

"Chanson de guerre" (Kanakan), translated into French by Louise Michel, Part 2, Chapter 6.

"Le Chêne," Part 1, Chapter 7. Translated as "The Legend of the Oak," pp. 43–44.

"La coupe est rougie," Part 1, Chapter 8.

"Dans les mers polaires," Part 2, Chapter 6. Prose translation, p. 93.

"Entendex-vous tonner l'airain?" Part 1, Chapter 8. Translated as "Do you hear the brazen thunder," p. 53.

"La Grilla rapita," Part 1, Chapter 2.

"Le Lai du troubadour," Part 1, Chapter 8. Translated as "Lay of the Troubadour," p. 42.

"La Manifestation de la paix," Part 1, Chapter 13.

"Marie Ferré," Part 2, Chapter 11. Translated as "In Memory of Marie Ferré," pp. 137–38.

"Moi, je suis la blanche colombe," Part 1, Chapter 8. Translated as "Me, I am the white dove," p. 53.

"Les Oeillets rouges," Part 1, Chapter 13.

"L'Oiseau noir du champ fauve," translation into French by Louise Michel of patois poem, "L'Agé na deu champ fauvé," Part 1, Chapter 4. Translated as "The Black Bird of the Fallow Field," p. 18.

"Pour mes premiers jouets . . . ," Part 2, Chapter 6. Translated as "As my first toys," p. 91.

"Les Roses," Part 1, Chapter 17.

"Le *Takata*, dans la forêt," Kanakan chant of Andia, translated into French by Louise Michel, Part 2, Chapter 9. Translated as "The *Takata*," pp. 113–14.

"Toute l'ombre a versé ses ténébreuses urnes," Part 1, Chapter 12. Last two stanzas translated as "Criminals and Whores," p. 49.

"Les Veilleurs de nuit," Part 1, Chapter 13.

"Vent du soir . . . ," Part 1, Chapter 3.

"Volez, oiseaux . . . ," Part 2, Chapter 6. Translated as "Soar high in brilliant whiteness, birds," p. 93.

"Le Voyage," Part 2, Chapter 1. Translated, with stanzas rearranged, as "The Voyage," p. 15.

Poems by Other Persons

"A des antiquaires," by Etienne-Charles Demahis, Louise Michel's grandfather, Part 1, Chapter 3.

"L'Agé na deu champ fauvé," patois poem translated into French by Louise Michel as "L'Oiseau noir du champ fauve," Part 1, Chapter 4. Translated as "The Black Bird of the Fallow Field," p. 18.

"Air de 'Malbrough [sic],' " by friends of Louise Michel in collaboration, Part 1, Chapter 8.

"A ma voisine de tribord arrière," by Henri Rochefort, Part 2, Chapter 6.

"Eut qu'elle aimot," traditional folksong, Part 1, Chapter 10. Translated as "He whom she loved," p. 16.

"La Mort," by Louise Porcquet Demahis, Louise Michel's grandmother, Part 1, Chapter 3.

"Paris sanglant, au clair de lune," ["Au peuple," second stanza], by Victor Hugo, Part 2, Chapter 9. Second stanza translated as "To the People," p. 192.

Index

The first names of minor figures, when given, must be treated as only tentative, unless the name also appears in the Memoirs.

Adouéke (New Caledonian herb), 113–14
"Agé Na Deu Champ Fauvé, L' " (patois folksong): text, 17; translated into French by Louise Michel, text, 18
Alchemy, 20, 29, 97
Alcohol, use of, 104, 105, 175, 177
Alençon, Duke of, 123
Aleyron, Colonel and Governor of New Caledonia, 95, 98, 99, 101, 126
Allix, Jules, 136
Amiens, Workers' Union of, 129–30
Amnesty of 1880, viii, 120
Amouroux, 191
Anarchism and Anarchists, ix–xi, 1, 33, 130, 131, 132, 140, 148, 151, 154–57, 160, 161, 162, 167, 169, 183, 187, 198, 200
"Anarchists, Manifesto of the," ix; text, 155–56, 160
Anarchists, Trial of the Sixty-eight, at Lyon, 1883, xiv, 154–57, 158
Andia the Takala (Kanakan), 112–13
Andrieux, Louis, xiv, 131, 132, 133
Animals, cruelty toward, xvi, 24–25, 28, 29, 93, 195. *See also* Oppression and exploitation
Antwerp, socialist press in, 144
Anvers, Belgium, 147
Appert, General, 78
Arras, prison at, 78
Armand (pardoned deportee at Nouméa), 119
Arnal, P., 183
Arnold, Blanche, 110
Arson(ists), 57, 67, 85
Aryans, in Oceana, 116
"As my first toys," poem by Louise Michel, text, 91
Assi (Communard), 76
Ataï (Kanakan leader), 112–14
Atavism, 16, 17. *See also* Legends and history
Atlantis (legend), 92
Auberive prison, 35, 89, 153, 202
Auclert, Hubertine, 136
Audeloncourt, Haute-Marne, xiii, 8, 32, 33, 34, 35
"Avengers, The," song by Louise Michel, 83
Avronsart, 61

Babeuf, "Gracchus," ix
Bagne, Le, lost manuscript by Louise Michel, 202
Bakhunin, Mikhail, ix
Balandreau, Maître, 167
"Ballad of the Skeleton," from *The Dream of the Witches' Sabbath* by Louise Michel, text, 41
"Ballade en l'honneur de Louise Michel," by Paul Verlaine: cited, xi; quoted from, 198
Balloons, 65
Balzenq (deportee), 96
Barinage, miners of, 144
Bariol, 183
Barot, Odysse, 74–75, 183
Barthélemy-Saint-Hilaire, Jules, 126
Bataille, La (periodical), 183
Bâtard impérial, Le, by Louise Michel and Grippa de Winter, 202
Batignolles, Seventeenth Arrondissement, Paris, 63, 81
Baudelaire, Charles, 66, 91
Bauër, Henry, 97, 111
Belleville, Nineteenth Arrondissement, Paris, 63, 82
Bernard (defendant, Trial of the Sixty-eight Anarchists), 154
Besson (at Lyon), 156
Beths, Mme (educator at Chaumont), 31
Bias, Mme Camille, 135, 136, 179
Bilhoray (Communard), 76
"Black Bird of the Fallow Field, The" (patois folksong), translated into French by Louise Michel, text, 18
"Black Marseillaise, The," poem by Louise Michel and Vermorel, 53
Blanc, Louis, 191
Blanche, Place, women's barricade at, 67
Blanqui, Louis-Auguste (and Blanquists), ix, 62, 83, 97, 130; last speech of, 191–92; funeral, 183; anniversary of death, demonstration on, xvi, 134
Bloody Sunday, Russia (1905), 201
Bloody Week, Commune of Paris, 67
Boeuf, 118
Boire, Marie, 194
Bonaparte (and Bonapartism), x, 32, 36, 38, 46, 48, 51, 52, 56, 57, 63, 168, 169, 186; Louise Michel instructs pupils to

boycott prayer for, xiii, 35; Louise
  Michel plans assassination of, x, 54. *See
  also* Empire, Second
Bonaparte, Eugénie, 53
Bordat (defendant, Trial of the
  Sixty-eight Anarchists), 154
Bordeaux, France, 130
Bordeaux Assembly, 63, 65
Bossuet, Jacques Bénigne, 19
Botanical experiments, xii, 97–98, 105–06
Boulanger, General Georges (and
  Boulangism), 198, 199
Bourail, New Caledonia, 95
Bourgeois (executed with Ferré), 77
Breton. *See* Brittany
Brideau, Gabriel, 56
Brittany (and Bretons), 90, 93, 151, 198;
  Breton mobiles, 61
Brussels, Belgium, 143, 147, 191
Bunant (deportee), 97
Burgraves, by Victor Hugo, 19
Burlot (deportee), 61, 97
Butte de Montmartre. *See* Montmartre,
  Butte de
Buzenval, battle at (19 Jan. 1871), 61

Cadolle, Mme, 73, 136
Café Terminus Bombing (1894), Paris,
  200
Cailleux, Marie, 101
Caissaigne, Lieutenant, 74
Caldelar, Adèle, 202
Calle, Antonio de la, 183
Callot, "The Beggars" (painting), 152
Canary Islands, 91–92
Cannon, 63, 67
Cape of Good Hope, 93
Carr, E. H., x
Cartegena, Spain, 183
Cassation, Court of, 79
Caubet (socialist), 184
Cayenne (prison colony), 36, 37, 73, 172,
  195
Centrale Prison, Clermont, xv, 28–29,
  172, 174, 179, 180
Chabert, 187
Chagot, victims of, 144
Chalon-sur-Saône, 144
Champy (Communard), 76, 97, 183, 187
Chantiers Prison, Versailles, 71, 172–73
Châté païot, 11
Château-d'Eau, rue de (Mme Vollier's
  school in Montmartre), 38

Chaudey, General, 61
Chaumont, Haute-Marne, 10–11, 31, 32,
  35, 36
Cheminat, Mlle (of *Journal d'Education*),
  202
Cholera, 180, 181
Christ (Communard), 61
Cipriani (Communard), 100, 126
Citoyen, Le, 126, 127
Clamart, town southwest of Paris, 65, 66,
  84
Clefmont, Haute-Marne, xiii
Clemenceau, Georges, xii, 65, 74, 82, 182
Clément (Communard), 76
Clermont, France. *See* Centrale Prison,
  Clermont
Comète (ship), 90
Commune of Lyons, 65
Commune of Marseille, 65
Commune of Narbonne, 65
Commune (and Communards) of Paris,
  viii, xii, xiv, 28, 52; first proclaimed,
  60; Chapter 9, "The Commune of
  Paris," 63–68; Chapter 10, "After the
  Commune," 69–80, 81, 83, 84, 85, 86,
  89, 90, 109, 112, 120, 121, 123, 124,
  126, 136, 158, 168, 169, 172, 184, 194
Commune, Wards of the, 81
Conscience, La, lost manuscript by Louise
  Michel, 202
Constans (Minister of Interior), 199
Contes d'enfants, by Louise Michel, 106
Convict Deportation in New Caledonia,
  Inquiry into the System of, by
  Chamber of Deputies, 126
Coq rouge, Le, drama by Louise Michel in
  Nouvelliste, 202
Courbet (Communard), 76
Cournet, Frédéric, 130, 183, 191
Court-martial(s), 74–76, 79–80, 81–87,
  194
Cri du peuple, 84, 86
Criminals, women, 173, 174
"Criminals and Whores," poem by Louise
  Michel, text, 49
Croiset, Père (Communard), 97, 99, 107
Cyclones (in New Caledonia), 107–09,
  115

Dailly, Captain, 81, 87
Danel's musical notation, 48
Daoumi (Kanakan), 96, 112, 116; brother
  of, 116

Déjardin, Surgeon-Major, 77
Delambre (of Amiens), 130
Delaporte, Colonel, 81
Delarue (prosecution witness, 1871), 195
Delescluze, Charles, 65, 159; sister of, 137
Demahis, Etienne-Charles, viii, xiii, 4–5, 7, 13, 15, 21–22, 23, 90
Demahis, Laurent, viii, 188
Demahis, Louise Porcquet, xiii, 5, 7
Demahis family papers, 19
Demonstration(s): in Dec. 1870, 60; on 22 Jan. 1871, xiv, 35, 61–62, 151; on Blanqui Anniversary, 1882, xvi, 134; at Versailles, September 1882, 151; at les Invalides, 9 March 1883, xi, xv, 158; Chapter 21, "The Trial of 1883," 158–71; at Père Lachaise, 130, 182; on May Day, 1890, 199
Deneuvillers (journalist), 144, 183
Deportees, xiv, 95–123, 126–27, 147
Deputies, Chamber of, bombing (1893), 200
Deraismes, Maria, 58
Dereure, Mme, 173
Deschamp (Communard), 76
Desfossés, Adèle, 101
Diableries of Chaumont, 202. See also Legendary Haute-Marne; Diabolism
Diabolism, 10, 11, 19, 20
Dieppe, France, 122
Digeon (anarchist), 187
Discours sur l'histoire universelle, by Jacques Bénigne Bossuet, 19
Dombrowski, Jaroslav, 67
Dreyfus Affair, 200
Du Camp, Maxime, 126, 193
Ducos Peninsula, New Caledonia, xiv, 115, 183. See also Numbo; West, Bay of the
Dumollard, Mme (prisoner), 153
Dupré, Mme (deportee), 101
Duval, Mme (of Lagny), 31–32
Duval, Nathalie. See Lemel, Nathalie

École des femmes, L', by Molière, 21
Écrègne(s), xviii, 25, 26, 28, 33
Education, 20, 30, 33, 34, 47, 48, 117, 118, 142, 155; of schoolmistresses, 31, 32, 38, 39, 40, 46, 51, 172
Eighteenth Arrondissement, Butte-Montmartre, Paris. See Montmartre

Eighteenth Arrondissement, Revolutionary Sentinel of (organization), 183
Elementary Education, Society for, 51
Élysée-Montmartre, 123
Empire, Second, 34, 53, 54, 56, 57. See also Bonaparte
Encyclopédie enfantine, by Louise Michel in Journal d'éducation, 202, 203
England, 148, 194, 199. See also London, England
Enjolras (pseudonym of Louise Michel), 51, 202
Erasmus, Praise of Folly, 159
Esquiros, Adèle, 45, 53, 57, 202
Étendard, L', 202
Eudes, Émile, xiv, 56
Eudes, Mme. See Louvet, Victorine
Evolutionary socialists. See Possibilist socialists
Excommunié, L', (periodical), 202

Fabreguettes (prosecutor, Trial of the Sixty-eight Anarchists), 156
"Farewell, my dreaming retreat in the manor," poem by Louise Michel, text, 23
Favre, Jules, 50
Fayet (Rector, departmental academy, Haute-Marne), 36, 128
Feltereau (of Villeneuve), 195
Feminism, xv, 20, 39, 52, 58, 59, 60, 64, 67, 73, 83, 122, 124, 130; Chapter 18, "Women's Rights," 139–42; 148, 172, 173, 177, 191. See also Prostitution
Femme à travers les âges, La, by Louise Michel, 202
Ferrat (Communard), 76
Ferré, Mme (mother of Marie and Théophile), 74–75
Ferré, Marie, xiv, xvi, 74–75, 76, 77, 78, 104, 107, 121, 122, 129; Chapter 17, "The Death of Marie Ferré," 135–38; 153, 182, 185, 195; Louise Michel's poem on, text of, 137–38
Ferré, Marie, Association (Lyon), 136
Ferré, Théophile, xvi, 9, 61, 74–77, 79, 84, 86, 135, 136, 137, 178, 185, 195
Figaro, Le, 121
Flags: black, of anarchy or of demonstrations, 161, 162, 193, 194; red, of revolution, 57, 62, 65, 90, 112, 168, 183, 184, 185, 186, 193, 194, 195

Fleurville, de (inspector of Montmartre schools), 106–07
Florentin (police chief, Eighteenth Arrondissement), 184
Flourens, Gustave, 76
Forçat, Le (Lille), 202
Forty-third bastion. *See* Thirty-seventh bastion
Fountain of the Ladies. *See* Three Washerwomen, legend of
Foutriquet ("Little Squirt"). *See* Thiers, Adolphe
Franco-Prussian War (1870–71), 23; Chapter 8, "The Siege of Paris," 56–62, 63
Free School, 34
Freemasons, 146–47

Gallifet, General Gaston Gabriel Auguste de, 69, 123, 126, 167
Gambetta, Léon, 184
Garde républicaine, 184
Gaulet, Major, 74
Gaulois, Le, 127
Gauthier (at Amiens), 130
Gauthier de la Richerie, Governor of New Caledonia, 95, 97, 98
Gautier, Émile, xiv, 132, 136, 154; author of "Manifesto of the Anarchists," quoted, 154–56
Gaveau, Major, 74, 79, 195
General strike, the, 129, 199
Gérard, 124
German (and Germany), 178, 191, 194. *See also* Franco-Prussian War
Ghent, Belgium, 144
Ghi, Elisabeth de, 195
Ghost-in-Flames, legend of, 11, 25, 26
Gourget (co-defendant, 1883), 170
Government of National Defense, xiv, 56, 58, 60, 61
Grafford Hall, Paris, 124, 152
Granger, 183
Grévin Museum, 152
Grousset (Communard), 76
Guanches, 92
Guesde, Jules, ix, 150, 198
Guetré, Jean. *See* Tynaire, Mme
Guibert, Capt. de, 74

Hamet (of Amiens), 130
Hardouin, Mme Céleste, 73
Harmodius of Athens, 54

Haussman, Maître, 81, 87
Haute-Marne, xvi, 23, 24, 25; legends and history of, 9–11, 17, 32; patois of, poem in, 17. *See also* Audeloncourt; Chaumont; Écrègne(s); Vroncourt; Millières
Hautefeuille, rue, Paris (site of center for education), 47, 48, 50, 51, 52
Haute-Marne, Prefect of, 36, 57
Hautes Bruyères, attack at, 66
Henry, Lucien, 120
Henry, Mme (Mme Rastoul), 100, 101, 120
Hernani, by Victor Hugo, 19
"He whom she loved," folksong, text, 16
Holland, 146
Houdon, rue de, school on, 46
Hughes, Clovis, 136
Hugo, Victor, xi, 9, 19, 20, 36, 52, 54, 172, 173, 191, 192, 193; *Burgraves,* drama, 19; *Hernani,* drama, 19; "Harmodius," poem, quoted from, 54; "Louise Michel," poem published as "Viro Major" ("More than a Man"), quoted from, xi; "To the People," poem, quoted from, 173, text, 192
Humbert, Alphonse, 183

"Illegal Candidacy, The," article by Louise Michel, text, 124–25
Imperialism, 111–13, 117, 118, 130
Improvement of Working Women Through Their Work (organization), 82
Indian Ocean, 93
"In Memory of Marie Ferré," poem by Louise Michel, text, 137–38
Interior, Minister(s) of, xv, 180–81, 199
International, First, 154, 158, 199
International, Second, 199, 200
Intransigeant, L', 119, 134, 143, 144, 147, 151, 158, 183, 186
Invalides, les, demonstration at, 1883, xv; Chapter 21, "The Trial of 1883," 158–71
Issy, fort of, 65, 84

Jacobins, 149
Jacqueline, Mme (painter), 179
Jaundice, plant, 98
Jeunesse, La (periodical), 52
Joffrin, 122, 183
John Helder (ship), 120

Jourde (Communard), 76
Journal de la Jeunesse, 202

Kanaka, xv, 96, 111–14, 116–18, 140;
  Kanakan Rebellion, 1878, xiv, 111–14;
  Kanakan war chant, "The Takata,"
  translated into French by Louise
  Michel, text, 113–14. *See also* Andia the
  Takala; Ataï; Daoumi; Naïna; Segou
Keva, Mme (publisher), 203
Kropotkin, Prince Peter, ix, xiii, xiv, 154,
  157, 186, 200

Labbat, Warrant Officer, 74
Lacour (deportee), 96
Lafargue, Paul, 198
Lagny, France, 8, 31, 123
Laguerre, Maître, 167
Lamartine, Alphonse de, 9
Lambeth (district of London), 148
Lamennais, Félicité Robert de, ix, 9
Langlais. *See* Ghi, Elisabeth de
Langlois (deportee), 99
Laumont of Bourmont (physician), called
  Big Laumont, 6, 20
Laumont of Ozières (schoolteacher),
  called Little Laumont, 6
La Villette, Nineteenth Arrondissement,
  Paris, 82
"Lay of the Troubadour," from *The
  Dream of the Witches' Sabbath,* by Louise
  Michel, text, 42
League of Women, 60
Lecomte, General, 64, 82, 84, 85
"Legend of the Oak, The," poem by
  Louise Michel, text, 43–44
Legendary Haute-Marne, by Louise Michel,
  xvi; quoted from, 9–11
Légende du barde, La, by Louise Michel,
  202
Légendes canaques, by Louise Michel, 202,
  203
Legends and history, x, xii, 16, 17, 26,
  44, 45, 50, 146, 196; at Écrègnes,
  25–26; *Diableries of Chaumont,* 10–11;
  Dream of the Witches' Sabbath, 41;
  folksongs showing, 16, 17–18;
  Ghost-in-Flames, 11, 25, 26; Kanakan,
  112–13, 116; of the *Naglfar* (ship), 91;
  of the Haute-Marne, 9–11, 16, 24, 32;
  of the oath of the oak tree, 32, 43; of
  the Three Washerwomen, 9, 19, 26.
  See also Atavism

Léger, Second Lieutenant, 74
Lemel, Nathalie (Duval), ix, 101, 102,
  103, 194
Léo, André, 57
Léo, André, Mme, 57
Lesurques affair, 86
Levallois-Perret (suburb of Paris), 74;
  cemetery of, xvi, 136, 183, 185–87, 201
L'Homme, Caroline, 46
Libre-Pensée (periodical), 183
Lille, France, 153
Lisbonne, Maxime, 159, 170
Lissagaray, Hippolyte-Prosper-Olivier,
  183, 190
Literacy, rural, 6, 8, 27, 33; urban, 46
Littérature au crochet, by Louise Michel,
  202
Livre des morts, Le, lost manuscript by
  Louise Michel, 202
Livre d'Hermann, Le, by Louise Michel,
  202
Locamus (town councilor, Nouméa, and
  attorney), 119, 159
London, England, 121, 122, 132, 135,
  149, 156, 200. *See also* Lambeth
London, (Kropotkin's) Congress of, July,
  1881, xiii, 132, 134
Longchamps, Julie, xiii, xv, 32, 37, 38,
  39, 45
Louise, Mme, 195
"Louise Michel," poem by Victor Hugo,
  retitled "Viro Major" ("More Than a
  Man"), quoted from, xi
Louise Michel Association (Lyon), 136
"Louise Michel at the Graffard Meeting
  Hall" (painting by unknown artist),
  152; (painting with same title by
  Tynaire [*sic* Tinayre]), 153
Louvet, Victorine (Mme Eudes), xii, xiv,
  43, 44
Lucien, Henri, 110
Lucipia, 183
Lullier (Communard), 76
Lyon, France, 154, 156
Lyon, France, Commune of, 65
"Lyon, Manifesto of," 1883. *See*
  "Anarchists, Manifesto of the"
Lyon, Trial of the Sixty-eight Anarchists
  at, 1883. *See* Anarchists, Trial of the
  Sixty-eight

MacMahon, Marshal Patrice de, 123
Magasins pittoresques, 9

Mahis, de. *See* Demahis
Malézieux, "Père," 62, 96, 97, 100, 147, 191, 192
"Manifesto of Lyon." *See* "Anarchists, Manifesto of the"
"Manifesto of the Anarchists." *See* "Anarchists, Manifesto of the"
Marchais, Joséphine, 73, 78, 172
Marchand, Maître, 75
Maret, Henri, 183
Mareuil, Eugène, 160, 161, 162, 163, 165, 170
Marie Ferré Association (Lyon), 136
Mariguet (member of court-martial board), 74
Marseille, France, 200; Commune of, 65
Marseillaise, 30, 34–35, 56, 122
Marxism, ix, 199, 200
Mas (of Anvers), 147
Masons. *See* Freemasons
"Me, I am the white dove," poem by Louise Michel, fragment quoted, 53
Mémoires d'Hanna la nihiliste, by Louise Michel, 202
Memoirs of Louise Michel, The Red Virgin, xii, xiii, xiv, xvi, 1, 18, 22, 74; editors' system for reorganization of, xvii–xviii, Appendix I; second volume of, never written, xviii; smuggled from prison, 2; sources used in, xvi–xvii, 2, 7, 76–77, 89, 122, 152
Méprisées, Les, by Jean Guetré, Mme Tynaire [*sic* Tinayre], 203
Merlin, Colonel, 74, 195
Meurice, Mme Paul, 59, 61
Meusy, 158, 167
Michel (a schoolteacher not related to Louise Michel), 12–13
Michel, Louis (pseudonym of Louise Michel), 51, 202
MICHEL, LOUISE
—described, xi–xii, 5, 11, 21, 38, 52, 62, 81, 88, 144, 153, 179, 197, 200
—life (chronologically): born illegitimate, 29 May 1830, vii, 84, 188; begins school at Vroncourt, 11; has suitors, 20–21; inherits land, 23; meets Victor Hugo, 36; receives teacher training, 31; teaches at Audeloncourt, xiii, 32, 34; teaches at Paris, xiii; tries to start schools in Audeloncourt and Clefmont, but fails, xiii; joins with Julie Longchamps in Millières, 37; goes to

Paris, xiii, 37; becomes schoolmistress at Mme Vollier's, 38; gets partnership in school, rue du Château d'Eau, 39; buys day school in Montmartre, 45; begins studies for baccalaureate, 47; unites school with Mlle Poulin's on rue Houdon, 46; first arrest, 57; presides over Women's Vigilance Committee, 58; responsible for schoolchildren, xii–xiii; second arrest, 60–61; Demonstration of 22 Jan. 1871, 61–62; school on rue Oudot, 83; climbs Butte of Montmartre 18 March 1871, 64; member, National Guard, xiv; President, Club of the Revolution, 83; surrenders, 69; confined, Bastion 37 [*sic* 43], 69; moved to Satory, 70; moved to Chantiers prison, Versailles, 71; moved to Versailles reformatory, 73; moved to Arras, 78; trial, 81–88; sentenced on 16 Dec. 1871 to deportation to a fortified place, 87; moved to Auberive prison, 89; sails to New Caledonia on *Virginie*, xiv, 90; converted to anarchism, ix; lands at Numbo, 96; moved to the Bay of the West, 103; involved in Kanakan Rebellion, xiv, 112; goes to Nouméa, 1879, and teaches, 114; Amnesty of 1880, 120; sails to Europe via Sydney, 120–21; arrives Paris, 9 Nov. 1880, 122; first speech after return, 123–24; refuses to testify to Chamber of Deputies, 126; London Conference, 143; candidate, Chamber of Deputies, 124; writes for *La Révolution sociale*, 131–33; arrested after Blanqui demonstration, 1882, tried, convicted, 134–35; death of Marie Ferré, 23–24 Feb. 1882, 135; travels and speeches in France and abroad, 143–54; attends Trial of the Sixty-eight Anarchists, Jan. 1883, Lyon, 154–56; accepts "Manifesto of the Anarchists," ix, 160; Demonstration at Les Invalides, 9 March 1883, 158; tried, 160–70; convicted, 170; Centrale Prison, Clermont, 172; transferred to Saint-Lazare prison, Dec. 1884, xv, 181; mother dies 3 Jan. 1885, 182; pardoned, Jan. 1886, 198; arrested, convicted, and pardoned, summer 1886, 198; attempt to assassinate her,

Michel, Louise, continued
198; arrested 1890, 199; goes to
England, 199; dies, Marseille, 9 Jan.
1905, 200
—and feminism, xv, 20, 39, 52, 58, 59,
60, 67, 83, 122, 125, 130, Chapter 18,
"Women's Rights," 139–42, 148, 173,
191
—finances of, 23, 27, 31, 38, 39, 40, 45,
106, 127–28, 143, 147, 153, 199–200
—and music, 6, 19, 20, 37, 40–42, 48, 51,
83, 93, 96, 111–12, 118
—opinions on various subjects not
indexed otherwise (alphabetically):
antisemitism, 200; art, 30; battle, love
of, 66; books, 31, 32, 40; capital
punishment, 25, 27; children, 25;
courts and legal codes, 83, 86;
discipline, 33; freedom, 190; heroism,
65, 66, 139; history, x, 5, 16, 17, 18,
20, 51; honor, 166; justice, 168, 182;
marriage, 16, 20–21, 39, 44, 139;
mental institutions, 191, 199; merit, 13;
militarism, 200; nationalism, 168, 169,
173; politics, 52; prescience, 22, 91;
racism, xvi; religion, xiii, 8, 9, 12, 19,
27, 28, 31, 35, 42, 83, 86, 135;
revenge, 26, 142; scholars, 14, 105;
science, x, 29, 98, 118, 141, 149;
slanders, 119; suffrage, 125, 129, 130;
treason, 112
—and prostitution, 49, 121, 141, 142,
173–77
—and revolution: general, 1, 14, 28, 42,
48, 52, 54, 55, 59, 60, 64, 128–29, 130,
133–34, 139; origins of her
revolutionary feeling, 5, 9, 16, 18, 24,
25, 28; revolutionary theory, ix–xi, xv,
xvi, 9, 29, 51, 55, 122, 123, 128–29,
139, 140, 147, 155, 160, 169, 198, 203;
revolutionary acts of, x, xiv, 31, 36, 45,
54, 58, 82–85, 86, 128, 151, 163;
revolutionary dreams of, 30, 54, 71,
128, 131, 171, 193, 196, 197
—as a teacher: in Haute-Marne, xiii, 34,
35, 47; in Paris, 51, 83; in Nouméa,
34–35, 114, 116–19; education and
training of, 31–32, 47, 51; of Kanakas,
xv, 114, 116–19; methods and theories
of, 14, 20, 51, 117–18; pupils of, xiii,
xv, 34, 38, 40, 48, 88, 108–09; personal
satisfaction of, 40. *See also* Education
—trials and arrests of: gallows speeches,

xii, 18; arrests (1870), 57, 60; Trial of
1871, xii, xiv, 1, 38, 80, 158, 160; Trial
of 1871, transcript of, 81–87; Trial of
1871, observations upon, 87–88;
Second Trial (1882), xv, 134, 161;
Trial of 1883, ix, 59, 159–60, 179;
Trial of 1883, transcript of, 160–70;
Trial of 1883, observations upon,
170–71; Trial of 1886, 198; arrest
(1890), 199
—writing of, xiii, xvi, xvii, 4, 17, 36, 40,
52, 198; in collaboration with others,
53, 128, 202–03; under pseudonyms,
51, 202
—writings of, mentioned or quoted in
text (alphabetically): "As my first toys,"
poem, text, 91; "The Avengers," song,
83; *Le Bagne,* lost manuscript, 172–73,
202; "Ballad of the Skeleton," poem,
text, 41; *Le Bâtard impérial,* with Grippa
de Winter, 202; "The Black Bird of
the Fallow Field," poem, text, 18; "The
Black Marseillaise," poem with
Vermorel, quoted from, 53;
["Candidacy"], article, text, 125–26; *La
Conscience,* lost manuscript, 202; *Contes
d'enfants,* 106; *Le Coq rouge,* drama,
202; "Criminals and Whores," poem,
text, 49; *Diableries de Chaumont,* 202. *See
also Legendary Haute-Marne. Dream of the
Witches' Sabbath,* opera, 40–42;
Encyclopédie enfantine, 202, 203;
"Farewell, my dreaming retreat in the
manor," poem, text, 23; *La Femme à
travers les âges,* 202; "In Memory of
Marie Ferré," poem, text, 137–38;
"The Illegal Candidacy," article, text,
124–25; "Lay of the Troubadour,"
poem, text, 41; "The Legend of the
Oak," poem, text, 43–44; *Legendary
Haute-Marne,* xvi, quoted from, 9–10;
La Légende du barde, 202; *Légendes
canaques,* 202, 203; *Littérature au crochet,*
202; *Le Livre des morts,* lost manuscript,
202; *Le Livre d'Hermann,* 202;
["Manifesto"], text, 82–83; "Me, I am
the white dove," quoted from, 53;
Mémoires d'Hanna la nihiliste, 202; *La
Misère,* with Mme Tynaire [*sic* Tinayre],
202; *Nadine,* drama, with Grippa de
Winter, 202; *Naughty Deeds of Helen,* 6,
11; *Océaniennes,* 202; ["Piano with
bows"], article, 51, 202; "Silence the

Michel, Louise, continued
 Villain," article, text, 132–33; "Soar
 high in brilliant whiteness, birds,"
 poem, text, 93; "The Strike of the
 Conscripts," article, text, 128–29; "The
 Takata," translated Kanakan war chant,
 text, 113–14; "To M. Andrieux." *See*
 "Silence the Villain." *Universal History,*
 20; *Vroncourt,* quoted from, 9; "The
 Voyage," poem, text, 15; *The Wisdom of
 a Madman,* 50–51, 202. *See also*
 Appendix II, 207
Michel, Louise, Association (Lyon), 136
Michel, Louise, extended family of, 5, 6,
 8, 15, 18, 19, 31, 32, 33, 38, 88, 90,
 183
Michel, Louise, *Memoirs* of. *See Memoirs of
 Louise Michel*
Michel, Marguerite (maternal
 grandmother of Louise Michel), 5, 23,
 44, 46, 188
Michel, Marie Anne, also Marianne, also
 Myriam (mother of Louise Michel):
 described, 5, 187–88; emotional life of
 Louise Michel connected to, xvi, 89,
 115, 138, 195, 197; life of
 (chronologically): childhood, 188; gives
 birth to Louise, viii, 188; guardianship
 over Louise, 31; accompanies Louise to
 Lagny, 1851, 31; vacation of 1856, 44;
 stays in Haute-Marne when Louise
 goes to Paris, 38; sends Louise money,
 39; visits Louise, 40; sells land to
 finance school, 45; moves to
 Montmartre after death of Marguerite
 Michel, 23, 46; lives with Louise,
 53–54; period of Commune, 64, 66,
 67; government threatens to shoot, 69;
 visits Louise at Chantiers prison, 71;
 lives near Auberive prison, visits
 Louise, 89; lives in Paris during
 Louise's exile, 90; writes letters to
 Louise in New Caledonia, 104, 106,
 107; health declines, 107, 120; after
 return, 121–22, 127, 128, 129, 134,
 153; threats against, 167; forgery sent
 to, 11; Chapter 23, "My Mother's
 Death," 179–89 (dies 3 January 1885,
 xv, 182; funeral described, 182–87);
 not revolutionary, 115
Millière, de (revolutionary), 159
Millières, Haute-Marne, school at, xiii, 37
Minck (or Mink), Paule, 60, 65, 124

Miot (Republican), 54
Misère, La, by Mme Tynaire [*sic* Tinayre]
 and Louise Michel, 202
Moïse, Charles, 183
Molière (Jean-Baptiste Poquelin), 5, 21,
 139
Montmartre (Paris), viii, 38, 45, 58, 61,
 63, 64, 84, 136, 182, 184
Montmartre, Butte de, 63, 67, 82
Montmartre, National Guard, battalions
 of, 61
Montmartre Vigilance Committee (men's),
 Chaussée Clignancourt, 58; (women's),
 rue de la Chapelle, xii, 58; work of,
 58–59, 136
Montretout, battle at (19 Jan. 1871), 61
Morceau, Armand, 147
Moreau (alias Gareau), 170
"More Than a Man" ("Viro Major"), by
 Victor Hugo, quoted from, xi
Morphy, 126
Moulin de Pierre, fighting at, 66
Moulineaux, fighting at, 84
Muette, Château de la, 70
Murget (or Murger), grave of, 67
Muriot (deportee), 110
Musées des familles, 9
Music, 6, 20; Arab, 96; Danel's notation
 for, 48; *Dream of the Witches' Sabbath,
 The,* opera by Louise Michel, 40–42;
 Jewish, 42; Kanakan, 96, 112, 118;
 methods of instruction in, 118; of
 Brittany, 90, 93; by piano with bows,
 51, 202; *Robert the Devil,* opera
 performed in New Caledonia, 111–12;
 scoring in, 41–42

Nadine, drama by Louise Michel and
 Grippa de Winter, 202
Naglfar (legendary ship), 91
Naïna (Kanakan), 112
Napoleon III. *See* Bonaparte
Narbonne, France, Commune of, 65
National Guard, xiv, 60, 61, 63, 64, 75,
 81, 82, 86, 167
Naughty Deeds of Helen, The, by Louise
 Michel, 6, 11
Ndié Bay, New Caledonia, 110
Nemours, Duke de, 123
Netherlands. *See* Holland
New Caledonia, viii; Chapter 13,
 "Numbo, New Caledonia," 95–103;
 Chapter 14, "The Bay of the West,"

104–14; Chapter 15, "Nouméa and the Return," 115–18; 181, 192. *See also* Aleyron; Cyclones; Ducos Peninsula; Gauthier de la Richerie; Kanakas; Nou Island; Nouméa; Numbo; Ribourt, Admiral; Rochefort; West, Bay of; Western Forest

Newspapers, 63, 75, 121, 147–48. *See also* newspapers under titles

Nihilists, 122, 124, 178

Noir, Victor, 82, 84, 186

Northern Forest, Ducos Peninsula, New Caledonia, 100

Nou Island, New Caledonia, 107, 109, 110, 111, 114, 152, 183

Nouméa, New Caledonia, xv, 35, 95, 100, 114; Chapter 15, "Nouméa and the Return," 115–20

Nouméa, Board of Municipal Public Instruction, 119

Nouméa, Journal de, 100

Nourny (deportee), 100

Numbo, New Caledonia, xiv; Chapter 13, "Numbo, New Caledonia," 95–103; 107, 110

Oak tree, oath of, 32, 43–44

Oceana, jade axe of, 52

Oceanic tribes, Aryanism in, 116

Océaniennes, by Louise Michel, 202

Oddin, 187

Opportunists (properly "Opportunist Republicans," a political faction) and Opportunism, 123, 125, 128, 129, 149, 187, 198

Oppression and exploitation: of animals, xvi, 24–25, 29; by Bonaparte and under Second Empire, 54, 186; in Bible, 27; not eased by charity, 27; of children, 47; at night in city, 49; in dramas, 18; of Greeks, 27; of Kanakas, 111; of peasants, 25, 26, 28; of people, 13, 196; of the poor, 27; when power not shared, 131; of powerless, xv; of prisoners, 98–99; of prostitutes, 173; through rent, 39, 40; will bring revolution, 29, 171, 193; by rich, 155; by Rome, 27; in Russia, 28; symbolized by spider, 106; in statecraft, 65; of women, 125, 139–42, 153–54, 176–77; of workers, 125. *See also* Animals, cruelty toward; Bonaparte; Feminism; Kanaka; Prisons; Prostitutes;

Revolution; Social Revolution

Orleanists, 163

Orleans, House of, 123, 168

Otterbein (of Brussels), 147

Oudot, rue, school on, 83

Pain, Olivier, 96, 122

Pall Mall Gazette, 148

Palmas, Las, Grand Canary Island, 91

Papavoine, Eulalie, 73, 172

Papayas, vaccination of, xii, 97

Pardons, Board of, 76, 87

Parent (Communard), 76

Paris: attraction of, 35, 37; condemns school, 45; Hôtel de Ville of, 57, 60, 61, 62; Siege of, xiv, 35, Chapter 8, "The Siege of Paris," 56–62. *See also* Commune of Paris

Paris, Count and Countess of, 123

Parliamentarianism, 65, 187, 196

Paroles d'un croyant, by Félicité Robert de Lamennais, 9

Passedouet (deportee), 110–11

Peasants, 24, 26, 27, 28

Pelletan, Eugène, 50

Penand, Mme (schoolmistress, New Caledonia), 35

Pépinière Barracks, Le, Paris, 184

Père Lachaise Cemetery (properly Cimetière de l'Est), 151, 182

Perle, de la, Meeting Hall, 152

Perronet barricade, Neuilly, 28, 66, 96

Perusset (deportee), 107–08, 115

Pichon, S., 183

Place, Henry, 99, 202

Place, Théophile (infant), 99, 110

Plebiscite, May 1870, 56

Poe, Edgar Allan, 22, 91

Poirier (Communard), 194

Police, xii, 51, 77, 85, 145, 146, 150, 164, 165, 182, 184. *See also* Andrieux, Louis

Popular Front, 201

"Possibilist" Socialists, 198, 199, 200

Pottery (police spy), 184

Pouget, Jean-Joseph-Emile, ix, 160–65, 167, 170

Poulin, Malvina, 46, 47, 51, 59, 67

Power, nature of, x, 49, 50, 52, 71, 131, 155, 169

Prisons (and prisoners), xiv–xv, 2, 28–29, 71, 73, 88, 95, 96–97, 98, 102, 126, Chapter 22, "Prison," 172–78, 193. *See also* Arras; Auberive prison; *Bagne, Le;*

Centrale Prison; Chantiers Prison;
  Saint-Lazare prison; Satory, detention
  area at; Thirty-seventh Bastion;
  Versailles, reformatory of
Pritzbuer, Captain de, 100
Progrès musical, Le, 51, 202
Prostitution, 39, 49, 59, 121, 125, 129,
  141–42, 173–78
Proudhon, Pierre Joseph, ix, 110–11,
  142, 167
Provins (deportee), 97
Provisional Government. *See* Government
  of National Defense
Prussia. *See* Franco-Prussian War
Publishers, 40, 128
Puech (merchant, Nouméa), 119
Pyat, Félix, 124

Quesnay de Beaurepaire, Avocat-général,
  167

Racism, xvi
Radical, Le, 183
Radical des Alpes, Le, 183
Raison, La, 202
Ramé, Judge, 160
Ranvier (child), 71
Rastoul (Communard), 76
Rastoul, Mme. *See* Henry, Mme
Ravanchol (anarchist), 200
Razoua, Eugène, 61
Regère (Communard), 76
Reinsdorff (German), 194
Religion, 8, 12, 42, 145
Relingue's house of prostitution, 175
Republic (and Republicans), 31, 35, 36,
  45, 50, 56, 57, 63, 64, 73, 75, 123, 168.
  See also Commune of Paris;
  Opportunists; Revolution
Republicans, Fraternal Association of, of
  the Basses-Alpes, Vaucluse, and Var,
  183
Retif(fe), Elisabeth, 73, 78, 172, 195
Retz, Gilles de, 29
Revolution (and Revolutionaries), ix, 1, 9,
  24, 28, 39, 42, 46, 52, 53, 56, 57, 58,
  59, 63, 64, 65, 69, 86, 125, 128, 130,
  131, 133, 136, 138, 147, 148, 151, 158,
  160, 165, 166, 170, 193, 197
Revolution, Club of, 83
Revolutionary Sentinel of the Eighteenth
  Arrondissement (organization), 183

Révolution sociale, La, xiv, 131, 132, 133,
  143, 202. *See also* Andrieux, Louis
Revue scientifique, 164
Ribourt, Admiral, 99, 101, 126
Richerie, de la. *See* Gauthier de la
  Richerie, Governor of New Caledonia
Rigault, Raoul, 159
Rights of Man, Club of, Vaucluse, 183
Rights of Women (organization), rue
  Thévenot, 59
Robert the Devil (opera), 111
Roche, Ernest, 185
Rochefort (city), 90
Rochefort, Henri, xvi, 57, 92, 95, 96, 98,
  114, 116, 122, 136–37, 143, 152, 167,
  179, 183, 184, 198, 199–200
Rosiers, rue de, 64, 82
Rossel, Louis-Nathaniel, 77, 137
Rossel, Mlle, 137
Rouillon, 167
Royer, Mme (educator at Chaumont), 31
Russia (and Russian Revolutionaries), 27,
  28, 52, 58, 59, 178, 191, 194, 200
Russo-Japanese War, 200

*Sagesse d'un fou. See Wisdom of a Madman,
  The*
Saint Antoine, faubourg, Paris, 45, 63
Saint-Just, Louis de, 131
Saint-Lazare prison, xv, 2, 11, 173, 179,
  181, 191
Sand, George, 19
Santa Catarina, Brazil, 92
Sapia (demonstrator), 62
Satory, detention area at, 70–71, 77, 78,
  79, 80, 86, 87, 124, 151, 152, 172, 193,
  194
Saxe-Coburg-Gotha, Prince and Princess
  of, 123
Schmi(d)t, Marie, 101, 195
Second Empire. *See* Empire, Second;
  Bonaparte
Sedan, Battle of, 54, 56, 57, 168, 169,
  192, 193
Segou (Kanakan traitor), 113
Seine District, Superior Court of, 160–70
Senart, Captain, 74
Serr(e)aux (pseudonym of Egide
  Spilleux), 131, 132, 133
Shaw, George Bernard, x
Siege of Paris. *See* Paris, Siege of
Sifou, New Caledonia, 96

"Silence the Villain," article in *La Révolution sociale* by Louise Michel, text, 132

Silkworms, 105–06

Simon (acting mayor, Nouméa), 118, 119

Simon, Jules, 51

Simon, Mme Jules, 59

Simond, Victor, 183

Sivry, Charles de, 42, 51

Sixth Arrondissement, Luxembourg, Paris, 63, 165

Sixth Court-martial Board, 81–87

"Soar high in brilliant whiteness, birds," poem by Louise Michel, text, 93

Socialists, German, 178

Socialists, plea for unity among, 187

Socialists, "Possibilist." *See* "Possibilist" Socialists

Social Revolution, x, xi, xv, 82, 85, 122, 123, 124, 151, 165, 184, 199, 200

Soldiers, 61, 70, 73, 74, 75, 128–29, 184. *See also* Commune of Paris; Franco-Prussian War; Paris, Siege of

"Song of the Shirt, The," by Thomas Hood, 149

Stenography, 47

Strasbourg, France, 57, 58

Strasbourg, Statue of Our Lady of (Paris), 57

"Strike of the Conscripts, The," article by Louise Michel, text, 128–29

Strike(s), 128, 150, 153–54. *See also* General strike

Suétens, Léontine, 172

Suez, Isthmus of, 121

Suffrage, 129, 130, 194

Susini, 198

Sydney, Australia, 100, 101, 108, 115, 120

"Takata, The," Kanakan war chant of Andia, translated by Louise Michel, text, 113–14

Tenth Arrondissement, Entrepôt, Paris, 82

Terrorism, x, 200

Théleni, 183

Thévenot, rue, school on, 51

Thierry (co-defendant, 1883), 170

Thiers, Adolphe, x, 84, 86, 123, 143; statue of, 133

Third Military Court-martial, 74–76

Thirty-seventh [*sic*] Bastion, properly the Forty-third, 69

Thomas, Clément, General, 64, 82, 84, 85

Thomas, Edith, xv, xvi

Three Washerwomen, legend of, 9, 19, 26

Tiffault, Eugenie, 110

Tinayre. *See* Tynaire, Mme

Titard, 183

"To M. Andrieux," original title of "Silence the Villain," article by Louise Michel, text, 132–33

"To My Neighbor, Starboard Aft," poem by Henri Rochefort, cited, 92

"To the People," poem by Victor Hugo: cited, 173; text, 192

"To the People's Army" (pamphlet), 163–64

Tomb, name of Demahis chateau, Vroncourt, 4, 5, 7, 15, 18, 22, 23

Tortelier, Joseph, 187

Tour Saint Jacques, square of, 61

Transnonain, 124

Trials. *See* Michel, Louise, trials of; Anarchists, Trial of the Sixty-eight

Trinquet (Communard), 76, 124

Trochu, General Louis Jules, 56, 57, 151

Turpin, 64–65

Tynaire [*sic* Tinayre], Mme (pseudonym of Jean Guetré), 202–03; son of, 128

Tyrannicide, x, 128

Union des poètes, L', 52, 202

Union of Women, Central Committee of, 82

Union of Women for the Defense of Paris and the Care of the Wounded, 82

Universal History, by Louise Michel, 19, 20

Urbain, Raoul, 76

Usury, 26

Vaccination, xii, 98

Vaillant, Edouard, 183

Vallès, Jules, 84, 159, 193

Valley of the Sorcerers, legend of, 26

Var, France, 183

Varlet, 147

Vaucluse, France, 183

Vaughan, Ernest, 158, 167, 183

Verdet, Marie, 9, 10, 11, 19, 26

Verdure (Communard), 76, 109–10
Verlaine, Paul, xi, 198
Verlet, 99
Vermorel, 53, 159
Versailles, Demonstration at, September 1882, 151
Versailles, reformatory of, 73
Versailles Government, 63, 64, 65, 76, 89
Viard, 147
Victims of the War, Society for, 59, 60, 61
Vigilance, Committees of, 60, 63, 82. *See also* Montmartre Vigilance Committees
Virgil (Publius Vergilius Maro), 23, 27
Virginie (ship), ix, xiv, 13–14, 90, 91, 93, 95
"Viro Major," by Victor Hugo, quoted from, xi
Vitellius, 127
Vollier, Mme, 32, 38, 39, 40, 45–46
Voltaire (François Marie Arouet), 5, 20
Voltaire, Le, 144
Vosges, Place des, 63

"Voyage, The," poem by Louise Michel, text, 15
Vroncourt, by Louise Michel, quoted from, 9
Vroncourt, Haute-Marne, viii, 4, 9, 12, 43

Wagram, Parc, 63
West, Bay of the, xiv, 98, 101, 103; Chapter 14, "The Bay of the West," 104–14
Western Forest, New Caledonia, 95, 104–05, 106
Winter, Grippa de (pseudonym of Jean Winter), xvii, 202
Wisdom of a Madman, The, manuscript by Louise Michel, 50–51, 202
Wolowski (deportee), 112
Women. *See* Feminism
Women, League of, 60
Workers' Union of Amiens, 129, 130
Workhouses, 148